The Evolution of Foreign Banking Institutions in the United States

The Evolution of Foreign Banking Institutions in the United States

Developments in International Finance

Faramarz Damanpour

Foreword by Terri Sohrab

Q

QUORUM BOOKS

New York • Westport, Connecticut • London

Library of Congress Cataloging-in-Publication Data

Damanpour, Faramarz.
   The evolution of foreign banking institutions in the United States: Developments in
International Finance / Faramarz Damanpour.
     p. cm.
   Includes bibliographical references.
   ISBN 0-89930-371-4 (lib. bdg. : alk. paper)
   1. Banks and banking, Foreign — United States. I. Title.
HG2491.D36   1990
332.1′5′0973 — dc20   89-10692

British Library Cataloguing in Publication Data is available.

Library of Congress Catalog Card Number: 89-10692
ISBN: 0-89930-371-4

First published in 1990 by Quorum Books

Greenwood Press, Inc.
88 Post Road West, Westport, Connecticut 06881

Printed in the United States of America

The paper used in this book complies with the
Permanent Paper Standard issued by the National
Information Standards Organization (Z39.48–1984).

10 9 8 7 6 5 4 3 2 1

To
My father, Ali, and my mother, Afzal

Contents

Tables

Foreword

The complexities of international banking and world financial affairs are presented in this book in a concise and erudite manner. The evolution of foreign banking in the United States reflects the changes in the mosaic of banking practices that Faramarz Damanpour elucidates to give us a vision of the future, based on experience.

I welcome this book and encourage all those with interest in international banking and finance to read it. It is a useful text for both banking practitioners and educators. I am especially pleased with the comprehensive presentation of the modern international banking environment, and the indication that banks have achieved enormous progress while adjusting to the changes of the time. Given the recent shifts in the world credit markets, this is a positive message.

This book is carefully laid out to blend the application of international banking and lending agencies with other segments of the economy, commerce, and national policies. Such a complete study of the intracacies of foreign banking in the United States can contribute to one's lifelong learning process and enlighten all of us on the wisdom of future cooperation.

Terri Sohrab
Vice President
Chemical Bank

Preface

International banking has historically been the major component of world trade and monetary exchange activities. The early banks were merchant banks engaged in the remittances of money and the settlement of accounts. Development of money centers in Europe facilitated foreign investment and deposit-taking activities. International banking houses provided loans and served as agents of underwriters for foreign bond issues.

The international monetary development of the mid-twentieth century changed the direction of historical trends in the banking and the financial system. The U.S. dollar became a means of international exchange, a store of value, and the prominent world currency. New York replaced London and Paris as the most prominent financial center. As a result, the United States became a dominant force in the world's currencies and trade.

Foreign banks sought to capitalize on growing international trade and lending opportunities in the United States. Their rush to take advantage of these circumstances resulted in an increasing number of foreign banks. The sharp escalation in foreign bank presence produced a heated debate about the motivation, competitive effect, and monetary implications of the presence of these institutions. Various legislation was enacted to calm concerns and to place foreign banks on a more equal footing with U.S. banks.

The lack of international banking textbooks that address the overall status of foreign banks in the United States, and at the same time spell out the structural components of international banks and lending institutions in one place, encouraged this author to attempt this effort. This book is intended to serve two constituents. It is intended as a textbook for graduate and undergraduate students in banking, international business, and finance programs. More importantly, though, it is for the banking community at large.

For the first time, this book draws together in one place a substantial amount of information and data not readily available to the general public and libraries. The book is also a potentially useful source for American historians and the general public interested in learning about America's international financial exposure and dependency, and foreigners' banking investments, as evolved over the years.

What is intended here is to present, in lay language, important background information about the historical development of foreign banking activities in the United States, including their market structure and activities, areas of specialization, legal environment, as well as their motivation, impact, and future prospects. It also contains information about international banking and its institutional structure, international financial markets, and lending agencies. In addition, the study sheds light on the interrelationship between international trade financing and banking development, and summarizes country and regional participation in U.S. banking/financial markets.

Substantial amounts of time and effort have been devoted to the collection and statistical calculation of the tables. For the purpose of uniformity and in order to minimize errors, the study relied on two major sources of information and data: the Board of Governors, Federal Reserve System, Structural Data for U.S. Offices of Foreign Banks; and *American Banker*, special reports on foreign banks in the United States. I give special thanks to Susan Cash and Gudrun Meyer of the Research Library of the Federal Reserve Bank of Richmond for their patience and supply of valuable information.

In writing this book, I have also benefited from the advice and counsel of many others. Michael Benigni helped by reading the entire manuscript and providing valuable advice in presenting this book in a stylish manner. I am also indebted to many other colleagues who provided valuable advice and comments throughout the course of writing this book. However, the major credit should go to my wife, Jill, for her enormous contributions in providing assistance in editing, calculating statistical illustrations, designing tables, and preparing and typing the final copy of the book. My research time was aided by the Faculty Educational Leave granted by James Madison University for the spring of 1989.

Abbreviations

ACU	Asian Currency Unit
ADB	Asian Development Bank
AFDB	African Development Bank
AID	Agency for International Development
ATM	Automated Teller Machine
BHC	Bank Holding Company
BIC	Business Income Coverage
BIS	Bank for International Settlement
C&I	Commercial & Industrial
CIRR	Commercial Interest Reference Rate
DCL	Discretionary Credit Limit
ECI	Export Credit Insurance
ECU	European Currency Unit
EEC	European Economic Community
EFTA	European Free Trade Association
EIB	European Investment Bank
FCIA	Foreign Credit Insurance Association
FDIC	Federal Deposit Insurance Corporation
FHLBB	Federal Home Loan Bank Board
FINE	Financial Institutions and the Nation's Economy
GNP	Gross National Product
IADB	Inter-American Development Bank

IBA	International Banking Act
IBF	International Banking Facilities
IBRD	International Bank for Reconstruction and Development
ICSID	International Centre for Settlement of Investment Disputes
IDA	International Development Agency
IDCA	International Development Cooperation Agency
IFC	International Financial Corporation
IMF	International Monetary Fund
LIBOR	London Interbank Offered Rate
MIGA	Multilateral Investment Guarantee Agency
OECD	Organization for Economic Cooperation and Development
OPIC	Overseas Private Investment Corporation
P/E	Price/earnings Ratio
PEFCO	Private Export Funding Corporation
S&L	Savings and Loan
SBCL	Special Buyer Credit Limit
SDR	Special Drawing Rights
SIBOR	Singapore Interbank Offered Rate
UCP	Uniform Customs & Practices for Documentary Credits

The Evolution of Foreign Banking Institutions in the United States

1 Evolution of Foreign Banking

For nearly two decades, foreign banking activities in the United States have been the topic of much discussion. Many questions have been raised about foreign banks' expansionary activities via acquisitions of domestic banks and the advantages these institutions have over their counterparts in this country. The 1970s saw a sharp escalation in foreign bank presence in the United States. The number of offices tripled, while assets increased by 600 percent. Federal and state banking agencies expressed heightened levels of concern with regard to increases in the size and number of foreign banks locating in U.S. money-center cities. Of major concern was the fact that these institutions were under no federal government control, because the existing legislation did not cover foreign banks. With control of over 10 percent of the U.S. banking assets at that time, it was feared that foreign banks could end up redirecting domestic banking activities and having an impact on overall monetary policy.

Prior to 1972, no official collective data were published about foreign banking structural activities in the United States. There were legitimate questions about the extent of U.S. regulators' knowledge and the adequacy of information about foreign banking here, and whether there was adequate control over foreign ownership interests. Mounting pressure finally resulted in congressional passage of the 1978 International Banking Act (IBA) and the ruling on Regulation K and Edge corporations. The establishment of the international banking facilities in 1981 was another signal from authorities about their readiness to strengthen the U.S. banks in competition with foreign institutions and provide them an opportunity to participate in money market activities similar to the Euromarket overseas.

The question remains as to what impact foreign banking institutions have had on the international banking industry in the United States — whether competitively, with their greater growth superiority, or geographically, with their market concentration penetrating to dominate the U.S. banking market. The following information indicates that such domination has not yet occurred, because of the dimension, diversity, and strength of American banking; but the foreign success, especially among Japanese banks, is alarming.

INTERNATIONAL BANKING DEVELOPMENT

The origins of modern banking can be traced back to the thirteenth century. The early banks were merchant banks, engaged in trade and money-exchange activities. Their deposit-taking activities were exclusively in the exchange of coins and the settlement of accounts. The merchant bankers traded goods internationally and held assets at different points along the trading routes, via agents located in other cities and foreign countries. The extent of their activities was limited to the region in which trading partners were located.

Banking historians point to Italy as the major center of early banking and international transactions. From the thirteenth to mid-fifteenth century, international banking bloomed as merchant banking houses were busy financing exports-imports and trading foreign currencies and coins. Even industrial and trade venture loans were common; however, they were limited to reputable manufacturers and merchants of high renown. The advanced form of security financing did not exist until the nineteenth century. International banking activities declined sharply from the mid-fifteenth century until the eighteenth century, in part due to the difficulties of merchant banks involved in international trade and lending activities. Bad loans, poor management, and lack of coordination among merchant banks caused a shortage of cash and financial stress for some large merchant houses.[1]

These difficulties, while slowing the activities and development of the merchant houses, boosted development of "money centers" in Europe. These centers, mainly short-term and wholesale markets in nature, were involved in providing "drafts" and "bills of exchange" between private bankers, traders, and governmental agencies. Investment activities by wealthy individuals and merchants in money centers were advanced, boosting deposit-taking activities of various natures and terms. By the late-sixteenth century, the money centers paved the road for a new type of customer, the European governments who needed to finance their war chests.[2] At the time, the banks involved in these money-center activities were mainly family-owned operations. Most deposits originated from wealthy noblemen, clergy, and wealthy individuals and businessmen. The loans and trade financing were short- and medium-term loans to reputable merchants and industrialists.

The growth of mercantilism, nationalism, political turmoil, and war in Europe changed the shape of international banking in the seventeenth and eighteenth centuries. First, the dominant money centers of Europe shifted from northern Italy and western Holland to France and England. Then, with the French Revolution, England became the rising star of Europe, as the foremost center of finance, a safe country, free of war and eager for advancement. Herbert Feis, writing about British banking activities in the nineteenth century, has noted, "There were few governments in the world to which the English people did not make a loan."[3]

Colonial domination and adventurous attitudes made it natural for British foreign investment to be widely scattered. The borrowers in the early stage were Spain, Portugal, Greece, Germany, Austria, Hungary, the Scandinavian countries, Russia, and Turkey.[4] Most of these investment-lending activities were in government and railroad securities. One of the sidelines of the international banking houses at the time was to serve as agents of underwriters for the foreign bond issues. The British public was eager to purchase foreign bonds from almost any country. The enthusiasm backfired by the late eighteenth and early nineteenth centuries, as many borrowers defaulted. Among others were governments and private businesses of Russia, Egypt, Peru, Spain, Bolivia, and other developing nations.[5]

INTERNATIONAL BANKING DURING THE TWENTIETH CENTURY

The twentieth century has been a takeoff stage for international banking. Banks from various countries have advanced in international financial affairs to create a new era in banking development. Pioneering the field were Great Britain, France, Germany, and Spain. British interests in the early twentieth century were primarily with colonies and the affiliated countries of Australia, Canada, and South Africa. As Britain expanded its activities with other countries, it paid special attention to North America, China, and Japan. Of the nearly £3.8 billion British capital investment in the early twentieth century, approximately 47 percent was within the British Empire, 20 percent in the United States, and 20 percent in Latin America. Investment in Europe was small, accounting for only 5.5 percent of the total investment. China, Japan, and Egypt similarly received nearly 5 percent of Britain's capital investment.[6]

French international banking activities blossomed in the early twentieth century with a very few strong banks sponsoring the majority of the investments and loans. French international financial activities quadrupled from 1886 to 1908 to a record high of F1.5 billion. Unlike those of the British, French banking investments were very selective. However, like the British, the French were first inclined toward railroad bonds, but quickly turned their attention to other forms of long-term investments. The majority of their investments were with the French colonies, Russia, and European countries. As a result, one may conclude that the French were more conservative and less adventurous with their business investments, and more inclined toward the familiar nearby markets of Europe. Nearly one-half of their total investments were with European countries, one-fourth with Russia, and only 3 percent with North America. By 1914 their investments reached F45 billion, continuing to follow the historical trend without any visible significant change.[7]

Germany's banking structure at mid-nineteenth century consisted of a very large number of banks. The structure changed in the twentieth century, as a few dominant banks prevailed. Half of Germany's investments were in Europe and the other half spread in Africa, Asia, Latin America, and North America. The size of the investment was relatively small, approximately DM24 billion. From the total, DM3.7 billion, or 16 percent, was invested in Canada and the United States.[8] Like France and Great Britain, Germany's early investments were in governmental and railroad securities.

Other prominent banking countries such as Japan, Hong Kong, Italy, and Switzerland were not influential in the early twentieth century nor historically expansionary in nature. Italy was a shining star in the thirteenth to fifteenth centuries, but faded away until the mid-twentieth century. Japan was a small island with limited political, economic, and financial power. Like Russia, Japan was a borrowing nation at first. Foreign capital contributed enormously in building the Japanese infrastructure, especially in railroad and large-scale industry. The British were the first arrivals in Japan, followed by the French, and then by the Germans on a small scale. Japanese interest in international investment in the early part of the century was limited to China, Korea, and a few Southeast Asian nations. Japan, as a world investor, sparked in the 1960s and took off in the 1970s with the successful invasion of the U.S. market.

Russia historically was a borrowing country, the largest of prewar Europe. Foreigners contributed and financed from 30 to 48 percent of Russia's appropriated budget in the nineteenth and early twentieth centuries.[9] Hong Kong's and Switzerland's international financial activities sparked in the late nineteenth century, exclusively in banking-related activities. Today, their success may be attributed to their ability to manage their portfolios in the traditional, conservative manner, diverting themselves from high-risk lending activities.

During the first half of the twentieth century, two events changed the formation and direction of international banking and investments: first, the financial crisis of the "gold standard" system and the establishment of "free convertibility" of currencies; and second, World War II and the resulting economic collapse of Europe, causing progress and industrialization to move toward the United States. The Bretton Woods Agreement of 1944 established a new monetary system centered around the International Monetary Fund and the International Bank for Reconstruction and Development (World Bank). The objective of this system was to facilitate the expansion of world trade and to use the then powerful dollar to provide liquidity and relatively inflation-free stability with the more traditional use of gold as a standard of value.

After World War II, the United States was the only significant holder of wealth and producer of goods. The Bretton Woods Agreement further enhanced the importance of the U.S. dollar as a means of exchange and store of value. Moreover, the Marshall Plan to rebuild Europe opened an avenue for U.S. banks to operate subsidiaries abroad. New York replaced London and Paris as the most prominent financial center. By the late 1950s and in the 1960s, European international banking interest surged toward the new frontier, as the United States became a dominant force in the world's currencies and trade.

The most attractive factor behind the European decision to invest in the American markets was the size and diversity of the U.S. financial-banking industry, along with the stable and low-inflationary economy. The development of Eurodollar and Eurocurrency markets further strengthened both sides' interest to operate subsidiaries in U.S. money-center cities and in the European money centers of Zurich, Paris, London, and Frankfurt. The United States' banks rapidly expanded their foreign branches and subsidiaries abroad to take advantage of opportunities in the Euromarkets and to serve the needs of their multinational clients abroad.

The U.S. balance of payment and trade deficits in the early 1970s, along with two devaluations of the U.S. dollar in 1971 and 1973 and the oil energy crises of 1973 and 1979, reversed the trend as foreign expansion in the United States accelerated. Banks became easy targets for foreign investors. Lack of federal banking regulations on foreign acquisitions and depressed banks' stock values provided unprecedented opportunities for foreign bankers to enter U.S. markets. Continued deterioration in the U.S. trade balance, especially with Japan during the 1980s, further encouraged foreigners to invest vast amounts of their surpluses in this land of opportunity.

INTERNATIONAL MONETARY SYSTEM

International monetary developments of the mid-twentieth century changed the direction of the historical trends in banking and the financial system. The Bretton Woods Agreement shifted the center of activities and means of exchange for international trade from Europe to the United States. The U.S. dollar became the major vehicle currency in foreign exchange and trade transactions. Since foreign exchange rates are one of the key variables in determining prices of products and services, their availability and stability play a key role in international business decisions. The fluctuations in these rates over time cause difficulties for international bankers and portfolio managers in analyzing foreign exchange risk.

In essence, the international monetary system is a structural system to price and stabilize foreign exchange rates and international capital flows and trade, as well as to provide a tool for balance-of-payment adjustments. Although this system in theory is organized and conducted by governmental authorities, it is practiced by international bankers and other organizations involved in international financial affairs. For that reason, a study of the international monetary system is essential to understand the international banking field.

Gold Standard Valuation (Prior to 1944)

Historically, gold was used as a medium of exchange and a store of value. The major countries of the world attempted to secure exchange-rate stability by linking their currencies to gold (known as the classical gold standard). The United States joined the gold standard in 1879. Under the gold standard, deficits or surpluses in a country's balance of payments situation were expected to provide internal adjustments and restore stability. The primary emphasis was on domestic price and income changes to achieve equilibrium. In effect, countries were expected to subordinate their national economic interests to their external economic and monetary relations. The gold standard worked adequately until World War I, when trade patterns were interrupted and primary trading countries suspended their operations.

Immediately after World War I, the industrialized nations allowed their currencies to fluctuate over a wide range in terms of gold and each other. A form of limited flexible exchange rate mechanism was adopted. However, as in the gold standard system, the supply and demand for a country's exports and imports were expected to provide internal adjustments and equilibrium in the foreign exchange market. Unfortunately, flexible exchange rates did not work in equilibrium. On the contrary, the free flow of trade was disrupted more than ever before, creating disorder in exchange rate stabilization. The major problem was created by speculators' reactions to occurrences in international currency trading markets. To reduce risk, portfolio managers sold weak currencies short, causing further declines in value, and automatically boosting strong currencies' values more than warranted by real economic factors.

The net result was that the volume of world trade did not grow in proportion to world gross national product (GNP) and declined to a very low level with the advent of the Great Depression. The collapse of a large number of banks and the stock market from 1929 to 1933 and the failure of the Austrian banking system in 1931 caused most nations to reform their monetary standards by returning to a modified form of the gold standard system. The United States returned to a modified gold standard in 1934. Gold was priced at $35 per ounce but was sold only to foreign central banks, and not to private citizens. From 1934 to the end of World War II, exchange rates were theoretically determined by each currency's value in terms of gold, yet only the dollar was convertible into gold. However, in practice, intervention in exchange rates occurred to stabilize an individual country's economic condition.

Par Value System: Bretton Woods Agreement (1944–71)

After World War II, the United States was the only significant holder of wealth and producer of goods. Recognizing the need to restructure the international monetary system, the 44 representatives of the free world countries gathered in New Hampshire in 1944 and agreed to establish a new systematic monetary order that centered around the International Monetary Fund (IMF) and the International Bank for Reconstruction and Development (IBRD) or World Bank. The object of this system was to facilitate the expansion of world trade and to use the then powerful dollar as a standard of value to provide liquidity and relatively inflation-free stability.

Under this agreement, all countries were to fix the value of their currencies in terms of gold. Only dollars remained convertible into gold at $35 per ounce. All other currencies would fluctuate vis-à-vis the dollar. Within this system, all countries had par values for their currencies that fluctuated by 1 percent in each direction or by a total spread of 2 percent. Any appreciation or depreciation in the value of the dollar would be adjusted by central banks, buying dollars at a lower limit and selling dollars at an upper limit. Devaluation was discouraged as a competitive trade policy, but a 10 percent devaluation was permitted without IMF approval if the currency became too weak to defend or if the pricing mechanism caused severe disruption in the trade and internal economy of a country. Larger devaluations required IMF approval.

International Monetary Fund (151 members). The IMF was established to promote international currency stability, to eliminate exchange restrictions, and to render temporary assistance to countries trying to defend their currencies against cyclical, seasonal, or random occurrences. The IMF can also assist a country having structural trade and balance-of-payment problems if the country agrees to take necessary steps to correct its problems. However, if persistent deficits occur, the IMF cannot save a country from eventual devaluation.

Each member of the IMF, upon joining the organization, negotiates a quota. The size of the quota serves three functions at once:

- Determines how much the member must contribute to the common pool.
- Determines how much the member may borrow from the common pool.
- Determines the member's voting power within the organization.

In contributing to the common pool, members are required to make 25 percent of their quota contribution in the form of gold or U.S. dollars. The remainder is made in the member's own currency, in the form of a bank account set up in the member country to the credit of the IMF. Any member can borrow up to its original 25 percent gold or convertible currency (gold tranche) in any twelve-month period, plus 100 percent of its total quota (credit tranche). Thus a member could conceivably borrow up to 125 percent of its quota. Recently, IMF loan allocations have been liberalized by permitting borrowing up to 150 percent of the quota, or up to 450 percent during a three-year period. The IMF imposes restrictions on borrowing beyond the first 25 percent of the quota to ensure that steps are being taken to correct the borrower's currency problems. Control of the IMF is maintained by votes according to member quotas. The United States has approximately 19 percent of the votes, United Kingdom 7, and the European Economic Community (EEC) together near 20 percent. Since a country's "gold tranche" can be withdrawn automatically from the IMF, countries consider it part of their reserves. The IMF system, sometimes called the system of the adjustable peg, seeks to assure maximum exchange-rate stability yet facilitate orderly changes when needed, thus avoiding competitive devaluations like those occurring during the 1930s.

World Bank (151 members). The International Bank for Reconstruction and Development (IBRD) or World Bank was actually established to provide financial assistance for postwar reconstruction and development of war-torn countries. The first two years of activity of this organization were dominated by reconstruction loans to the four European countries of France, Denmark, Netherlands, and Luxemburg. After these commitments were disbursed, the IBRD began functioning as a worldwide institution, lending to both developed and developing nations. By 1968, the bank's function virtually reversed its original intent by terminating its lending policy to developed countries and concentrating instead on developing countries of the world, whose numbers had increased rapidly in the second half of the twentieth century. From 1956 to 1988 the bank acquired four affiliates:

- The International Finance Corporation (IFC) was established in 1956 to stimulate private investment in developing countries. The IFC finances business projects mainly in the manufacturing and processing fields, either through loans or guarantees. It provides a multinational source for financing international enterprises but has not played a broad role in influencing the international business environment.
- The International Development Agency (IDA) was created in 1960 for making soft loans — that is, loans with long-maturity, relatively low rates of interest, and easy repayment terms — to the developing countries. Nearly all early IDA loans have been established for a term of 15 years, with a 10-year initial grace period and no interest charge, but requiring a small annual service fee. Such loans are made to member governments exclusively for developmental purposes.

- The International Center for Settlement of Investment Disputes (ICSID) was created in 1966 to review and rule on possible international investment disputes. The idea was to provide a place for the arbitration of investment disputes between member countries and to promote a climate of mutual confidence among investors. The ICSID tries to alleviate the friction between developing countries through advice, mediation, and arbitration. In addition, it attempts to increase the flow of resources to developing nations.

- The Multinational Investment Guarantee Agency (MIGA) was created in 1988 to encourage the flow of investments for productive purposes among its member countries. MIGA is intended to enhance mutual understanding between host governments and investors. To fulfill this purpose the agency will guarantee eligible investment losses resulting from noncommercial risk and carry out research and promotional activities. The four types of risk covered are the risk resulting from host government restrictions on currency conversion and transfer, the risk of loss from host governmental legislative or administrative action to deprive foreign investors of ownership or control, the risk of armed conflict and civil unrest, and finally, the repudiation of investors or contractors or unreasonable delay in contractual action by the host government with no forum for any judicial action.[10]

Smithsonian Agreement (1971–73)

With the steep deterioration in the U.S. balance of payments, the growing reluctance of foreigners to hold dollars, and the excessive demand for gold, the United States was forced to suspend its gold sales except to official parties during 1968, which resulted in a two-tiered system of official and free gold prices. On August 15, 1971, the United States ceased exchanging gold for dollars even with official parties and, in effect, floated the dollar in a series of measures intended to force both a change in the dollar parity and a review of the entire IMF system. As a result, the Smithsonian Agreement in December 1971 was constituted. Ten major industrial countries from the IMF convened at the Smithsonian Institution to form a new agreement, named after the institution. They created a new central rate around which the market rate would fluctuate within the bounds of 4.5 percent, a 2.25 percent upper limit and a 2.25 percent lower limit. As a result, the Bretton Woods limit of ±1 percent changed to ±2.25 percent around the central rate.

With the Smithsonian Agreement of December 1971, virtually all major industrial countries revalued their currencies against the dollar, resulting in an effective dollar devaluation of 10 percent (the price of gold was reset at $38 per ounce). The exchange crisis was renewed again early in 1973 with the increase in dollar sales against major strong currencies. As a consequence, a second 10 percent dollar devaluation was announced in February 1973, increasing the gold price to $42 per ounce. The impasse in monetary regulations continued, since neither the U.S. government nor foreign authorities offered to support the dollar through the sale of gold. By March 1973, every major currency was floating without much formal discipline. This period set the foundation for the development of the free floating system of the second half of the 1970s.

Managed Float (1974-present)

Today the industrial countries permit their currencies to fluctuate based on supply and demand considerations. However, these fluctuations are controlled by the monetary authorities of the individual countries. The central banks intervene in the exchange markets, "managing" or "dirtying" the float to preserve what they construe to be orderly foreign exchange markets and appropriate exchange-rate relationships. This intervention counters unwarranted currency speculation and prevents currency movements that might precipitate competitive currency devaluations among the countries. Thus a system of multilaterally managed float has emerged. While the discipline is less rigid and formal than under the fixed-rate Bretton Woods arrangement, it nonetheless exists.

Despite the adoption of a floating exchange rate by the industrial nations, developing countries' exchange rates remain fixed in relation to the currencies of principal trading partners in industrial countries. The purpose is to seek a stable rate with their most important economic partners, to facilitate desired trade, and to stimulate investment patterns. Nevertheless, there have been important changes in the way exchange rate values are determined among the trading countries. These changes are the by-products of both independent actions taken by individual countries and decisions reached through collective discussion at monetary meetings in Rambouillet, France, in 1975 and in Jamaica during 1976.

FOREIGN BANKING IN THE UNITED STATES

The exact date of the first appearance of foreign banks in the United States is unclear and widely disputed. Current literature includes nearly a half-dozen dates. One source dates the origin of foreign banking presence as early as 1818 when the Bank of Montreal set up its agency in New York to manage the money positions of its parent organization.[11] Another source indicates that foreign banking interest began when Darmstadler Bank of Germany acquired an interest in a New York City bank in 1854.[12] A third source records the origin as being in the 1870s when Japanese and Canadian banks set up operations in California, Oregon, and Washington State.[13] The directory of foreign banking in America indicates that the first foreign bank was the Bank of Montreal, established in 1859 in New York.[14] Various other sources cite different times.

Bank historians agree that foreign banks have been a peripheral part of the American banking scene for years, used primarily to facilitate trade and the flow of long-term investments between the United States and other countries. The first British bank to open in the United States was the Hong Kong and Shanghai Banking Corporation in San Francisco in 1875, before the bank moved to New York in 1880.[15] Most early British investment in the United States was in railroad bonds; however, the mismanaged and troubled American railroad system in the nineteenth century proved to be a disappointment to British investors and bankers. The situation changed in the early twentieth century as the United States improved its railroad system and communications and transportation between cities. Later, when the U.S. government joined the gold standard system and moved toward industrialization of manufacturing goods via mass production, foreign interest resurged. The British showed initial interest, followed by the Canadians, French, Dutch, and Germans.

The year 1913 is known as the top year for British investment in the United States. Nearly one-third of all investments outside the empire were in the United States. Early investments, in addition to railroad bonds, were in land and cattle in Texas, Oklahoma, Arkansas, and the Dakotas. French investments, on the other hand, were exclusively in railroad bonds from the eastern states of Pennsylvania and New York. The two cities of St. Louis and San Francisco also benefited from French capital funds flow. German bankers were interested only in government and railroad securities. Table 1.1 lists the early foreign banking settlers in the United States. From the 25 foreign banking establishments, 21 selected New York City, 2 San Francisco, 1 Los Angeles, and 1 Charlotte, North Carolina.

The first state to pass a law permitting foreign banking was Massachusetts in 1906, followed by Oregon in 1907, California in 1909, and New York in 1911.[16] The post–World War I era brought many foreign banks into the United States. The Great Depression halted the expansion of foreign banks for nearly 15 years, but interest in U.S. financial markets was revitalized after World War II. However, the growth of foreign banks in the United States during the late 1940s and in the 1950s was very moderate. The major push occurred in the late 1960s, with a subsequent takeoff in the 1970s. In the 1960s, interest in foreign banking expansion in New York City was intensified by the new state law, effective January 1, 1961, that allowed foreign banks to open branches.[17] Table 1.2 shows the stages of development in the foreign banks in the United States.

U.S. BANKING ACTIVITIES ABROAD

Historically, the American industrial machine has produced for internal consumption. The banking activities of its history followed the path of industrial production. The U.S. banks stayed home to finance the rapidly

Table 1.1
Foreign Banks in the United States in Early Years

Family Bank Name	Country	Year of Estab.	City
Bank of Montreal	Canada	1859	New York
Canadian Imperial Bank of Commerce	Canada	1864	New York
Canadian Imperial Bank of Commerce	Canada	1864	San Francisco
Bank of The West	France	1874	San Francisco
Hong Kong & Shanghai Banking Corp.	Hong Kong	1880	New York
Lloyds Bank	U.K.	1886	New York
Royal Bank of Canada	Canada	1899	New York
National Westminster Bank	U.K.	1905	New York
Bank of Nova Scotia	Canada	1907	New York
Banco di Napoli	Italy	1907	New York
Union Bank	U.K.	1914	Los Angeles
Sumitomo Bank	Japan	1916	New York
Philippine National Bank	Phil.	1917	New York
Credito Italiano	Italy	1917	New York
Banca Commerciale Italiana	Italy	1918	New York
Toronto Dominion Bank	Canada	1919	New York
French American Banking Corp.	France	1919	New York
Barclays American Corp.	U.K.	1919	Charlotte
Mitsubishi Bank	Japan	1920	New York
Banco di Roma	Italy	1921	New York
Israel Discount Bank of N.Y.	Israel	1922	New York
IBJ Schroder Bank & Trust Co.	Japan	1923	New York
Atlantic Bank of New York	Greece	1926	New York
Banco National de Mexico	Mexico	1929	New York
Banco Central of New York	Spain	1929	New York

Source: Derived from information provided by **Institutional Investor**, September 1987, pp. 303-325, and September 1988, pp. 259-289.

growing domestic market. The National Banking Act of 1863 prohibited member banks (national banks) from opening branches overseas and from participating in accepting drafts, bills of exchange, or bankers' acceptances arising from imports or exports of goods and services. The only active participants in international banking abroad were state-chartered banks, with a limited number of foreign branches. The Federal Reserve Act of 1913, for the first time, permitted national banks to branch overseas. Therefore

Table 1.2

Historical Stages of Foreign Banking Development Based on the Year of Establishment

Year	Number of Banks	Year	Number of Banks
Before 1930	25	1961-1970	36
1931-1940	6	1971-1980	164
1941-1950	8	1981-1988	143
1951-1960	23		

Source: Calculated from information provided by the **Institutional Investor**, September 1987, pp. 303-325, and September 1988, pp. 259-289. The 1988 data are derived from the Board of Governors of the Federal Reserve System, **Structural Data for U.S. Offices of Foreign Banks**, December 31, 1988. Data exclude acquisitions and mergers.

international banking, until early in the twentieth century, was largely dominated by European banks.

The first foreign branch of a U.S. national bank was established in Buenos Aires by Citibank of New York in 1914. At that time, there were 26 U.S. state-chartered banks operating foreign branches in comparison to nearly 2,000 overseas branches of European banks. The number increased rapidly to 181 branches in 1920, to 457 branches in 1969, and to 779 branches in 1980, with total assets of $290 billion. Table 1.3 shows the number, assets, and geographical distribution of U.S. overseas branch banks in selected years prior to 1980.

Three factors contributed to U.S. branch banking expansion overseas. During World War I, the European countries were unable to provide for their own needs and supply customers in foreign markets. This vacuum provided an impetus for U.S. international banking expansion. Money-center U.S. banks opened offices to channel funds and to finance American foreign commerce. The expansion paralleled the growth in trade, as exports-imports rose from $4.3 billion in 1914 to $13.5 billion in 1920.[18] A second impetus further accelerated the branching expansion when in 1919 the Federal Reserve Act, Section 25(a), was amended to aid financing and stimulation of foreign trade. The amendment, known as the Edge Act, authorized establishment of Edge corporations to engage in international deposit-taking and investment activities, under specified rules, governed by the

Table 1.3

Assets, Numbers, and Geographical Distribution of Overseas Branches of U.S. Banks

	Number of Branches				
	1914	1920	1939	1950	1969
Europe	7	29	28	15	104
Latin America	6	122	61	60	265
Far East	13	30	21	20	81
Africa and Middle East	–	–	–	–	7
World Total	26	181	110	95	457

Year	Number		Total Assets (Billions of Dollars)	
	Overseas Branches	Edge Act Corporations	Overseas Branches	Edge Act Corporations
1970	532	77	52.6	4.6
1973	699	103	108.8	6.9
1976	731	117	174.5	11.1
1979	779	132	290.0	16.3

Source: P. Henry Mueller, "A Conspectus for Offshore Lenders," **Offshore Lending by U.S. Commercial Banks**, Robert Morris Associates, 1981, pp. 3-4.

Federal Reserve Board. These rules were revised in 1963, 1979, and 1985, under Regulation K, to broaden the scope and activities of Edge corporations in trade financing, foreign investment, foreign branch establishment, and foreign ownership of Edge corporations.

The third factor that aided in the expansion of U.S. overseas branches in the late 1960s and early 1970s was the market force of competition and the desire of U.S. banks for diversification. The European and Latin American markets provided a new opportunity for expansion into the diversified and attractive markets of the friendly nations. Between 1970 and 1979, the total assets of U.S. overseas branches of American banks increased from $52.6 billion to $290 billion, an expansion unmatched by any country active in international banking at that time.

Major factors contributing to this expansion were the restoration of the value of the dollar as the standard of value in currency exchange-rate fluctuations after World War II, and the successes of the Marshall Plan in Europe and the Bretton Woods Agreement of the 1940s. The expansion has had its greatest impact on foreign credit, as the recycling of petrodollars has provided an abundant supply of dollars via Eurocurrency markets. The foreign credit of U.S. overseas branches increased at an annual average of 22 percent from 1960 to 1972, and thereafter by 36 percent until 1979.[19] This annual growth rate far exceeded growth in assets by a margin of 2 to 1 and growth in the number of offices by a margin of 6 to 1.

RATIONALE AND FINANCIAL GOALS

Modern international banking did not develop until the 1960s. The United States in the 1930s and 1940s, faced with the Great Depression and World War II, did not develop a significant movement in the banking arena. Similarly, the decade of the 1950s was a transitional period. Three factors played a key in the expansion of international banking in the 1960s: the rapid growth of Europe and Japan, the emergence of the Eurodollar market, and the increased internationalization of businesses outside the home-market area. In the 1960s, U.S. banks moved abroad. In the 1970s, foreign banks came to the United States for the same reasons, namely, financial opportunities, favorable government regulations, risk diversification, and expansion into new territories. These factors provided a rationale for the internationalization of banking expansion and the progression toward multilateral trade financing. Certainly profit motivation and, in some respects, saturation of the domestic market played a key role in persuading banks to consider investments abroad.

The combined incentives for the U.S. banks to expand their overseas operations were: (a) Regulation Q, an interest rate ceiling on deposits in the United States, and the reserve requirement on domestic deposits, which caused a heavy toll on domestic banking operations in the relatively high rate period of the second half of the 1960s; (b) the rapid progress and development of the Eurodollar market; (c) the relative strength of the U.S. dollar, stimulating investment abroad; and (d) the voluntary credit restraint program of 1965, which imposed restrictions on U.S. companies' foreign direct investment, and foreign loans by U.S. financial institutions. In the 1960s, 8 U.S. banks had 131 overseas banking offices; in 1987, 153 Federal Reserve member banks maintained over 902 offices abroad. Their assets grew from $3.5 billion in 1960 to $350 billion in 1987.[20] By one estimate, in the 1980s, the U.S. banking assets abroad represented approximately 20 percent of total U.S. banking assets.[21]

The rationale and financial goals of the U.S. banking expansion overseas and foreign banks' expansion in the United States are associated with the economic reality at the time. Since the foundation was initiated and developed in the decades of the 1960s and 1970s, the focus of discussion here should be centered on those periods. From 1960 to 1980, the real GNP of the major industrial countries of France, Germany, Japan, the United Kingdom, and the United States grew at an average rate of 3 to 7 percent.[22] This rapid economic expansion required investment of a large sum. In some cases the funding was not available domestically. Thus, expansion into foreign markets to raise the needed funds was required. In other cases, surpluses provided a means for banks to seek customers abroad. As a result, banks were forced to expand beyond home markets.

A summary of data on the global network of banking presence for the period 1960 to 1979 is presented in tables 1.4 and 1.5. As indicated in table 1.4, the United States had only 8 banks in operation overseas in 1961, compared with 17 for the United Kingdom and 16 for France. However, by 1970, the U.S. banking presence increased to 68, and France's to 19, while

Table 1.4
Number of Foreign Banks by Country of Origin, Major Industrialized Countries

Country of Origin	1961	1970	1978
France	16	19	24
Germany	2	2	12
Japan	6	11	23
United Kingdom	17	13	20
United States	8	68	136

Home Country	Banks Among the World's 50 Largest		
	1959	1969	1979
France	3	3	4
Germany	3	4	8
Japan	6	10	14
United Kingdom	5	4	4
United States	20	14	6

Source: Diane Page and Neal M. Soss, "Some Evidence on Transnational Banking Structure," **Foreign Acquisition of U.S. Banks**, The Comptroller of the Currency, and Robert F. Dame, Inc., 1981, p. 145 (the first half of the table). And Dwight B. Crane and Samuel L. Hayes III, "The Evolution of International Banking Competition and Its Implications for Regulation," **Journal of Bank Research**, 1983, p. 49 (the second half of the table).

Table 1.5
Number of Foreign Bank Branches and Agencies

Country	By Country of Origin			By Host Country		
	1961	1970	1978	1961	1970	1978
France	361	179	226	39	72	142
Germany	2	5	47	16	46	86
Japan	27	65	131	34	38	79
United Kingdom	4,184	4,192	1,114	40	127	467
United States	128	467	670	34	63	239
Others	585	1,207	2,150	5,124	5,769	3,325
Total	5,287	6,115	4,338	5,287	6,115	4,338

Source: Diane Page and Neal M. Soss, "Some Evidence
on Transnational Banking Structure,"
Foreign Acquisition of U.S. Banks, The
Comptroller of Currency, and Robert F. Dame,
Inc., 1981, pp. 144-145.

the presence of U.K. banks decreased to 13. No other country showed significant growth of such magnitude as the United States.

Table 1.5 similarly shows the number of foreign banks' branches and agencies by country of origin. U.S. banks' branches and agencies in other countries grew from 128 in 1961 to 670 in 1978, while the number of branches and agencies of other countries' banks in the United States grew from 34 in 1961 to 239 in 1978. Dominant banking countries of the eighteenth and nineteenth centuries, such as Italy, Germany, France and the United Kingdom showed weakness in their global performance, as their presence slowed down or decreased during the second half of the twentieth century.

Overall, it appears that the key loser was the United Kingdom, as its dominant financial empire collapsed due to the loss of the colonies, economic difficulties at home, and stronger competition abroad. The U.S. progress of the 1960s and 1970s was also overshadowed by the Japanese financial strength of the 1980s. The United States, once the record holder with 20 banks among the world's 50 largest banks, relinquished its position with only 4 banks, whereas the Japanese expanded their dominance to 20 of the world's 50 largest banks by the end of 1988. As indicated in the second half of table 1.5, subtitled "by host country," the major industrial countries were the donors and the developing countries were the recipients of the foreign bank branches from 1961 to 1978. The flow is in accordance with the wealth of the nations and the pattern of trade.

NOTES

1. These merchant houses included some giants like the Medicis in Italy, Fuggers and Welsers in Germany, and Jacques Coeur in France.

2. Antwerp, Belgium, was known as a prominent place for European governments to finance their war chests. For a century, Antwerp advanced via trade and war financing to become a prestigious money center in Europe.

3. Herbert Feis, *Europe: The World Banker, 1870-1914*, W. W. Norton and Company, New York, 1965, p. 19.

4. Ibid., pp. 22-33.

5. Yoon S. Park and Jack Zwick, *International Banking in Theory and Practice*, Addison-Wesley Publishing Company, Reading, Mass., 1985, p. 3.

6. Feis, p. 23.

7. Data provided here were derived from Feis, pp. 44 and 51, and from Paul H. Emden, *Money Powers of Europe in the Nineteenth and Twentieth Centuries*, Garland Publishing, London, 1983, and other historical notes.

8. Feis, pp. 63-68, and Emden, pp. 1-63. Feis, on page 63 of his book, estimated the number of banks in Germany in 1872 at about 130. Others recorded 135 and 141 banks at approximately the same time. The four dominant ones are The Deutsch Bank, Diskonto-Gesellschaft, the Dresdner Bank, and the Darmstadler Bank. These four are known collectively as the four Ds.

9. Feis, p. 210.

10. "World Bank Policies and Operations," *The World Bank*, Annual Report, 1988, p. 80.

11. Kang Rae Cho, Suresh Krishnan, and Douglas Nigh, "The State of Foreign Banking Presence in the United States," paper presented to the Academy of International Business, London, England, 1986, p. 1.

12. Klaus Peter Jacobs, "The Development of International and Multinational Banking," *Columbia Journal of World Business*, Winter 1975, pp. 33-39.

13. Sarkis J. Khoury, *Dynamics of International Banking*, Praeger Publishing Company, New York, 1980, p. 86.

14. "The 1987 Foreign Banking in America Directory," *Institutional Investor*, September 1987, p. 306.

15. Khoury, pp. 86-88.

16. Ibid., pp. 87-88.

17. Prior to this period, the foreign banks could operate agencies, representative offices, and subsidiaries, but not branches in New York.

18. United States Bureau of Census, *Historical Statistics of the United States, Colonial Time to 1957*, Washington, D.C., 1960, pp. 550-552.

19. Josephine F. Polomski, "Voluntary Foreign Credit Restraint Program Spurs Foreign-Based Activities of U.S. Banks," *Business Review*, Federal Reserve Bank of Philadelphia, June 1973, p. 8.

20. James V. Houpt, "International Trends for U.S. Banks and Banking Markets," Staff Study No. 156, Board of Governors of the Federal Reserve System, May 1988.

21. James C. Baker and John K. Ryan, Jr., "An Evaluation of U.S. Federal Regulation of Foreign Bank Operations," *Issues in Banking Regulation*, Spring 1987, p. 28.

22. International Monetary Fund, *International Financial Statistics*, various issues.

2 Institutional Structure of International Banking: Foreign Banking Offices in the United States

The type of organizational office of multinational banks reflects their worldwide strategy. The international banking activity of these institutions is determined by their policy objectivity and the extent of their desire to participate in international financial transactions. A multinational bank must decide whether it is advantageous to be physically present outside the home market or to select a correspondent form of international banking. A correspondent banking relationship requires neither an establishment nor an acquisition of a local banking entity, nor does it require physical presence abroad. On the other hand, physical presence in the form of a local entity necessitates provision of a wider range of services. At the same time, the entity accommodates a good foundation for further expansion.

The organizational form chosen by foreign banks is influenced by the front-office cost of a new banking establishment, the state and federal laws of the host country, and the objective of the home office in defining the principal purpose of the expansion. If the expansion is for the penetration of a new market, then physical presence in the host country is essential. However, if the purpose is to facilitate international transactions of the home country's clients and involvement in the international currency market, then correspondent banking or transactions via "shell" banks may be the proper operational procedure.

Foreign banks generally gain access to the U.S. banking market either by establishing their own offices or by acquiring interest in existing financial institutions. Foreign banks in the United States choose one of seven organizational forms: agency, branch, subsidiary, representative office, investment company, international banking facility, and Edge corporation. The major difference between an agency and branch bank is that an agency does not accept deposits. Subsidiary banks are heavily oriented toward the domestic market and retail banking. Representative offices perform no banking functions at all, providing only information and advice to clients. Edge corporations engage in international trade financing and depository operations. All investment companies located in New York City engage in investment and financial activities related to commerce. International banking facilities (IBFs) are involved in money market transactions and offer daily time deposits to nonbank residents.

FOREIGN BANKING DEVELOPMENT IN THE UNITED STATES

During the decade of the 1970s, foreign banks grew in terms of both total assets and number of offices. As shown in table 2.1, from 1972 to 1988 the total number of foreign banking offices (excluding representative offices) increased from 105 to 674. Branches gained substantial strength at the ex-

Table 2.1
Number of U.S. Banking Institutions Owned by Foreign Banks

Year	Agencies	Branches	Subsidiaries	Investment Companies	Edge Corp.	Total
1972	53	24	25	3	–	105
1973	62	27	27	3	–	119
1974	75	52	30	3	–	160
1975	82	60	33	4	–	179
1976	91	67	33	5	–	196
1977	115	93	34	5	–	247
1978	140	110	39	6	–	295
1979	164	125	39	6	–	334
1980	178	152	44	6	10	390
1981	185	194	46	7	23	455
1982	190	233	52	8	31	514
1983	182	272	56	8	35	553
1984	176	305	66	10	39	596
1985	182	315	76	11	–	584
1986	195	324	79	12	33	643
1987	201	334	86	9	30	660
1988	206	346	84	10	28	674

Source: Calculated from Board of Governors of the Federal Reserve System, **Statistical Release**, 1972–79; and **Structural Data for U.S. Offices of Foreign Banks**, 1980–88. The total for 1985 excludes Edge banks.

pense of agencies, as agencies' numbers declined from 1983 to mid-1986. Other forms of foreign banking offices experienced slow but steady growth. With 362 representative offices in the United States in 1988, the grand total number of foreign banking offices has reached 1036.[1]

The total assets of foreign banking institutions grew from $26 billion in 1972 to $198 billion in 1980, an increase of seven and one-half times. The growth in assets continued in the 1980s, to a record high of $653 billion, with branches and subsidiaries as major beneficiaries. Table 2.2 illustrates this trend. The offices of foreign branches control nearly 66 percent of all the assets of the foreign banking offices in the United States. The three offices of agencies, branches, and subsidiaries together control 99 percent of all foreign banks assets and 94 percent of all foreign bank offices. The preferences of foreign banks are revealed in the types of offices they select for conduct of international banking activities.

FOREIGN BANKING OFFICES

This discussion of foreign banking offices concentrates on the major components of these institutions in the United States. The six major offices of foreign banks are representative office, agency, branch, subsidiary commercial bank, investment company, and Edge corporation. The following discussion describes the characteristics of each institution, the choices of business forms, assets size, and the number and growth of offices in recent years.

Representative Offices

The primary function of foreign bank representative offices in the United States are to attract business for the parent bank and to develop correspondent relationships with local U.S. banks. They provide a convenient and inexpensive means of establishing a presence in a new location. These offices are prohibited from engaging in general banking activities, but are permitted to receive checks for forwarding to the home office and to handle the signing of loan papers.

Representative offices are regulated by state law and must be registered with the secretary of the treasury, normally within 180 days after opening. These offices are not required by the state to secure a license, except in California. A simple form of registration with state banking regulatory offices is sufficient. Since the basic function of these offices is to provide information, advice, and local contacts for the parent bank's clients, their contributions could fall into four categories. First, they act as liaisons between the parent bank and the local domestic banks. This function includes advising clients from the home country with an interest in overseas investment and establishing local contacts for the customers with any local businesses within the area

Table 2.2
Total Assets of U.S. Banking Institutions Owned by Foreign Banks
(Millions of U.S. Dollars)

Year	Agencies	Branches	Subsidiaries	Investment Companies	Edge Corp.	Total
1972	14,421	5,676	4,646	1,362	–	26,105
1973	21,752	7,081	5,922	1,858	–	36,612
1974	28,790	12,330	11,955	2,320	–	55,395
1975	27,875	12,675	13,386	2,753	–	63,689
1976	30,086	26,892	15,544	2,323	–	74,845
1977	28,999	43,190	18,291	2,216	–	92,695
1978	39,751	62,546	22,779	2,510	–	127,585
1979	54,102	84,928	26,375	2,983	–	168,388
1980	58,079	89,654	50,207	–	175	198,115
1981	51,134	120,890	75,708	2,896	590	251,218
1982	52,297	155,096	89,348	3,023	1,257	301,021
1983	52,349	175,609	100,789	3,258	1,332	333,337
1984	56,613	215,265	105,555	–	881	378,314
1985	61,018	250,387	125,842	3,274	–	440,521
1986	79,220	317,575	123,919	3,888	2,333	526,935
1987	86,599	374,095	127,962	3,402	2,423	594,481
1988	83,600	430,154	132,348	4,213	2,928	653,244

Source: Calculated from Board of Governors of the Federal Reserve
System, **Statistical Release**, 1972-79; and **Structural
Data for U.S. Offices of Foreign Banks**, 1980-88.

of the representative office residence. Second, the representative offices serve as an information center, collecting and analyzing business data, and providing advice to businesses interested in obtaining specific information about host-country business and cultural affairs. Third, they provide credit analysis of local firms and economic and political intelligence about the host country. And, finally, representative offices often serve as forerunners for other forms of activities, such as the opening of an agency or a branch office.

The main advantage of these offices is their inexpensive formation. A representative office is usually small, often consisting of one or two executives, a few clerks, and general office workers. Since the representative office does not transact banking business, it can be licensed easily with a relatively low budget. Also, it can easily be closed or changed to another form of banking establishment. The major disadvantage of a representative office is its limited ability to conduct general banking activities. Because of its smallness, it may lack the breadth and depth that a larger establishment could provide, and may also lack the managerial skill required in the updating and collection of data and other necessary information essential to address the complex world of the banking industry.

Accurate data about the number of representative offices in the United States, in the early stage, are difficult to obtain. By the year 1972, the number of these offices is estimated to have been nearly 120. The numbers increased to 280 by 1980 and to 362 by year-end 1988.[2] The representative offices' functions and depth of activities have not changed over time, because basically they cannot make loans, take deposits, issue drafts and letters of credit, or even deal in the Eurocurrency market. However, they have served their primary function of being a relatively inexpensive means of establishing a presence in a new location.

Agencies

An agency is established in a host country by a parent bank to carry on normal banking services and activities and to finance international trade. In accordance with the IBA of 1978, an agency cannot accept deposits from U.S. citizens or residents if they are not engaged in international activities. An agency, in addition to being prohibited from taking deposits, is also prevented from selling certificates of deposit and activities related to trust functions. It may, however, elect to be state or federally chartered. The latter falls under the chartering supervision of the comptroller of the currency.

One of the primary roles of an agency is to finance trade for the home office customers and to serve as a fiscal agent for the home-country government. Agencies may arrange commercial and industrial loans; finance trade; issue letters of credit; accept, buy, and collect drafts or bills of exchange; conduct foreign exchange activities; and deal in the Eurocurrency market. Despite the fact that they are barred from accepting deposits from host-country citizens, they may instead keep "credit balances," which consist of receipts from transactions and undisbursed loan balances, and in fact serve the same purposes as short-term transaction accounts. Agencies also can borrow from parent and affiliate banks.

Foreign Agencies in the United States. Traditionally, agencies in the United States were free to operate interstate bank lending and borrowing. They have been relatively inexpensive to establish and operate, as they do not require a separate capital base, and they have generally been licensed where foreign banks have been unable to establish branches. Since agencies do not take deposits, they are held neither to the Federal Reserve requirements that specify the amount of funds needed in the cash balance, nor to the 10 percent maximum loan requirements for an individual customer, thereby allowing them to make larger loan contributions. One other noticeable advantage is that most foreign bank agencies operate with low overhead costs, because they do not require extensive office facilities.

The growth in the number of U.S. agencies of foreign banks was briefly halted between 1983 and 1986, but progress resumed thereafter. As revealed in table 2.3, in 1988 there were 206 active foreign banking agencies in the United States, with total assets of $83.6 billion. The majority of these offices are small, with assets of less than $250 million, but the large-sized asset agencies are increasing. Most agencies are state chartered, with 38 percent grandfathered under IBA. Nearly half of these offices are located on the West Coast, in Los Angeles and San Francisco.

Because agencies deal mainly with international financing, U.S. domestic banks have not been concerned about their progress and competitive ability. In California, agencies are barred from any form of trust activity, but are allowed to accept foreign deposits once they secure approval from the state regulatory authorities. In New York, agencies are required to maintain 100 percent reserves in U.S. assets against their liabilities to the public. This action has not been interpreted as a requirement to keep reserves against their deposits, but as a safeguard against risky loan activities, as well as a way to limit foreign bank agencies from strongly competing with local banks in the area of international loan activities.

Historically, agencies allocate one-third of their assets for transactions with the parent bank while one-fourth is in the form of industrial and commercial loans. However, this allocation varies among banks of different countries. For example, Canadian agencies allocate nearly 45 percent of their banking assets activities with the parent and only 25 percent for commercial and industrial loans.[3] Of the total number of agencies in the United States, 85 percent are from Canada, Japan, and Western Europe.

Branch Banks

A foreign branch bank is a legal and operational part of the parent charter bank. A branch is not a separate legal entity; instead its assets, liabilities, and credit policies are those of the parent bank. Foreign branch banks are subject to two sets of banking regulations: home and host-countries' regulations. They carry on complete domestic and international banking operations, subject to the constraints of local regulations and the extent of activities desired by the parent bank. Branches may conduct a full range of banking services and are subject to the laws of taxation at home. Their activities include, but are not limited to, deposit taking, credit extension and lending, participation in money market activities, trade financing, and other banking activities related to the pursuit of home-country clients and competition with the host countries' local banks. A foreign branch has three major advantages. First, it has the full faith and credit of the parent bank. Second, its services to customers are on a worldwide basis, thus providing a larger market base. Third, because most branches are located in key international money centers, they have access to a larger capital base and may tap deposits from interbank or Eurocurrency markets. The key disadvantage is that a branch's parent bank can be sued at the local level for the debt of the branch. Despite this negative characteristic, bankers have found it more advantageous to set up branches abroad than any other form of entity for the conduct of their international business operations.

Foreign Branch Banking in the United States. In the United States, a foreign branch bank is an integral part of the parent bank, established under state or federal laws. It provides the opportunity to develop complete banking operations, with the added capacity of full deposit-taking powers. Prior to the IBA of 1978, branches of foreign banks were not subject to Federal Reserve requirements but were free to operate in more than one state. Currently, foreign branches have the option to obtain a federal license from the comptroller of the currency, but may not establish an office in a state whose laws prohibit foreign bank branching operations. A federally licensed branch has limitations and activities similar to national banks and may participate in all activities permitted by law for domestic banks, including fiduciary activities. In addition, federal branches accepting retail deposits must be insured by the FDIC and subject to all the requirements of capital equivalency on deposits as a Federal Reserve member bank. Branch banks that are not involved in retail banking and deposit taking from the general public, and state-chartered branches that accept only deposits permissible for Edges, are not required to carry FDIC insurance for daily operations.

A review of the structural components of the foreign branch banks in the United States (table 2.4) reveals that there are 346 foreign branches with total assets of $430 billion. More than one-third of these offices have assets exceeding $500 million. In comparison with other forms of foreign banking offices in the United States, branches are larger in assets size and financial strength.

These offices are more prevalent in the eastern part of the United States, with nearly 65 percent selecting New York City as the home base. They are very progressive in establishing international banking facilities (IBFs), and a large number of them elect to be federally chartered, to accommodate their general business activities.

Lending Activities and Behavioral Trends. Foreign branches have traditionally focused their lending operations on home-country clients. However, in recent years, they have become increasingly involved in the U.S. corporate banking market. Most are engaged in wholesale banking and business lending. Their other activities include trade financing, foreign exchange transactions, investment in dollar resources, and activities related to overseas funds transfers and participation in issuance of certificates of deposit and banker's acceptances.

Data from the Federal Reserve Bulletin on assets and liabilities of U.S. branches and agencies of foreign banks indicate that foreign branch banks allocated nearly one-third of their assets to commercial and industrial loans, one-fifth to interagency activities with U.S. institutions and foreign agencies

Table 2.3
U.S. Agencies of Foreign Banks

Year	No. of Bank Offices	Total Assets ($M)	Number of Offices in Assets Size ($M)						Largest Assets Size ($M)	Smallest Assets Size ($M)
			<100	100-250	250-500	500-1000	>1000	Not Reported		
1980	178	58,079	88	38	19	16	16	1	4,543	1.1
1981	185	51,134	93	39	16	19	14	4	2,653	1.2
1982	190	52,297	91	43	21	20	11	4	2,576	0.3
1983	182	52,349	81	46	20	13	17	5	2,615	0.3
1984	176	56,613	80	36	23	15	16	6	2,768	0.3
1985	182	61,018	75	46	18	14	19	10	3,346	0.3
1986	195	79,220	81	50	21	12	24	7	4,621	0.0
1987	201	86,599	74	59	24	10	25	9	6,211	0.0
1988	206	83,600	74	54	30	20	18	10	6,637	0.0

Number of Offices

Year	Los Angeles	New York	San Francisco	Miami	Atlanta	Houston	F	G	S	X
1980	56	61	32	13	9	–	5	132	173	–
1981	60	52	36	21	9	–	9	117	176	48
1982	61	44	36	28	11	–	9	110	181	99
1983	59	33	35	32	12	–	8	97	175	105
1984	57	27	33	33	13	–	8	90	168	104
1985	59	30	31	33	13	2	7	87	175	105
1986	62	29	30	36	14	10	9	86	186	106
1987	62	31	31	36	14	12	10	84	191	107
1988	65	33	29	36	14	13	12	79	194	100

Dominant Cities – Number of Offices

Source: Calculated from Board of Governors of the Federal Reserve System, **Structural Data for U.S. Offices of Foreign Banks**, 1980-88.

a Less than $100,000.

Definition of Codes:

F-National Charter

S-State Charter

I-Insured by FDIC

G-Grandfathered under IBA   X-Entity established as IBF

Table 2.4
U.S. Branches of Foreign Banks

Year	No. of Bank Offices	Total Assets ($M)	Number of Offices in Assets Size ($M)						Largest Assets Size ($M)	Smallest Assets Size ($M)
			<100	100-250	250-500	500-1000	>1000	Not Reported		
1980	152	89,654	45	23	26	15	33	10	5,825	1.2
1981	194	120,890	65	37	18	24	39	11	5,790	2.0
1982	233	155,096	73	46	30	16	52	16	7,093	2.5
1983	272	175,609	85	60	35	27	49	16	8,874	0.0
1984	305	215,265	97	72	31	29	57	19	8,960	0.0
1985	315	250,387	92	70	39	27	64	23	10,691	0.2
1986	324	317,575	96	55	46	30	71	26	15,304	1.2
1987	334	374,095	79	62	50	31	80	32	17,516	0.8
1988	346	430,154	79	65	53	33	92	24	21,610	0.6

Dominant Cities - Number of Offices

Year	New York	Chicago	Los Angeles	Seattle	Boston	San Francisco	F	G	I	S	X
1980	92	32	0	8	4	1	8	143	23	144	–
1981	122	36	2	10	5	1	26	135	31	168	81
1982	147	42	9	10	5	1	45	137	32	188	139
1983	178	43	12	11	5	5	64	137	34	208	169
1984	199	44	17	11	5	9	80	138	38	225	195
1985	206	46	18	11	5	10	87	135	39	228	202
1986	214	47	18	10	7	10	88	135	39	236	207
1987	220	53	20	10	8	9	85	135	39	249	212
1988	224	54	25	9	8	8	84	134	53	262	213

(Number of Offices)

Source: Calculated from Board of Governors of the Federal Reserve System, **Structural Data for U.S. Offices of Foreign Banks**, 1980-88. See definition of codes in Table 2.3.

a Less than $50,000

abroad, and only 2 to 3 percent to retail banking. Nevertheless, despite this historical trend toward wholesale banking, their retail banking activities have been increasing in recent years.

Naturally, not all foreign branches behave alike. Their behavior depends largely on the duration of their presence in the United States, the nationality of the owners, their office location, and the banking regulations in the state in which they decide to open an office as a home base. For example, in California until the passage of IBA in 1978, a foreign branch could not accept deposits unless it carried FDIC insurance. This requirement prevented foreign branches from entering into the California banking market. New York State, on the other hand, has permitted foreign branching since 1961, including deposit taking, but has required the branches to keep liquid, short-term, money market instruments equivalent to their liabilities for safety reasons. The same is true about the Illinois state banking law that has permitted branching only in the Chicago area with 100 percent of the liabilities in liquid securities, to defend against unforeseen occurrences.

Based on the nationality of the foreign branches, different preferences can be deduced. Western European banks prefer the eastern part of the United States and wholesale banking services. Canadian banks, on the other hand, prefer the eastern states and are very active in retail banking. Both Canadian and Western European banks show heavy involvement in transactions with parent banks to pursue the parent's obligations and those of the affiliated organizations. Japanese banks are a mixed bag of wholesale and retail banking. They select western states as their home base of activities, are more inclined toward retail banking, and are less involved than European and Canadian banks in dealing with parent banks.

Limited Branching. Limited branching developed pursuant to the International Banking Act of 1978, to provide not only flexibility but also regulatory control over the specific activities of the foreign branches. Like a full branch, the limited branch office is subject to the regulatory authority of the Federal Reserve System and is subject to the comptroller of the currency for federal chartering, or state banking authorities for a state charter. From the lending point of view, its power is parallel to a national bank. Therefore, branch offices can participate in both retail banking and international lending activities. However, their deposit-taking activities are limited to international operations and they are barred from interstate operations. Limited branches are neither required to become a member of the Fed nor required to be insured by the FDIC. Similarly, they are barred from nonbanking activities contained in the Bank Holding Company Act.

Subsidiary Banks

A subsidiary bank is a separate, legally incorporated bank chartered in the host country under the local laws of the land. It is owned entirely or in major part by a foreign parent, to conduct general banking business. A foreign-owned subsidiary is a full-service bank, involved in both domestic and international business. It is the closest form of foreign bank office to a national bank in regard to the services rendered on a day-to-day basis. A subsidiary bank may be either a state or national bank. National banks are chartered by the comptroller of the currency, while the state banks are governed by the state banking authorities. Subsidiaries are normally created when foreign branches are prohibited by state law or when retail banking is the focus of operation. One may establish a subsidiary via acquisition of an existing bank or by opening a new one. A national charter must be a member of the Federal Reserve and be insured by the FDIC.

As U.S. corporations, subsidiaries are subject to all the regulatory requirements and restrictions imposed upon U.S. banks, including geographic restrictions to one-state operations, lending limits based upon size of capital base, prohibition from further acquisitions in other states (Bank Holding Company Act), and the requirement for the parent organization to divest itself of investment banking (Glass-Steagall Act). A subsidiary is subject exclusively to the laws of the host country and the majority of the directors of the national charter must be U.S. citizens. One key advantage of a subsidiary over a branch or agency is its local flavor. Due to the fact that the majority of the directors are U.S. citizens and thus are extensively involved in retail banking and deposit taking, in the eyes of customers a subsidiary is a U.S. bank. Thus, most have no difficulty in attracting local customers.

Foreign Subsidiaries in the United States. Table 2.5 shows the activities, location, and assets size of the foreign subsidiaries in the United States in the 1980s. After branches, this form of office is the most popular among foreign investors today. Nearly 55 percent of subsidiary bank offices have assets exceeding $250 million, with 26 percent controlling over $1 billion. The largest foreign bank office in the United States, Marine Midland Bank of North America, a subsidiary of Hong Kong and Shanghai Bank, has assets exceeding $20 billion. The majority of these offices are insured by the FDIC, due to the nature of their retail banking activities. Proportionally, a larger percentage of the subsidiary banks are federally chartered, with California and New York State as their likely main home base. Subsidiary banks, like branches, have advanced at the expense of agencies, as more foreign banking institutions have shown interest in retail banking transactions. New York City is the major beneficiary of the subsidiaries' office expansion in recent years.

Two key elements separating subsidiary banks from agencies and branches are the high front-office cost of establishment and the ownership nationality of these institutions. A subsidiary is the most expensive form of opening a bank office, requiring a large investment and an expert team of managers for the operation of a de novo office. Subsidiary banks are the favorite of non–Western European nations. The countries from east and south Asia

Table 2.5
U.S. Subsidiaries of Foreign Banks[a]

Year	No. of Bank Offices	Total Assets ($M)	Number of Offices in Assets Size ($M)						Largest Assets Size ($M)	Smallest Assets Size ($M)
			<100	100-250	250-500	500-1000	>1000	Not Reported		
1980	44	50,207	10	9	4	9	11	1	11,088	8.3
1981	46	75,708	6	10	4	9	15	2	19,893	11.6
1982	52	89,348	8	10	5	7	20	2	22,016	5.4
1983	56	100,789	9	11	6	6	22	2	21,304	11.9
1984	66	105,555	12	16	6	7	23	2	17,483	11.4
1985	76	125,847	16	17	8	5	26	4	17,815	6.7
1986	79	123,919	18	12	13	4	26	6	20,484	6.8
1987	86	127,963	19	13	15	6	27	6	20,344	6.3
1988	84	132,348	20	11	15	9	22	7	20,621	1.4

	Dominant Cities - Number of Offices			Number of Offices				
Year	New York	Los Angeles	San Francisco	F	G	I	S	X
1980	21	8	8	5	38	42	39	-
1981	21	10	10	6	37	44	40	21
1982	21	12	10	10	38	50	42	29
1983	21	13	10	12	38	54	44	29
1984	23	13	10	16	38	64	50	31
1985	23	14	9	25	37	70	51	34
1986	28	13	8	24	36	73	55	35
1987	36	13	8	24	36	79	62	38
1988	36	12	6	23	33	77	61	36

Source: Calculated from Board of Governors of the Federal Reserve System, **Structural Data for U.S. Offices of Foreign Banks**, 1980-88. See definition of codes in Table 2.3.

- U.S. commercial banks, more than 25 percent owned by foreign banks.

and Japan have selected the subsidiary type of banking office, and California has benefited most from this movement, because the state banking law prohibited branching without FDIC insurance in the 1970s, and because it has a large Chinese, Japanese, and Korean population. Similarly, Western European subsidiaries favored New York State and other East Coast locations.

Retail banking accounts for 40 percent of foreign subsidiaries' activities in the United States. These offices devote limited amounts of resources to parent-relationship activities, an average of 5 percent of their total assets. As with agencies and branches, commercial and industrial loans account for one-third of their total assets; but unlike agencies and branches, one area of strength of subsidiaries is trust activities. Their investment in this area is approximately 85 percent of all their activities in money and capital markets.[4] In general, foreign subsidiary office activities are very similar to those of a national bank, both for retail banking and international financing. Business loans account for two-fifths of the deposits at subsidiaries, indicating that a relatively smaller amount of the allocated budget and funds goes for business lending activities.

Affiliate Bank. One form of subsidiary bank is known as an "affiliate." An affiliate is a joint venture bank between two or more countries. It is locally owned in part, but not necessarily controlled by a foreign parent. An affiliate bank may be formed via acquisition of an existing bank or a newly formed de novo office. Three key advantages of an affiliate bank are (1) the financial risk diversification with joint ownership, (2) its access to the expertise of several owners with different international experiences, and (3) the international connection as various nationalities join to form an organization. This last factor expands the scope of the bank's activities and provides more flexibility in its market participation and its conduct of international business activities. The drawbacks of a joint venture are two: (1) related to ownership-policy decisions and (2) related to the way capital, resources, management, and staffing must be allocated and planned. Owners from different nationalities and backgrounds may present conflicting styles of leadership and detract from uniformity of managerial-policy decisions, thus possibly having an impact on the progress of an affiliate bank. Similarly, the allocation of resources and staffing procedures may cause conflicts and impediments in the decision-making process and the advancement of this form of banking office.

Foreign Investment Companies

Investment companies are in the venture capital business, dealing with small and medium-size companies in existing capital markets or new territories. Their activities include high-risk trade financing, acceptances and remittances of funds, foreign exchange transactions, and the provision of short- and medium-term loans. Due to the nature of their activities, most investment companies are located in or near money-center cities. In the United States, all ten investment companies that are majority owned by foreign banks are in New York City. New York State provides these institutions with tax incentives to attract their attention in the early stage of development.

Prior to the passage of the IBA of 1978, foreign branches and agencies that were not under the Federal Reserve's jurisdiction could become involved in investment banking activities and the purchase of nonbank investment companies The IBA stipulated that, until December 31, 1985, a foreign bank could continue to engage in nonbanking activities in the United States, in the state in which it was lawfully engaged on July 26, 1978. Thus, a foreign bank could retain ownership or control of any voting shares of any domestically controlled office engaged in the business of underwriting, distribution, or trade of securities. However, after the above date, new foreign banks had to choose between investment company and commercial banking activities. In reality, before the 1978 act, the Glass-Steagall Act did not apply to foreign bank nonbanking activities.

As a result, the new provision limited the growth of investment companies by forcing them to choose between the activities related to commercial banking and investment banking. Historically, these institutions invested approximately 50 percent of their loan portfolio in commercial and industrial (C&I) loans. The transactions with parent and affiliates accounted for only 10 percent of their assets. Funds tapped from demand and time deposits were nearly one-third of their total liabilities and equity. Security investment made up 10 percent of their assets, and borrowing was evenly split between the interbank market and other related institutions.[5]

Investment Companies' Performance. New York investment companies are chartered under the New York State Investment Company Act, Article XII, to engage in international or foreign banking activities. Like agencies, New York investment companies cannot accept deposits from U.S. citizens or residents except for credit balances, but may be involved in the conduct of full-scale lending operations, the issuance of acceptances and remittances of funds, foreign exchange transactions, and related activities. As presented in table 2.6, of the ten investment companies operating in New York, half have assets under $250 million; only one has assets exceeding $1 billion. Their smallness limits their progress and restricts the area of their activities to investment banking.

The three largest investment companies in the United States are French-American Banking Corporation with assets of $2.3 billion, PK Banken International with assets of $622 million, and DNC American Banking Corporation with assets of $571 million.[6] Some recent large acquisitions in investment company-related activities include the purchase of the Boston Stock Exchange by Dresdner Bank and the Hope-Bank of Munich, and the

Table 2.6
New York State Investment Companies, Majority Owned by Foreign Banks

Year	No. of Bank Offices	Total Assets ($M)	<100	100-250	250-500	500-1000	>1000	Largest Assets Size ($M)	Smallest Assets Size ($M)
			Number of Offices in Assets Size ($M)						
1980	6	-	-	-	-	-	-	-	-
1981	7	2,896	1	3	0	1	1	1,140	92.8
1982	8	3,023	2	2	2	1	1	1,087	26.1
1983	8	3,258	2	1	3	1	1	1,061	21.9
1984	10	-	-	-	-	-	-	-	-
1985	11	3,274	4	1	5	0	1	1,211	6.6
1986	12	3,888	3	3	4	1	1	1,426	6.5
1987	9	3,402	3	3	1	1	1	1,665	6.2
1988	10	4,213	4	2	1	2	1	2,259	5.7

Year	Number of Offices G	S
1980	6	6
1981	6	7
1982	6	8

Year	Number of Offices G	S
1983	6	8
1984	5	10
1985	5	11

Year	Number of Offices G	S
1986	5	12
1987	5	9
1988	5	10

Source: Calculated from Board of Governors of the Federal Reserve System,
Structural Data for U.S. Offices of Foreign Banks, 1980-88. See
definition of codes in Table 2.3.

1986 purchase of Goldman, Sachs and Company for $500 million (equivalent to the 25 percent ownership limit set by the Fed) by Sumitomo Bank of Japan.

Edge Act and Agreement Corporations

At the beginning of the twentieth century, U.S. national banks were prohibited by law from engaging in international operations. State-chartered banks, on the other hand, were free to participate in foreign banking operations if they chose. To stimulate U.S. trade and commerce, Section 25 of the Federal Reserve Act was amended in 1916 by Congress to allow national and state member banks with capital assets and surpluses of $1 million or more (the minimum has now increased to $2 million) to invest up to 10 percent of their capital and surpluses in subsidiaries incorporated under state or federal law in order to conduct international banking. However, banks had to reach an "agreement" with the Federal Reserve Board as to the type of their activities, restrictions, and the limitations of their operations. Thus the agreement corporation was created.

Unfortunately, the arrangement did not work out as expected. In 1919, Senator Walter E. Edge of New Jersey proposed and amended the Edge Corporations Act to enhance a broader scope of activities and to specify a clearer definition of the distinction between "Edge" and "agreement" corporations. Both types of corporation were permitted to be involved in activities related to international banking, trade, and financing. The difference between the two was based on the origination of their chartering authority and the extent of their activity abroad. Agreement corporations are normally state-chartered agencies engaged primarily in international or foreign banking. Edge Act corporations are federally chartered agencies, which are also permitted to engage in other forms of foreign financial transactions.

Regulatory Environment. The IBA of 1978 extended the Edge Act privilege to foreign banks operating in the United States. In 1979, the Federal Reserve expanded Edge Act corporations' interstate banking power to permit them to select a "home" in a state, with the right to branch their activities into other states. The interstate activities were limited to international-related businesses. In the most recent Regulation K revision of October 24, 1985, an Edge Act corporation has been defined as a U.S. corporation engaged directly or indirectly in activities in the United States that are permitted by the sixth paragraph of Section 25(a) of the Federal Reserve Act and are incidental to international or foreign business. These activities include receiving deposits from foreign governments and foreign persons, or any person in the United States, if such deposits are to be transmitted abroad, or to consist of funds to be used for payment of obligations abroad, or to consist of the proceeds of collection abroad or other related activities permitted in Regulation D. The deposit accounts may consist of transaction accounts, savings and time deposit accounts, and issuance of negotiable certificates of deposit.

Legally, both member banks and bank holding companies can establish Edge Act corporations. While the corporation is physically located in the United States, it can have overseas branches, subsidiaries, and investments. Edge corporations first boomed in the 1920s, but most were liquidated in the 1930s. Stagnation continued until the late 1950s, when in 1957 the Federal Reserve Board amended Regulation K to allow Edge corporations to participate in banking and investment activities. Investment Edges were permitted to hold stock in companies, but not to engage in banking. The distinction was made to retain the separation between commercial and investment banking. However, in 1963, Regulation K was revised to eliminate this distinction. Both Edge and agreement corporations are now subject to organizational requirements, investment restrictions, and the liability limits of Regulation K and the Federal Reserve Act.

Edge Corporations in the United States. By the end of December 1988, there were 22 offices of banking Edge or agreement corporations in the United States, majority owned by foreign banks (table 2.7). Two-thirds of these offices are small, with assets of less than $100 million. Nearly one-third have established international banking facilities.

An Edge corporation may receive bills, checks, drafts, acceptances, bonds, and other instruments for collection abroad, and may collect such instruments in the United States for a customer abroad. The services may also include the transmission and receipt of wire transfers of funds and securities for depositors, foreign exchange activities, fiduciary and investment advisory activities for holding securities in safekeeping, buying and selling securities upon order, trustee activities, and investment and portfolio management advisory activities.

Other Types of Banking Offices

The type of organization a bank elects to establish for its foreign operations reflects its worldwide strategy, and is in response to the regulations and business opportunities abroad. Those who plan premiere foreign business operations choose agencies, branches, and subsidiaries. Others may choose less complex forms of organization for their conduct of banking abroad. These limited-service offices include correspondent banking, consortium banks, international banking facilities, and offshore banking offices.

Correspondent Banks. Correspondent banking relationships provide financial communication among banks in various countries and the money-center cities. The two-way link between banks, or between banks and financial or money-market centers, becomes crucial when a bank does not have any local offices, because local offices by law are not permitted to conduct certain transactions in the host nation, or because the volume of business is

Table 2.7
U.S. Offices of Banking Edge or Agreement Corporations, Majority Owned by Foreign Banks

Year	No. of Bank Offices	Total Assets ($M)	Number of Offices in Assets Size ($M)		Largest Assets Size ($M)	Smallest Assets Size ($M)
			<100	>100		
1980	10	175	10	0	47	0.44
1981	23	590	22	1	167	0.16
1982	31	1,257	25	6	249	2.30
1983	35	1,332	30	5	285	2.38
1984	39	881	39	0	84	0.61
1985	-	-	-	-	-	-
1986	33	2,333	24	9	532	0.20
1987	30	2,423	20	10	494	4.83
1988	28	2,928	17	11	535	2.57

Source: Calculated from Board of Governors of the Federal Reserve System, **Structural Data for U.S. Offices of Foreign Banks**, 1980–88.

not sufficient to warrant the front-office cost of establishing a branch or subsidiary office abroad. Correspondent banking normally starts when two banks maintain deposits in each other in local currency in return for banking services.

Correspondent services include accepting deposits and drafts; extending letters of credit and bankers' acceptances; processing securities; participating in foreign exchange transactions and trade dealings, safekeeping, and cash management services; and providing general advisory services and credit information reports. Correspondent banking may be used to settle third-party transactions via the affiliate office of the host correspondent bank office in the third country.

Consortium Banks. These banks first started in the early 1900s, as joint venture banks of different nationalities. They are similar to stock-ownership corporations, with each bank or owner acquiring stock ownership in proportion to its contribution to the common pool, under a subsidiary form of organization. Banking activities are with parent banks, as well as with other international business institutions. They tend to focus on certain activities, mostly international in nature, such as offering large and long-term loan syndication, underwriting securities, participating in medium-term lending in the Eurocurrency market, and engaging in investment and merchant bank activities.

The growth of consortium banks has slowed in recent years, because of the failure by some and the strong competition from subsidiary and merchant banks. Most consortium banks are in Europe, with a large proportion having a London base. The consortium bank infrastructure began in the United States in 1913 when the Federal Reserve Board allowed national banks to establish overseas branches. Among the early comers were the Continental Banking and Trust Company of Panama, the Mercantile Bank of America, the American Foreign Banking Corporation, and the Bank of Central and South America.[7]

International Banking Facilities. In order to attract Eurocurrency business, in June 1981 the Federal Reserve Board authorized, effective December 3, 1981, the establishment of U.S.-based international banking facilities (IBFs). IBFs are physically located in the United States, but are not subject to domestic reserve requirements, FDIC insurance premiums, or interest rate ceilings on deposits. They may offer time deposits to foreign nonbank residents, with a minimum maturity of two days. The minimum transaction size is $100,000. In addition, they can offer time deposits to foreign banks and foreign offices of U.S. banks with a one-day maturity. Loans can be made to foreign banks and residents as well as to other IBFs. Loans may not be made to U.S. residents. Transactions may be denominated in any currency, but most are expected to be in U.S. dollars. To attract IBFs, several states, including New York, Illinois, California, and Florida, have exempted these institutions from state and local taxes. The U.S.-owned IBFs are also exempt from federal taxes, but foreign-owned IBFs are subject to federal taxes.

In some ways, IBFs resemble offshore banks. They are basically free-trade zones for banking services inside a country. While IBFs are not separate entities, they maintain assets and liability accounts separate from their parent bank. The parent bank may be a U.S.-chartered depository institution, branch, or agency of a foreign bank or Edge Act corporation. Deposits may be accepted only from foreign residents, companies, governments, or other IBFs. No U.S. deposits may be accepted nor can funds be used to support U.S. economic activities. Thus, U.S. residents have been barred from holding deposits in an international banking facility, and these institutions have been prohibited from issuing negotiable certificates of deposit and bankers' acceptances.

The effectiveness of IBFs in capturing the Eurocurrency market and helping the United States compete worldwide can be seen in their recent rise in popularity. By December 1988, there were 468 IBFs in existence in the United States, nearly half of which were established by foreign branches.[8] IBFs have attracted a significant share of Eurodollar business away from other existing centers. Various reports have estimated the IBFs' accounts as exceeding $200 billion by the end of 1986. The beneficiaries have been the states of New York, California, and Florida. Japanese and Italian banks are especially interested in this form of banking because their home countries prohibit "shell" banking operations.

Shell Banks. A "shell" bank or, as it is known collectively, offshore financial center, is a network of financial communication developed to provide easy access to Eurocurrency and Eurobond markets. These centers are free of taxation and exchange controls, deal in currencies of countries other than the one in which the center is located, and are primarily for nonresident clients with worldwide access. A shell bank or shell branch has practically no office or extensive staff. It is typically established on a Caribbean island or other area with good air transportation and hotel facilities. Some examples of such locations are the Bahamas, Nassau, the Cayman Islands, Hong Kong, and Singapore.

Banking institutions have developed these centers to benefit from economies of scale in the international operations, without being subject to restrictive home-country regulations. Banks use shell branches to take advantage of the tax structure of offshore locations, but also use these offices to lessen the impact of tight monetary policies at home, to channel excessive surpluses abroad (outward), to channel funds into local areas (inward), and also to take advantage of low-cost, high-volume operations. Each center has its own specific characteristics and clients. For example, Americans prefer the Caribbean Islands; thus they conduct their shell banking activities there. Europeans and Australians are more active in the Singapore money center, while Korea, Japan, China, and other Southeast Asian countries are more inclined to utilize the Hong Kong financial center. Language, overlapping business hours, and banking specialization are also factors in determining the placement of funds within each market.

NOTES

1. The International Banking Act of 1978 extended the Edge privilege to foreign banks operating in the United States. Information on representative offices was acquired from *American Banker*, Special Report, March 6, 1989, p. A1.

2. These data and information were collected and adjusted from various newspapers and professional and governmental reports and "Foreign Banks in the United States," *American Banker*, March 6, 1989, for the year 1988.

3. Board of Governors of the Federal Reserve System, *Federal Reserve Bulletin*, 1978–88, and other statistical data published by the board.

4. Sarkis J. Khoury, *Dynamics of International Banking*, Praeger Publishing Company, New York, 1980, pp. 103–107; and the Federal Reserve Statistical Release and Bulletin.

5. Khoury, p. 110.

6. Board of Governors of the Federal Reserve System, *Structural Data for U.S. Offices of Foreign Banks*, December 31, 1988.

7. Yoon S. Park and Jack Zwick, *International Banking in Theory and Practice*, Addison-Wesley Publishing Company, Reading, Mass., 1985, p. 54.

8. Board of Governors of the Federal Reserve System, *Structural Data for U.S. Offices of Foreign Banks*, December 31, 1988.

3 Legal Environment

In broad principle, the United States accepts the market system. . . .
We are content to see economic policy work its way through relatively
impersonal market incentives.

Paul Volcker
Federal Reserve Chairman
International Monetary Conference
London, June 12, 1979

The United States seeks to maintain a public policy of general separation
between banking and commerce. Section 4(a) of the Bank Holding Company Act provides that no bank holding company shall acquire direct or indirect ownership or control of any voting securities of any company that is not
a bank. The purpose is clearly to separate commercial banking from other
commercial activities. The reasons stem from the economic and social history of the country, expressed and protected via antitrust laws, specifically the
Sherman and Clayton Acts. The major concerns are fear of increased concentration of economic power, unfair competition, and above all, the possible conflicts of interest between a bank's fiduciary responsibility to its depositors and its own economic interests derived from ownership of
nonbanking firms. At the same time, the U.S. policies accept the market
system and support free movement of capital as being in the national interest. Thus, the policymakers have adopted a more open attitude toward
foreign banking.

One of the significant aspects of the long debate that led to the International Banking Act (IBA) of 1978 was the response of Congress to the concerns expressed about foreign banks' rapid expansion and acquisition of large U.S. banks. Apprehension about foreign takeovers of large U.S. institutions centered around the point that U.S. institutions did not have equivalent opportunities. Concerns were expressed about the regulatory advantages that foreign banks in the United States had over domestic competitors in the areas of interstate banking, the Federal Reserve requirements, the unsoundness of foreign banks' financial operations due to their lack of required federal insurance, and others. The IBA was enacted to place foreign banks on a more equal footing with U.S. banks with respect to the limitations on interstate banking imposed by the McFadden Act and the Douglas amendment to the Bank Holding Company Act, and other banking-related concerns.[1]

PREVIOUS REGULATIONS

Previous regulations of foreign bank operations in the United States were lenient and inequitable. Foreign bank entry to the U.S. market was determined exclusively by state banking laws. These banks were affected by federal law only if they became members of the Federal Reserve System, were nationally chartered, or controlled a subsidiary bank of a holding company in which the Bank Holding Company Act applied. A state could regulate and supervise the activities of a banking office within its jurisdiction; but without federal regulation and supervision, and with different states' regulatory provisions, no coordinated oversight existed for a multistate banking organization's entire operation. In addition, since most U.S. offices of foreign banks were not required to hold reserves in Federal Reserve banks, and were able to branch across state lines, they seemed to enjoy several competitive advantages.

First, foreign banks were not subject to the Federal Reserve requirements. This advantage reduced foreign banks' cost of funds by an estimated average of 0.5 percent, subject to the size of their deposits and specialized activities. Second, foreign banks were not required to purchase FDIC insurance and were subject to lower, state-controlled, capital requirements. This in turn contributed to additional cost savings, providing foreign banks with a more favorable cost advantage. Third, foreign branches were allowed to operate interstate activities, a privilege denied to domestic banks under the McFadden Act of 1927. It is reported that by 1978 there were 65 foreign banks with branches and/or agencies in more than one state.[2] Fourth, foreign bank affiliates were permitted to operate securities and nonbanking activities, as opposed to their U.S. counterparts, which were prohibited from doing so under the Glass-Steagall Act of 1934 and the Bank Holding Company Act of 1956.[3] Fifth, foreign branches and agencies were free to make loans and to offer other domestic banking services that were denied U.S. banks under the Edge Act.[4] Finally, the absence of U.S. federal guidelines and examination of foreign banking practices further favored foreign banks over their domestic competitors. Furthermore, many foreign banks were subsidized by their own governments and had greater access to overseas money markets.

REGULATORY DEVELOPMENT

Early attempts to facilitate the operations of the U.S. banks in the international market and trade arenas were made at the federal and state levels, long before the influx of foreign banking in the U.S. national market. Edge Act legislation, initially passed in 1919 and further amended in 1957 and 1963, enabled subsidiaries of U.S. banks to cross state lines to engage in an array of international banking and financial activities.[5]

By the mid-1960s, the debate over the foreign banks' impact on credit market flows and the difficulties of central banks in achieving their monetary policy objectives were intensified. In July 1966, the Congressional Joint Economic Committee published a research report on foreign banking activities.[6] The study recommended two major changes. First, it recommended the inclusion of foreign banks' activities under the supervision of national banking authorities — namely the comptroller of the currency and the Federal Reserve System; second, it also proposed the extension of the option of federal chartering to include foreign bank affiliates.

Shortly after, the first bill dealing with these issues, S. 3765, was introduced in the Senate. This bill aimed at bringing foreign banking under federal control with the comptroller of the currency as the sole chartering and supervising authority for foreign banking activities. The main objective was to provide foreign banks roughly the same supervised environment as national banks, with the exception that they would be able to operate across state lines.[7] This action was strengthened by the 1970 amended version of the BHC Act, which sought to allow U.S. banks to cross state lines within operational areas considered reasonable and related to normal bank activities. The outcome was expected to enhance the market position of U.S.-owned banks, and somewhat limit foreign access to state credit markets. Meanwhile, the Federal Reserve recognized the importance of having detailed information on the financial activities of U.S.-based foreign banks; thus it instituted a data collection program in late 1972.[8] The realization of the greater need to control and implement economic policy and fair competition within the banking establishment aided the introduction of H.B. 11440 in 1973, which reinforced the need for a national policy change.[9]

In February 1973, the Federal Reserve Board set up a steering committee to review the regulatory aspects of international banking. The committee's work was drafted by the board in the form of a bill and sent to Congress in December 1974. The bill was revised and resubmitted on March 4, 1975, under the title Foreign Bank Act of 1975.[10] The goal of this bill was to establish a national policy toward foreign banking operations in the United States. It stated that all foreign banking facilities would be required to obtain licenses from the comptroller of the currency, regardless of their federal or state charter affiliations. The requirement of FDIC insurance then applicable to foreign subsidiaries would be extended to branches and agencies, and Federal Reserve membership would be required of all foreign banking operations in the United States whose parent organizations had worldwide assets in excess of $500 million. The act also provided some relief for foreign banks. Under the supervision of the comptroller of the currency, foreign ownership of national banks would be facilitated by allowing up to one-third of their directors to be foreign citizens. More importantly, foreign banks and their U.S. subsidiaries would be permitted to own controlling interests in Edge corporations, an arrangement that was then prohibited.[11]

Two features of this act were received favorably by U.S. bankers: first, the intention of the act, to create a nondiscriminatory environment between domestic and foreign banks; second, the section extending the BHC Act provision to cover branches and agencies of foreign banks, not just the subsidiaries, as was the case in the past. However, the grandfathering provision of this act neutralized the result somewhat in the area of interstate banking and investment company activities. The 1975 act allowed foreign banks to retain those interstate facilities in operation prior to December 3, 1974, the date when the proposed legislation was first introduced. Furthermore, New York investment companies and foreign consortia were also exempted when the parent company's ownership reached 25 percent or more of the bank's stock.[12]

Later in 1975, a study by the House Banking Committee, known as *Financial Institutions and the Nation's Economy (FINE)*, recommended, among other things, that foreign banking entities in the United States that accept domestic deposits should be required to function under the subsidiary form of organization. Grandfathering should not be permitted, and the underwriting and equity investment activities of foreign banking organizations should be forbidden as well. State chartering of foreign banking activities should be abolished, with the entire supervisory function transferred to a newly created federal agency, the Federal Deposits Institution Commission. The new FDIC would then be responsible for the chartering and examination of all federally chartered depository institutions, foreign and domestic, consolidating activities that were then divided between the comptroller of the currency, the Federal Reserve System, the FDIC, the Federal Home Loan Bank Board (FHLBB), and the National Credit Union Administration.[13] However, this revolutionary idea, while receiving the admiration of academicians and some bankers, met with resistance from the staffs of regulatory agencies.

INTERNATIONAL BANKING COOPERATION

A major step toward international banking supervisory cooperation was taken in 1974 with the formation of the Committee on Banking Regulations and Supervisory Practices at the Bank for International Settlement (BIS). The committee was formed by the central bank governors from the Group of Ten[14] major industrial countries and Switzerland, to improve the coordination of supervision of international banking activities. This committee was initially called the "Basle" or "Blunden" Committee after its first chairman, George Blunden of the Bank of England. The International Banking Cooperation was an extension of the Basle Agreement on currency fluctuations, formed on April 24, 1972, among the members of the European Economic Community. The Basle Agreement of 1972 was formed to narrow the band of fluctuations among the currencies and to create the European Monetary Cooperation Fund. In 1974, the same supervisory cooperation was extended to international banking activities among the major industrial countries.

In 1977, Blunden was succeeded by Peter Cooke, also from the Bank of England; the committee name was then changed to the Cooke Committee. The cooperation was expected to provide an avenue for developing personal working relations among national banking authorities in monitoring the activities of their foreign banking offices, and to facilitate rapid and effective cooperative action should banks experience difficulties. The cornerstone of the action was based on the premise that the national authorities would be willing to cooperate in harmony in monitoring the activities of overseas operations of their own national banks and the local operations of foreign banks.

The committee's view or "concordat" was based on the principle that the supervision of foreign banking activities should be the joint responsibility of both host and home authorities. The concordat's guidelines separated the supervisory responsibilities of host and home country by assigning different aspects of monitoring responsibility to each. The supervision of liquidity of all foreign branches and solvency of subsidiaries abroad was regarded as the primary responsibility of the host-country authorities. The supervision of solvency of foreign branches was considered to be primarily in the hands of home-country authorities. The coordination among the country's authorities would be facilitated by the transfer of information between responsible authorities.

Despite the considerable progress that has been made within the European community in regard to the international exchange of supervisory information, the overall result does not signal a great success. The major obstacle to the success of the concordat has been the failure of the members to receive worldwide endorsement. It has been further weakened by the unavailability of timely data and information necessary for the supervisory process, and the assumption that the national authorities are willing and able to supervise the international activities of their banking activities. Events in Argentina, Chile, Iran, and Poland have shown that the reciprocal treatment from foreign sovereigns may not result.

In May 1983, the committee published a revision to the 1975 concordat. The revision subjugated the holding companies and nonbanking companies active within the banking group to the 1975 concordat version and changed supervisory issues concerning the solvency of subsidiaries and the liquidity of branches. The changes now require host and parent countries to participate jointly in the supervision of branches' liquidity and subsidiaries' solvency. In the 1975 concordat, both of these cases were subject to supervision of the host country only.

In recent years, in addition to the Cooke Committee, three other regional committees were formed to harmonize banking supervision. In 1977, the European Community adopted a "Banking Coordination Directive" to unify the international banking supervision of member countries. In the 1980s, the "Offshore Supervisor's Group" and the "Commission of Latin American and Caribbean Supervisors and Regulatory Bodies" were established. Both of these organizations are in their primitive developmental stages, and their working relationship should be evaluated after 1990.

ORGANIZATIONAL STRUCTURE BEFORE THE 1978 ACT

Foreign banks established a variety of organizational structures for conducting their business operations in the United States. These structures were tailored specifically to the laws of the states in which the foreign banks elected to operate. For example, California state law prohibited entry by foreign branches, but permitted the establishment of branches by foreign banks if they had FDIC insurance. However, because the FDIC Act did not then permit a branch to be eligible for deposit insurance, foreign banks had to establish separately chartered subsidiaries to take retail deposits, and agencies instead of branches to carry out the other nondepository activities of the parent bank. Due to this legal barrier, agencies outnumbered branches in California by a ratio of 4 to 1. An agency, by virtue of its organizational structure, can carry out international banking operations that are wholesale in nature, participate in money market activities, and make loans, but they cannot take deposits.[15]

In contrast to California law, the Illinois and New York state laws permitted foreign banks to operate branches and did not preclude them from taking deposits prior to 1978. Such deposits, however, could not be covered by FDIC insurance. New York state law required foreign branches to operate under the rule of reciprocity—the foreign national laws had to permit New York banks to operate branches in their home countries. Furthermore, New York state law did not allow foreign banks to operate both agencies and branches. The applicant had to choose one or the other form of affiliation to conduct its international business activities. These variations in the laws of the states caused discomfort and necessitated legal adjustments for foreign countries who wished to operate in the U.S. market. Canada, until the late 1970s, prohibited foreign bank branching operations in Canada; thus, Canadian banks were forbidden to establish branches in New York State. Instead they chose to establish an agency or subsidiary form of organization. Similarly, Australian banks were not able to form state-licensed branches in New York, because Australian law did not subscribe to the law of reciprocity. These problems were a direct result of the dual U.S. banking system whereby banks were chartered and operated at both federal and state levels. In most other countries, banks were licensed, regulated, and supervised at only the national level, under uniform laws.[16]

INTERNATIONAL BANKING ACT OF 1978

The International Banking Act of 1978, known as [H.R. 10899] Public Law 95–369, was enacted on September 17, 1978, to provide equal treatment of banking operations in the United States. Under this act foreign banks operating in the United States through branches, agencies, or commercial lending companies are to be subject to federal supervision and regulation in a manner similar to domestic banks. The act is a significant step toward applying the principle of national treatment, or nondiscrimination, to foreign banks operating in the United States. The foreign banks are subject to the same restrictions and privileges as domestic banks, and have the same rights as domestic banks to seek federal or state licenses. The comptroller of the currency is authorized to charter federal agencies and branches of foreign banks in a manner similar to domestic banks. The foreign banks are required to select a "home state" with either state or federally licensed agencies or branches, or establish or acquire full banking subsidiaries. They are not permitted to operate both agencies and branches in the same state or charter or to acquire subsidiaries beyond the home state.

More significantly, the IBA restricts expansion of interstate deposit taking by foreign banks, subjects foreign branches and agencies to the Federal Reserve requirements and interest rate regulation, requires deposit insurance for branches engaged in retail banking, and permits foreign banks to own Edge corporations. In addition, it allows agencies and branches access to the discount window and to payment services provided by Federal Reserve banks. However, it restricts foreign banks' nonbanking activities subject to the BHC Act on banks operating branches and agencies in the United States.

Although certain aspects of the act are self-implementing, others—specifically, Sections 9, 13, and 14—require administrative action by either the Board of Governors of the Federal Reserve System, the secretary of the treasury, the comptroller of the currency, or the FDIC. A summary highlighting key provisions of the International Banking Act of 1978 is presented here with minor exceptions, Sections 1, 2, 11, and 12. Section 1 is limited to the definitions and rules of restrictions governing the types of offices held by foreign banks. These terms will be defined appropriately within the contents of other sections, described later. Section 2 is a correction of Section 5746 of the Revised Statutes (12 USC 72), which redefines the authority of the comptroller of the currency regarding the citizenship requirement of the directors of the subsidiary of an affiliate of a foreign bank. This revision will be discussed, in part, in Section 3 on Edge Act corporations. Similarly, Section 11 extends Section 8(b) of the FDIC Act to Section 8(a) of the IBA Act, and to any subsidiary of a foreign bank or company in the same manner they apply to a bank holding company. The term "subsidiary" shall have the same meaning assigned to it as in Section 2 of the BHC Act of 1956. Section 12 of IBA addresses the Banking Act of 1933 by redefining territorial coverage of the act to include the United States, any state, territory, or district that engages in business under the law of the United States' control.[17]

Section 3: Edge Act Corporations

The purpose of this section is to eliminate or modify provisions in Section 25(a) of the Federal Reserve Act that discriminate against foreign-owned banking institutions or limit corporations organized under this section in competing with foreign-owned banking institutions in the United States or abroad. The rule provides Edge corporations with sufficient powers to compete effectively with similar, foreign-owned institutions in the United States or abroad. The legislation facilitates U.S. Edge corporations' participation in international finance and trade and strengthens their ability to promote exports. Furthermore, it stimulates competition and provides the Board of Governors of the Federal Reserve System with supervisory power to rule and regulate their activities as prescribed. Section 3(c) strikes out the citizenship requirement of the elected or appointed directors of the banks, thus permitting non–U.S. citizens to serve as directors of Edge corporations.[18]

Section 3 also removes the 10 percent minimum reserve requirement on the domestic deposits of an Edge corporation but rules that the domestic deposits of an Edge corporation will continue to be subject to the same reserve requirements as a member bank. Also, the majority of the shares of the capital stock of an Edge corporation shall at all times be held and owned by citizens of the United States or by corporations with "controlling interest" owned by U.S. citizens, under United States law. Notably, foreign banks under the law of the United States and with the approval of the Board of Governors of the Federal Reserve System may own and hold 50 percent or more of the shares of capital stock of any Edge corporation. The exception is subject to the same provisions of law as any other corporation organized under the Edge Corporation Act and its "controlling interest" shall be construed under Section 2 of the BHC Act of 1956.[19]

Section 4: Federal Branches and Agencies

With the approval of the comptroller of the currency, a foreign bank may establish one or more federal branches or agencies in any state in which it is not operating a branch or agency pursuant to state law. The comptroller shall take into account the effects of the proposal on competition in domestic and international commerce of the United States, the financial and managerial resources and future prospects of the applicant foreign bank, and the branch or agency, and the convenience and needs of the community to be served.[20]

The operation of a foreign bank at a federal branch or agency shall be conducted with the same rights and privileges as a national bank at the same location and shall be subject to all the same duties, restrictions, penalties, liabilities, conditions, and limitations that would apply under the National Bank Act to a national bank doing business at the same location, except that (1) the requirements of Section 5240 of the Revised Statutes [12 USC 481] shall be met with respect to a federal branch or agency if it is examined at least once in each calendar year; (2) any limitation or restriction based on the capital stock and surplus of a national bank as applied to a federal branch or agency shall be deemed to refer to the dollar equivalent of the capital stock and surplus for the foreign bank and to the aggregate of branches or agencies, if the foreign bank has more than one federal branch or agency; (3) a federal branch or agency shall not be required to become an insured bank as that term is defined in Section 3(h) of the FDIC Act.[21]

Sections 4(d), 4(e), and 4(f) also stipulate that neither may a foreign bank maintain both a federal branch and a federal agency in the same state, nor shall a foreign bank receive deposits or exercise fiduciary powers at any federal agency. Any branch or agency operated by a foreign bank in a state, pursuant to state law, including any commercial lending company controlled by a foreign bank, may be converted into a federal branch or agency with the approval of the comptroller of the currency. No foreign bank may maintain both a federal branch and a federal agency in the same state. The authority to operate a federal branch or agency shall terminate when the parent foreign bank is dissolved or its license is revoked or cancelled in the country of its organization.[22]

In November 1983, the Federal Reserve Board ruled that a state cannot prohibit foreign banks from establishing federally chartered interstate branches and agencies if the state permits foreign banks to establish state-chartered interstate branches and agencies. The ruling was in accordance with the belief that the construction of the International Banking Act was intended to accord foreign banks competitively equal treatment nationally with their domestic counterparts. Therefore, for the purpose of establishing additional offices in the home state, the foreign bank's initial home state office is equated with a domestic bank's principal office.[23]

Section 5: Interstate Banking Operations

The main thrust of Section 5 is to limit the acquisition of commercial banks and the establishment of deposit-taking branches by foreign banks outside their "home" states. Accordingly, no foreign bank may directly or indirectly establish and operate a federal or state branch or an agency outside of its home state unless its operation is approved by the state in which it is to be operated. It extends the restriction one step further to require that no foreign bank may directly or indirectly acquire any voting share of, interest in, or substantial majority of the assets of a bank located outside of its home state if such acquisition is prohibited under Section 3(d) of the BHC Act of 1956. Furthermore, deposits received by any federal or state branch, subject to the limitation of an agreement or undertaking imposed under this subsection, shall not be subject to any requirement of mandatory insurance by the FDIC. In sum, Section 5 of the International Banking Act of 1978, like Section 3(d) in the BHC Act of 1956, reinforces the restrictive pattern of the McFadden Act of 1927 that bars multistate branching by national and state member banks and extends that pattern also to foreign bank branching.[24]

A minor exception is when the foreign bank agrees with the Federal Reserve Board to forgo a domestic deposit business and to accept at the branch only deposits permissible for Edge Act corporations that are from foreign sources and international in nature. This is true also for commercial lending corporations and the investment companies organized under Article XII of the New York Banking Law to conduct essentially foreign or international operations.[25] Furthermore, Section 5(b) of IBA grandfathered from the above restrictions on interstate operations such activities that commenced, or for which applications were pending, on or before July 27, 1978. This is the date that the Senate Banking Committee bill was scheduled to be completed.[26]

On various occasions, the Federal Reserve Board has been forced to issue interpretive notes and decisions to clarify the content of different segments of the IBA of 1978. One ruling concerns Section 5 on interstate banking by foreign banks. The Federal Reserve Board stated that foreign banks may not operate branches in more than one state, unless interstate branches were opened prior to the effective date of the 1978 act. However, foreign banks may make a one-time change of home state and may acquire banks in other states where acquisition is not prohibited by state or federal laws. This order was made in reference to the case of the Allied Irish Bank, Ltd. on November 21, 1983.[27]

Section 6: Insurance of Deposits

Section 6 stipulates that no foreign bank may establish or operate a federal branch that receives deposits of less that $100,000 unless the branch is an insured branch as defined in Section 3(s) of the FDIC Act, or unless the comptroller of the currency determines by order or regulation that the branch is not engaged in domestic retail activities requiring deposit insurance protection. In the states that require deposit insurance for state-chartered banks, state banks that receive deposits of less than $100,000 must be insured. The foreign bank branches that are not subject to mandatory insurance may voluntarily apply for federal deposit insurance coverage. A branch that was established prior to the date of enactment must have obtained federal deposit insurance by September 17, 1979 (a year after the date of enactment), if the branch is subject to the mandatory insurance provisions. A branch established after the date of enactment is immediately subject to the act's provisions.[28]

Section 7: Authority and the Federal Reserve System

The act broadens the authority of the Federal Reserve System and the Federal Reserve Act to every federal branch and agency of a foreign bank in the same manner as for a member bank. The board, by either general or specific regulation or ruling, may waive the minimum or maximum reserve ratios prescribed under Section 19 of the Federal Reserve Act and may even prescribe any ratio, not more than 22 percent, for any obligation of any such federal branch or agency that the board may deem reasonable and appropriate. In their consideration, the board shall view the character of business conducted by these institutions and the need to maintain an air of competition between such institutions and member banks.[29]

Section 7(a)(2) subjects federal branches and agencies of foreign banks with total, worldwide, consolidated bank assets in excess of $1 billion to Federal Reserve requirements and interest rate limitations. In addition, the act authorizes the board to impose reserve requirements and interest rate ceilings on state branches and agencies of foreign banks after consultation and cooperation with state bank supervisory authorities.[30] The interest rate limitation of Section 7, as applied to Regulation Q, was eliminated in April 1986, in fulfillment of the requirement set by the Depository Institutions Deregulation and Monetary Control Act of 1980.[31]

Section 8: Nonbanking Activities

Before IBA enactment, a foreign bank that operated in the United States through a branch or agency, rather than a banking subsidiary, did not control a "bank," and consequently was not subject to the provisions of the

BHC Act. Such a foreign bank was not generally prohibited from engaging in nonbanking activities in the United States.[32] Section 8(a) subjects foreign banks operating branches and agencies in the United States to the nonbanking prohibitions of the BHC Act of 1956 and to Sections 105 and 106 of the BHC Act, thereby greatly increasing the number of institutions to which those prohibitions apply.[33] In addition, Section 8(a) revises the exemption contained in Section 2(h) of the 1970 act to permit a foreign bank holding company to own shares in any foreign company outside the United States, as well as a U.S. company so long as the latter is in the same general line of business. This exemption does not extend to companies engaged in the securities business in the United States.[34] This modification may be interpreted as unwillingness on the part of Congress to interfere with the nonbanking activities that foreign bank organizations may engage in abroad, so long as foreign activities do not violate the objectives of the BHC Act related to the structure and conduct of banking in the United States. This may be more sensible and in tune to today's realities concerning the conduct of international banking.

Until December 31, 1985, a foreign bank, or other company to which Section 8(a) applied on the date of its enactment, could retain direct or indirect ownership or control of any voting shares of any nonbanking company in the United States that it owned or controlled with power to vote on the date of enactment of this act or could engage in any nonbanking activities in the United States in which it was engaged on such a date. After December 31, 1985, a foreign bank could continue to engage in nonbanking activities in the United States in which, directly or through an affiliate, it was lawfully engaged on July 26, 1978. However, the board could terminate the activities if such action was necessary to prevent undue concentration of resources, decreased or unfair competition, conflicts of interest, or unsound banking practices in the United States. The above ruling on nonbanking activities also refers to ownership or control of any voting shares of any domestically controlled affiliate covered in 1978 that engaged in the business of underwriting, distributing, or otherwise buying or selling stocks, bonds, and other securities in the United States.[35]

Exemptions. Exemptions are known in legal terms as "grandfather" rights of companies or exemptions from the prohibitions on nonbanking activities of foreign banks, covered under Section 8(a) and 8(c) of the IBA of 1978. The rules permanently grandfathered nonbanking activities — including security activities — of foreign banks or affiliated companies covered by Section 8(a), or via an application to engage in such activities, for which the subject was lawfully engaged directly or indirectly, on or before July 26, 1978, or pursuant to a binding acquisition contract entered on or before that date. There is no clear indication in this ruling regarding the kind of applications contemplated. Presumably, it may be interpreted that any application to any federal or state authority to engage in particular nonbanking activities would qualify.

As used in this subsection, the term "affiliate" shall mean "any company more than 5 percent of whose voting shares are directly or indirectly owned, controlled or held with power to vote by the specific foreign bank or company," and the term "domestically controlled affiliate" covered in 1978 shall mean "any affiliate the majority of whose voting shares is owned by a company or group of companies, . . . foreign bank or group of foreign banks which do not own or control, directly or indirectly, 25 percent or more of its voting shares."[36]

Section 9: Study of Foreign Treatment of U.S. Banks

This section instructs the secretary of the treasury, in conjunction with the secretary of state, the Board of Governors of the Federal Reserve, the comptroller of the currency, and the FDIC, to report to Congress, within 90 days after enactment of this bill, a study of the extent to which bank organizations, under the laws of the United States, are discriminated against, or denied by law or practice of national treatment in conducting banking operations in foreign countries. Moreover, it instructs the secretary to report on the effects, if any, of such discrimination on U.S. exports to these countries.[37]

The purpose of this section is mainly educational, because U.S. laws and regulations prohibit U.S. banks from engaging in commerce either at home or abroad, and banking in the United States is under a dual system, involving federal and state regulations and supervision. On the other hand, most foreign countries' banking activities are regulated and supervised nationally, and the banks have the authority to engage in "universal" banking. Banks may engage in banking financial activities as well as commerce. This makes these institutions very formidable competitors of more restricted U.S. banking corporations.

Section 10: Representative Offices

A representative office performs no banking functions. It serves as a customer-information center and business-generating facility to assist bank clients. The act instructs the foreign banks' representative offices to register with the secretary of the treasury in accordance with rules prescribed by the secretary, within 180 days after the date of enactment of the act or the date on which the office is established, whichever is later, on or before March 16, 1979. This act does not authorize the establishment of any such office in any state in contravention of state law.[38]

Section 13: Regulation and Enforcement

The comptroller, the Board of Governors of the Federal Reserve, and the FDIC are authorized and empowered to issue rules, regulations, and clarifications as necessary in order to perform their respective duties and functions under this act and to administer and carry out the provisions and purposes of the act and prevent evasions thereof.[39]

Section 14: Report on McFadden Act

The president, in consultation with the attorney general, the secretary of the treasury, the Board of Governors of the Federal Reserve, the comptroller, and the FDIC, was ordered to transmit a report to the Congress containing recommendations concerning the applicability of the McFadden Act to the present financial, banking, and economic environments, no later than one year after the date of enactment of the act. The report was to include an analysis of the effects of any proposed changes on the structure of the banking industry, and on the financial and economic environment in general.[40]

REGULATIONS ON EDGE CORPORATIONS

An Edge corporation is chartered to engage directly or indirectly in activities in the United States that are permitted by Section 25(a) of the Federal Reserve Act and are incidental to international or foreign business. As a regulatory component of Regulation K, International Operations of U.S. Banking, Section 211.4 and 211.6(a), Edge corporations are supervised and regulated by congressional approval. The International Banking Act of 1978 requires the board to review and to revise Regulation K every five years to ensure that the purposes of the Edge Act are being served in light of prevailing economic conditions and banking practices. The regulatory authority over Edge corporations involves the following three major areas of permissible activities and limitations.[41]

Deposit and Foreign Exchange Activities

An Edge corporation may receive deposits from foreign persons or governments in the form of savings or time deposits, negotiable certificates of deposit, or any other form of deposits, to secure collateral abroad, or to finance payments of export or import bills, or any other transactions that are of an international character. The corporation may engage in foreign exchange activities to facilitate international trade or international money market activities. An Edge corporation may finance contracts, projects, or other credit activities related to the importation or exportation of goods to or from the United States, whether directly or through brokers or other intermediaries, including the shipment or temporary storage or repackaging of goods imported or to be exported. The payments and collections include the receiving and processing of checks, bills, notes, drafts, coupons, bonds, and other instruments for collection abroad, and in the United States for a customer abroad, including transmitting and receiving wire transfers of funds and securities for depositors.

Fiduciary and Investment Advisory Activities

An Edge corporation may hold securities in safekeeping, or buy or sell securities upon order and for account, provided that such services for U.S. persons pertain to foreign securities only. The corporation may act as a paying agent for securities issued by foreign governments or any other entities organized under foreign law, or as a paying agent with respect to any class of securities issued to finance foreign activities and distributed solely outside the United States. Except to the extent permissible for member banks under Section 5136 of the Revised Statutes (12 USC 24, seventh), no Edge corporation may otherwise engage in the business of underwriting, distributing, or buying or selling securities in the United States.

An Edge corporation may act as investment or financial advisor by providing portfolio investment advice and portfolio management with respect to securities, other financial instruments, real property interests, and other investment assets, and by providing advice on mergers and acquisitions, provided such services for U.S. persons pertain to foreign assets only. Similar to the activities of a representative office, an Edge corporation may participate in providing general economic information and statistical forecasting services, as well as industry studies and other related advisory activities, provided such services for U.S. persons are in conjunction with international transactions and usages.

Lending Limits and Capital Requirements

Effective October 24, 1985, Edge corporations are permitted to invest the lesser of $15 million or 5 percent of their capital and surplus without prior notice or approval by the Federal Reserve for activities permissible under the Federal Reserve Act.[42] The lending limitation ensures that an Edge corporation shall remain fully secured for all acceptances outstanding in excess of 200 percent of its capital and surplus, and all acceptances outstanding for anyone in excess of 10 percent of its capital and surpluses.[43] One exception to these limitations is when the excess represents the international shipments of goods for which the Edge corporation is fully covered by primary obligations to reimburse the contents, and is guaranteed by banks or covered by participation agreements from other banks.[44]

The total loans and extension of credit outstanding to any person by an Edge corporation engaged in banking and its subsidiaries may not exceed 15 percent of the Edge corporation's capital and surplus. The limitation does not apply to deposits with banks and federal funds sold and bills or drafts drawn in good faith against actual goods for which two or more unrelated parties are liable. The exemption is also extended to obligations secured by cash collateral, bonds, notes, certificates of indebtedness or Treasury bills of the United States, or loans and extensions of credit covered by participation agreements, or any obligations supported by the full faith and credit of the United States or any of its agencies and corporations, including the Export-Import Bank of the United States (Eximbank) and the Federal Credit Association, and international agencies, such as the World Bank, the International Finance Corporation, the African Development Bank, and other related agencies.

Protection is also extended to the Edge corporation capital account. Edge corporations' capital adequacy is measured in relation to the scope and character of their activities. In the case of an Edge corporation engaged in banking, its capital and surplus shall be no less than 7 percent of risk assets. For this purpose, subordinated capital notes or debentures, in an amount not to exceed 50 percent of nondebt capital, may be included for determining capital adequacy in the same manner as for a member bank. The risk assets are defined here as all assets on a consolidated basis other than cash, amounts due from banking institutions in the United States, U.S. government securities, and federal funds sold.

DEREGULATION AND MONETARY CONTROL ACT OF 1980

The overall objective of the "Depository Institutes Deregulation and Monetary Control Act of 1980" was to move the financial system toward a more competitive framework and to reduce the artificial barriers created by previous regulations among financial institutions via portfolio restrictions and interest rate ceilings. Deregulation aimed to increase competition by widening the sources of funds and expanding the uses of funds for financial institutions active in various aspects of depository markets. This act was the most comprehensive banking legislation since enactment of the Bank Holding Company Act of 1956.

 Two aspects of the legislation had an impact on foreign banks' activities in the United States. First, the act permitted foreign bank branches and agencies that maintained basic reserve balances at the central bank to become eligible to use Federal Reserve services. This provision provided foreign banks direct access to major Federal Reserve services, such as the discount window, federal funds, check clearing, and other beneficial activities. The beneficiaries of these provisions were mainly larger foreign banks with multidimensional activities in U.S. financial markets. Second, under Title IX,

"Foreign Control of U.S. Financial Institutions," the act set a moratorium on U.S. bank takeovers and acquisitions by foreign banks until July 1, 1980, during which time a commission would study the long-term implications of such takeovers.[45]

The concern came about in response to the belief that foreign takeovers of domestic banks were detrimental to the U.S. banking system. When foreign banks first began to enter the American market, it was through the opening of their own subsidiaries. The trend changed quickly in the 1970s, turning toward the acquisitions form of ownership. During the 1970s, 51 U.S. banks with assets exceeding $100 billion were purchased or taken over by foreign entities. The foreign bank assets rose from 4 percent to 10 percent of total American bank assets. In California and New York alone, foreign banks made more than 30 percent of all business loans. Most troublesome was the notion that foreign-owned banks were becoming a major new force in New York, the financial center of the nation.

The reason for the sudden wave of acquisition in the 1970s was very simple. U.S. banks were bargains to foreign buyers. The depreciations of the U.S. dollar in 1971 and 1973, along with the implementation of the floating foreign exchange system in 1974 and the depressed U.S. stock market values, caused banks and industries to be sold at less than book value. It was estimated that U.S. banks sold at an average market price of up to 30 percent below their book value, a bargain that foreign investors realized immediately and moved rapidly to take advantage of. The U.S. energy problems of the 1970s played an important role in creating depressed national currency and stock markets for American banks and businesses. Not surprisingly, the government banking regulations at the time also provided a positive environment for foreign acquisitions, expansion, and investment in the prestigious U.S. banking market.

The McFadden Act of 1927 prevented U.S. banks from branching across state lines. The Bank Holding Company Act of 1970 prohibited interstate banking by barring bank holding companies from acquiring banks in more than one state. These limitations, along with the antitrust law provisions, opened up the climate for the acquisition of U.S. banks by foreigners. The foreign banks were allowed to buy any size bank in any American market. When the FDIC auctioned off the assets of failed banks, it was foreign banks who frequently were the successful bidders. In addition to this peculiarity in American banking laws, the U.S. banks were unable to acquire domestic banks abroad, because no other nations' banking laws provided the simplicity and loopholes of U.S. banking laws. Due to these circumstances, the American bankers often bitterly complained that they were at a disadvantage in the world financial marketplace where foreign and U.S. banks compete with each other.

These concerns were the force behind the moratorium on foreign acquisition of banks, enacted under Title IX of the Monetary Act of 1980. Title IX defined "domestic financial institution" as any bank, mutual savings bank, or savings and loan association organized under the laws of any state of the United States. The term "foreign person" referred to any foreign organization, bank, or individual resident in a foreign country. The term "takeover" meant any acquisition of 5 percent or more of the stock or assets of any domestic financial institution. The act exempted foreign takeover from the moratorium under six specific circumstances:[46]

- If the takeover was necessary to prevent bankruptcy or insolvency of the domestic financial institutions.
- If the application was initially submitted for filing on or before March 5, 1980, the date on which legislation was proposed.
- If the domestic financial institution had deposits of less than $100 million.
- If the application related to a takeover of shares or assets pursuant to a foreign person's intrafirm reorganization or any application to establish a bank holding company pursuant to reorganization.
- If the application related to a takeover of the assets or shares of a domestic financial institution in which such assets or shares were owned or controlled by a foreign person.
- If the application related to the takeover of a domestic financial institution that was a subsidiary of a bank holding company under an order to divest by December 31, 1980.

THE MAJOR POLICY EFFECTS OF REGULATION

For the first time, under the International Banking Act of 1978, foreign banks operating in the United States have been subject to a comprehensive federal regulatory supervision. A basic premise of the act is that foreign banks are welcome in the U.S. market and will be treated as fairly and equally as U.S. domestic banks. It is the authorities' hope that the foreign branches of U.S. banks will be treated as the competitive equals of foreign banks in foreign countries without discrimination.

The equality provision subjected foreign banks to the same restrictions and the same privileges as domestic banks. In that respect, the foreign banking act restricts the expansion of interstate deposit taking by foreign banks, subjects foreign branches and agencies to Federal Reserve requirements and interest rate regulations, requires deposit insurance for branches engaged in retail banking, and extends the restrictions on nonbank activities of the BHC Act to foreign banks' branches and agencies operating in the United States. The act mandates presidential recommendations on the McFadden restrictions on interstate branching. However, the Federal Reserve amended the McFadden Act through the back door, by allowing Edge corporations to establish branches across state lines and to take domestic deposits.

A foreign bank may operate with a federal license in one state and a state license in another state. Interstate expansion of a foreign bank's deposit-taking activities generally is limited to accepting deposits related to international business, except in its designated "home state." In its home state the foreign banking unit's deposit-taking powers are not restricted by the provisions of the foreign banking act. At the same time, the regulatory authorities have mandated a liberalization of rules governing Edge corporations to enable U.S. banks to compete more effectively with similar foreign-owned institutions. As a result, U.S. Edge corporations are allowed to open branches nationwide and to expand their international banking services and deposit-taking ability. In keeping with the principle of equal national treatment, foreign banks are also permitted to own Edge corporations.[47] In addition, the imposition of reserve requirements has increased foreign banks' costs of various types of funds, forcing offices of foreign bank institutions to choose between higher loan rates or lower profit margins.

The notion of equal national treatment also requires domestic and foreign banks to operate under the same regulatory authority control on a day-to-day basis. Foreign branches and agencies choosing a federal license will be supervised by the comptroller of the currency. Those offices choosing state licenses and insurance will be supervised by the FDIC and banking authorities of the state in which the foreign bank operates. The offices that choose state license but are not insured by the FDIC will be supervised by the Federal Reserve and state authorities. The Federal Reserve is also authorized to conduct on-site examination of branches and agencies of foreign banks. Those who fall under the foreign bank holding companies' provision will continue to be regulated by the Federal Reserve.[48]

As part of the Monetary Control Act of 1980, foreign bank branches and agencies that maintain basic reserve balances at the central bank have become eligible to use Federal Reserve services, such as check clearing, ordering coin and paper currency, and transferring funds by wire through the central bank without an intermediary. They are also given the privilege of borrowing from the Federal Reserve discount window, under the same rule and at the same price as domestic depository institutions.

In recent years, foreign banks have complained about exclusion from some state interstate banking laws. The complaint is in regard to some of the state laws prohibiting foreign banks from participating in regional interstate banking even when the foreign bank's home state in the United States is located within the region. The foreign banks protested on the ground that the state laws are inconsistent with the national policy of "equal treatment" and the International Banking Act of 1978.

At the center of the dispute are state laws that, directly or indirectly, exclude foreign-owned or -controlled banks from interstate banking laws, a privilege granted state domestic banks and holding companies. State laws in

Florida and North Carolina directly, and in South Carolina, Georgia, and Indiana indirectly, contributed to this controversy. The controversy is derived in part from the policy changes of some states that welcomed foreign banks in order to take advantage of the inflow of funds in the 1970s, and then later on prevented their expansion by excluding them from interstate regional banking arrangements. However, the complaint has not boiled over largely because most foreign banks chose to house their main offices in

Table 3.1
International Banking and Monetary Control Acts

HIGHLIGHTS

The International Banking Act

Subjected foreign banks to comprehensive federal regulatory supervision and examinations.

Provided the agencies and branches of foreign banks with the option of federal licensing, but limited their interstate deposit-taking activities.

Imposed Federal Reserve requirements on foreign bank agencies and branches for monetary policy purposes and for competitive equality.

Required federal deposit insurance for branches of foreign banks engaged in retail banking.

Extended the restrictions on nonbank activities of the BHC Act to foreign bank branches and agencies.

Gave Edge corporations broader power to compete more efficiently with the agencies and branches of foreign banks; permitted foreign banks to own Edge corporations and international banking facilities.

The Monetary Control Act

Permitted foreign bank branches and agencies that maintain basic reserve balances at the central bank to become eligible to use Federal Reserve services.

---

either California or New York, two states usually excluded from regional banking arrangements.[49]

NOTES

1. The McFadden Act of 1927 allowed a national bank to establish branches in its office city only if branching was permitted there by state law. The Douglas amendment to the Bank Holding Company Act of 1956 prohibited a bank holding company from acquiring any interest in a bank located outside the applicant's "home" state (or open a branch) unless such acquisition was specifically authorized by the law of the target state. This provision, known as BHCA Section 3(d), carried the McFadden Act's branch bank restriction into the BHC Act by stipulating that out-of-state holding companies may acquire banks in other states only to the degree that state laws expressly permit them.

2. Gerard H. Anderson, "Current Developments in the Regulation of International Banking," *Economic Review*, Federal Reserve Bank of Cleveland, January 1980, p.6.

3. The Glass-Steagall Act separates commercial banking from investment banking, to increase the safety and soundness of the financial sector and to protect the consumer from conflict of interest abuses and other inequalities. Similarly, the BHC Act of 1956 prohibited holding companies of banks from acquiring, directly or indirectly, ownership or control of any voting shares of any company that was not a bank, or engaging in any business other than that of banking or of managing or controlling banks or of furnishing services to or for any bank of which it owned or controlled 25 percent or more of the voting shares. [Public Law 511, Section 4(a)(b), 70 STAT, May 9, 1956].

4. The Edge Corporation Act was passed in 1919 to permit domestic banks to establish subsidiaries (Edge corporations), which need not be in the same state as the parent bank. The Edge corporations are permitted to be involved only in international banking activities. Foreign banks were not permitted to establish Edge Act subsidiaries prior to the passage of IBA.

5. U.S. Congress, "An Act to Amend the Act Approved December 23, 1913, Known As the Federal Reserve Act," S. 2472, 66th Congress, 2nd Session, 1919, pp. 378–384. And Francis A. Lees, *International Banking and Financing*, New York: Holstead Press, John Wiley and Sons, 1974, pp. 25–27 and 138.

6. U.S. Congress, Joint Economic Committee, *Foreign Banking in the United States*, Economic Policies and Practices, Paper No. 9, by Jack Zwick, Washington, D.C., 1966.

7. S. 3765, 89th Congress, 2nd Session, 1966.

8. Board of Governors of the Federal Reserve System, "Data Series on Foreign-Owned U.S. Banks," *Federal Reserve Bulletin*, Vol. 60, No. 10, 1974, pp. 741–742.

9. H.R. 11440, 93rd Congress, 1st Session, 1973.

10. S. 958, 94th Congress, 1st Session, 1975.

11. Bruce J. Summers, "Foreign Banking in the United States: Movement toward Federal Regulation," *Economic Review*, Federal Reserve Bank of Richmond, January/February 1976, pp. 5–6.

12. Ibid., p. 6.

13. U.S. Congress, House Committee on Banking, Currency, and Housing, *Financial Institutions and the Nation's Economy (FINE) — Discussion Principles*, 94th Congress, 1st Session, Title VI, 1975.

14. The Group of Ten consists of Belgium, Canada, France, Germany, Italy, Japan, Holland, Sweden, the United Kingdom, and the United States.

15. James C. Baker and John K. Ryan, Jr., "An Evaluation of U.S. Federal Regulation of Foreign Bank Operations," *Issues in Bank Regulation*, Spring 1987.

16. Ibid., p. 29.

17. H.R. 10899, Public Law 95-369, 95th Congress, September 17, 1978, 92 STAT. 607, 608, and 624.

18. Ibid., Sections 3(a), 3(b), and 3(c), 92 STAT. 608 and 609.

19. Ibid., Sections 3(e) and 3(f), 92 STAT. 609 and 610.

20. Ibid., Sections 4(a) and 4(c), 92 STAT. 610 and 611.

21. Ibid., Section 4(b), 92 STAT. 610.

22. Ibid., Sections 4(d), 4(e), 4(f), 4(h), and 4(i), 92 STAT. 611 and 612.

23. United States Code Service, Lawyers Edition, 12 USCS Banks and Banking 2001–5000, May 1988, p. 181.

24. IBA 1978, Section 5(a), 92 STAT. 613–614.

25. 12 USC 3101(b)(1), 3101(b)(9), 3103(a)(3), and 3103(a)(4), S. Report No. 95–1073, August 8, 1978, p. 3.

26. IBA 1978, Section 5(b), 92 STAT. 614 and USC 3103(b); Congress Rec. S. 13396 (daily ed., August 15, 1978).

27. United States Code Service.

28. IBA 1978, Sections 6(a) and (b), 92 STAT. 614; USC 3104 and 1813.

29. Ibid., Section 7(a), 92 STAT. 620; USC 3105.

30. FDIC News Release, November 16, 1978. pp. 1–2.

31. Depository Institutions Deregulation and Monetary Control Act of 1980. Public Law 96–221, Title II, March 31, 1980.

32. Section 2(c) BHCA, 12 USC 1841(c)(1976), defines "bank" as follows: "Bank" means any institution organized under the laws of the United States, any state of the United States, the District of Columbia, any territory of the United States, Puerto Rico, Guam, American Samoa, or the Virgin Islands which (1) accepts deposits that the depositor has a legal right to withdraw on demand, and (2) engages in the business of making commercial loans. Such a term does not include any organization operating under Section 25 or Section 25(a) of the Federal Reserve Act, or any organization which does not do business within the United States except as an incident to its activities outside the United States.

33. IBA 1978, Section 8(a) 92 STAT. 622, 12 USC 1841 note, 12 USC 1850, 1971–1978. As amended in 1970, the BHC Act prohibited bank holding companies from holding shares of any company that is not a bank, with a limited number of exceptions. The exceptions included: (a) shares of any company with ownership interest of less than 5 percent, (b) shares in which national banks may by statute invest, (c) shares held in fiduciary capacity, (d) shares acquired in satisfaction of debts previously contracted, and (e) shares of premises and other companies providing operating services for subsidiary banks. The exception to the general prohibition was the one contained in Section 4(c)(8) of the act on permissible activities. The act conferred on the board the ability to determine which activities are closely related to banking and thus to allow bank holding companies to invest in companies engaged

in these activities. (Henry C. Wallich, statement before the Commerce, Consumer, and Monetary Affairs Subcommittee, House of Representatives, June 25, 1980, p. 2.)

34. Henry C. Wallich, Board of Governors of the Federal Reserve System, statement before the Commerce, Consumer, and Monetary Affairs Subcommittee of the Committee on Government Operations, House of Representatives, June 25, 1980, pp. 4–8. Section 2(h) and 4(c)(9) of the BHC Act, dating from 1966 and 1970 amendment, exempt nonbanking activities by foreign banks of a BHC when they were conducted exclusively outside the United States. The BHC Act of 1970 defines the foreign bank holding companies to which the exemption would apply as those companies "organized under the laws of a foreign country, more than half of whose consolidated assets are located or consolidated revenues derived outside the U.S." The rule also exempts (1) all activities conducted outside the United States, (2) activities conducted inside the United States incidental to international and foreign business, (3) ownership of companies principally engaged in the United States in financing or facilitating international or foreign transactions, and (4) ownership of up to 25 percent of the shares of any foreign company, in which more than half of whose assets or revenues are located or derived outside the United States.

35. IBA 1978, Sections 8(b) and 8(c), 92 STAT. 622–623, 12 USC 1841 note.

36. Ibid., 92 STAT 623, definition. For complete information regarding grandfathering or exemption on Section 8 of IBA, see Gruson and Weld, "Nonbanking Activities of Foreign Banks Operating in the United States," *University of Illinois Law Forum*, Vol. 129, 1980, pp. 121–162.

37. IBA 1978, Section 9, 92 STAT. 623–624, September 17, 1978, 12 USC 601 note. Rep. to Congress.

38. Ibid., Sections 10(a) and (b), 92 STAT. 624; Rule 12 USC 3107.

39. Ibid., 92 STAT. 624–625; 12 USC 3108.

40. Ibid., Section 14, 92 STAT. 625; 12 USC 36 note., 44 STAT. 1224.

41. Board of Governors of the Federal Reserve System, *Regulation K, International Banking Operation*, 12 CFR 211, Section 211.4, October 24, 1985.

42. Federal Reserve Press Release, September 30, 1985, p. 2.

43. These limitations apply only to acceptances of the types described in Paragraph 7 of Section 13 of the Federal Reserve Act (12 USC 372).

44. Regulation K, Edge Corporation, Section 211.6, October 24, 1985.

45. Depository Institutions Deregulation and Monetary Control Act of 1980, Public Law 96–221, March 31, 1980; 12 USC 226 note.

46. Ibid., 12 USC 3101 note, 94 STAT. 192–193.

47. Federal Reserve System, Fed Points 9 and 26.

48. Ibid.

49. For further information, see: Washington Financial Reports, Vol. 46, No. 1, January 6, 1986, p. 5.

4   International Financial Markets

Foreign investment decisions consist of a complex process that differs in many respects from domestic investment decisions. The complexity arises from different sets of strategic, motivational, and economic considerations far wider than a better known domestic market environment. Foreign investment is normally overshadowed by political and foreign exchange risk considerations, surpassed by longer process, cost overruns, and less familiarity with the participating market. What motivates a corporation to enter the foreign market is the intuition of higher earnings potential, the saturation of the domestic market, or the forces of market competition and customers' demand for a greater variety of services on a worldwide basis. Banks, like any other industrial corporation, are faced with a similar challenge. In fact, in some respects, they see a greater challenge than manufacturing or other service industries because the nature of the banking business requires far more liquidity than other business structures.

Today, international banking consists of more diversified activities far beyond the traditional form of trade financing, foreign exchange trading, or money market activities. A new element that has received quite a lot of attention in recent years is the area of investment banking and activities that have not been permissible for banks in the traditional form. Retail banking and entry into local banking markets have also become a prospect for foreign banks internationally, and in the United States exclusively. As a result, the growth of international banking has been accompanied by an increasing number of new foreign affiliate offices. This chapter will examine the strategic motives for foreign investment decisions, international money markets, and the establishment of international governmental agencies.

THE FOREIGN INVESTMENT DECISION

The traditional classical theories of international trade were formed on the basis of absolute or relative advantages in the production of goods and their distribution on a free trade basis. Free trade takes place because of the gain that a country can make from trade when it produces and consumes more in a free trade situation than it would without trade. The flow of trade arises from an economic advantage that one country or region may have over another in the output of particular goods and services. The advantages may lie in the differences in the cost of the factors of production, differences in technologies, economies of scale in production and distribution, or even differences of taste. In the second half of the twentieth century, theoreticians and practitioners tried to answer why an investor makes an attempt to establish direct facilities in foreign markets versus relying on correspondent relationships. In a broad sense, it is a distinction between foreign direct investment and acquisition via management contract, technology and licensing agreements, and financial loans.

The vast body of literature presents three motives for foreign direct investment. These motives consist of strategic, behavioral, and economic considerations. The strategic motive categorizes the investor as a seeker of markets, raw materials, production efficiency, technology, or political safety. The elements involved here are internal to the operation of the firm, and are derived from management policy seeking better strategies for the overall well-being of the organization. The behavioral motive, on the other hand, is subject to the external forces that drive the firm to take action to prevent market imperfections or loss of status due to lack of proper actions. This motive may include a fear of losing a market to the competitors, a need for the creation of new products, reaction to strong competition from abroad, and even a "band wagon" effect. The economic motive, based on market imperfection, consists of those activities and forces that stimulate financial well-being and profit-taking elements of a firm, causing the firm to expand into new environments for better economic results.[1] These elements may include oligopolistic advantage, superior managerial and marketing expertise, product differentiation, and financial strength, including the availability of large sums of capital and the desire for diversification to reduce risk. Above all, as a firm reaches a certain size, in order to grow, survive, and keep credibility, it must maintain a competitive advantage by receiving local identity. Thus, internationalization for a large-size firm becomes a key ingredient for future growth.

MODERN INTERNATIONAL ECONOMIC THEORIES

International economic theories have undergone a chain of revolutionary changes in the modern economic environment of the twentieth century. The changes can be traced back to the roots of classical theories of international movement of capital and the factors of production. The classical theory of international capital movement, based on the gold standard system, centered around trade imbalances and interest differentials for the securities of equal risk, given a purely perfect market condition. The trade and interest differentials were both self-correcting with an automatic mechanism that, over a period of time, would redistribute wealth and economic power from exporting nations to importing nations via price and income adjustments. For example, a trade imbalance would indicate that country A could produce and export at a cheaper rate than country B; thus, there would be a flow of revenue from B to A. Under the quantity theory of money, the increase in money supply in country A would lead to an increase in domestic prices and a decrease in interest rates. The opposite would occur in country B, where the lower prices would increase demand for products of this country, increase exports and redistribute wealth back to country B, given the completion of country A's progressive economic cycle. Similarly, the interest differentials would signal the imbalance between investment opportunities and resources available for investment among various countries. As a result, there would be a flow of capital investment from the lower-interest-rate market country to the one with more investment opportunities. While this theory indirectly recognizes market imperfections, it does not consider oligopolistic imperfection or regulatory interventions. Furthermore, the theory does not foresee the rise of prices along with higher interest rates, a situation that dominated the economic environment of the United States during the second half of the 1970s.

During the second half of the twentieth century, two events changed the structural formation of international economic trade theory. First, oligopolistic competition in imperfect markets replaced pure competition and monopoly. Second, with the adoption of the floating exchange rate (1974), independent economic policies among industrialized nations replaced the structurally set policy of the nineteenth century. Now national governments and multinational firms could pursue independent economic and trade policies via intervention and the creation of unique competitive advantages through product differentiation, tariff and other barriers, tax incentives, or capital market controls.

Foreign Direct Investment Theories

Economists credit the modern theory of foreign direct investment to Stephen Hymer (1960) and Charles Kindleberger (1969).[2] According to the Hymer-Kindleberger theory, foreign direct investment is a by-product of market imperfections, derived from oligopolistic industrial or market formation. For a multinational corporation to be effective in this environment, the market should be sufficiently large or protected, and economies of scale should exist to compensate for the disadvantage of not being familiar with local environments. Furthermore, the competitive advantage must allow the firm to earn a higher rate of return from foreign direct investment than otherwise would be earned by similar projects in the home market. If these conditions are not met, then a firm is better off producing at home and exporting abroad to be effective in its market participation approach.

The Product Cycle Model. The "product cycle" model presented by Raymond Vernon in 1966 describes three stages of development in a firm's production cycle.[3] In the "new product" stage, a firm produces at home and exports abroad. In this stage, technology is unknown or protected, and the manufacturer enjoys a monopolistic advantage. No foreign direct investment is needed in this stage of production. In the second stage, the "mature product" stage, the market reaches maturity, technology and know-how are commonly known, and goods are uniformly produced by competitors. Thus, foreign direct investment may appear to be a means for market expansion and a response to competition. In the third stage of development, the "standardized product" stage, foreign direct investment is initiated to aid a firm in better utilization of its resources and in becoming cost efficient as it faces the challenge to capitalize on market efficiency in pursuit of higher return on investment. Thus, multinational firms pursue foreign direct investment to take advantage of the opportunities abroad. American and British firms pursue this route, shifting production abroad to take advantage of lower wage rates in their attempt to become cost efficient, and at the same time to infiltrate new territorial markets for future expansion.

The Differentiated Products Model. In 1971, Richard Caves presented another version of Vernon's product cycle theory, based on differentiated products. Caves argued that multinational corporations that generate differentiated products at home may desire to market them worldwide to maximize return on investment and to compensate for the expenditures on research and marketing projects at home. The key to success here is the time lag that exists between the marketing of the original production and the time when such products may be copied by competitors abroad. An example of this situation is IBM. It took 25 years for competition to catch up with the technology of IBM, at a substantial cost. During this time, IBM enjoyed uninterrupted market domination and earned a substantial amount of profit by presenting differentiated products abroad.

Caves's differentiated products theory, like Vernon's product cycle theory, consists of three stages. In the first stage, the products can be marketed without any significant adaptation to local markets. Thus, mass production in the home country and exportation abroad is a prevailing choice. No foreign direct investment is needed in this stage of the production cycle. However, if the product does not enjoy mass production status, or the host country's government regulations require some form of local identification, then licensing may be a means of entry into a new market. Finally, if the host country's market differs in style and substance from the home country market, or the differentiated products are not the main competitive advantage of the exporting firm, then the expansion may take the form of foreign direct investment. Under the third option, the exporting firm has to maintain some form of oligopolistic advantage in the form of technology, know-how, managerial expertise, or even marketing superiority, in order to be seen as differing from other competitive market seekers.[4]

One example of market imperfection in which foreign direct investment may benefit participants is that of protected economies or communities. The formation of the European Economic Community (EEC) in 1957 and European Free Trade Association (EFTA) in 1958 provided opportunities for foreign direct investment. Under the EEC constitution, the members agreed to remove internal tariffs and coordinate monetary and fiscal policy. Similar opportunities developed when EFTA was established to facilitate trade and movements of goods and services among EEC member nations.[5]

THE THEORY OF INTERNATIONAL BANKING

The body of literature is not swollen with theories of international banking. Since 1975, various attempts have been made to explain the phenomenon of international banking. Most theoreticians based their argument on industrial organization theory, comparative cost advantage theory, trade theory, or even product differentiation theory. None of the existing theories provide production with a wide base application, nor do they show originality. The key failure here is the inability of theoreticians to provide data to support their meager research findings.

In 1970, Robert Aliber suggested that there is a connection between foreign direct investment and imperfection in the foreign exchange markets.[6] In other words, some foreign direct investment is motivated by imperfection in foreign exchange markets. Imperfection in foreign exchange markets develops when disequilibrium exists in the purchasing power parity and exchange rate between trading partners. Thus countries with overvalued currencies would engage in foreign direct investment in countries with undervalued currencies.

What is crucial to the Aliber theory is the timing of the investment. To achieve satisfaction, a firm should prepare the background and planning for investment, but start the process when a differential exchange rate occurs. A problem that may occur lies in the proper definition and interpretation of overvalued versus undervalued currency. More important is the fact that, under today's floating exchange system, a distinction between the two currency values is less a function of the purchasing power parity, but instead may be based more on other related factors. For example, it is true that the currently undervalued U.S. dollar has stimulated foreign investment in banking and other financial institutions. But the reason is not primarily the uncharacteristic differential in the foreign exchange rates. Instead it is a function of the large U.S. trade deficits, causing accumulation of substantial reserves of dollars by Japan and major European countries. Other factors involved are the U.S. budget deficits and high interest rates, bank failures, and the U.S. government's intention to keep the value of the dollar low to stimulate exports and discourage imports. Naturally, a multinational firm operating in the international market desires to manage its foreign exchange exposure to reduce foreign exchange risk; thus, an imperfection in foreign exchange rates may signal the timing for investment, if such an investment coincides with the firm's diversification policy and expansionary movements.

In 1976, Robert Aliber used the market imperfections theory to explain the phenomenon of international banking.[7] He based his approaches on trade and industrial organization theories, in an attempt to compare the efficiency of banks in different countries as an approach to successful international banking. Based on the free trade theory, international free movement of money would channel funds to banking institutions that pay higher interest rates and contribute to the demand for loans to those banking institutions that charge the lowest lending rate. Thus, the differential rate among banking institutions and international money centers indicates the direction of growth in international banking markets. On the other hand, based on the industrial organization theory, the spread between the interest rate paid on bank liabilities (deposits) and the yield earned on bank assets (loans) would determine the relative efficiency of banks in different countries. Assuming that the number of banks and profits are inversely related in a given market, the banks in a less saturated market would be more profitable than those with large numbers of banking establishments. Therefore, the countries with a lower concentration of banking offices would have a higher margin of profit and would receive international banking.[8]

According to a study by the Organization for Economic Cooperation and Development (OECD) in selected industrialized countries for the years 1968 and 1977, bank efficiency, measured by the earnings margin, is not necessarily correlated with the banks' concentration ratios and their international competitiveness. Instead the study reveals that the gross earnings margin of U.S. banks with a lower concentration ratio was higher than some other similar international banks from Australia, Germany, Italy, and Switzerland.[9] This result, along with the existing barriers in the free movement in money, contradicts Aliber's market imperfection theory due to the international differences in spread among borrowing and lending rates in international banking communities. Aliber's theory is based on free trade theory and international free movement of money. In today's financial environment, the free movement of money does not exist, because of the differential in exchange rates and prices, transaction and transfer costs, and governmental regulations. Thus the differential in spread between borrowing and lending rates may not be the determinant factor in international banking growth patterns.

In 1977, Herbert Grubel attempted to explain the phenomenon behind rapid expansion of international banking in the 1960s and 1970s.[10] Grubel sees a linkage between efficiency in international banking and the success some banks experienced in one or combined areas of retail banking, wholesale banking, and service banking. In the area of retail banking, product differentiation, in connection with management of technology and marketing know-how, would successfully transmit domestic uses to international uses, at lower marginal costs abroad. Furthermore, the product differentiation through different types of services, accompanied by advertising, branch office location, and automation could successfully protect skills applicable to foreign markets. Naturally, this scenario would occur if competitors failed to duplicate the result, a factor that historically has low probability in the banking industry.

The wholesale banking approach, based on comparative cost advantage theory, benefits from the application of economies of scale in funding and investment, and the spread of the overhead costs by international bankers among various countries. Access to international money markets would give the international bankers and money traders an advantage in cost efficiency that is not available to domestic banking activities. Similarly, service banking activities for multinational corporations and subsidiaries would build a positive relationship between corporate clients and banks. Such a relationship would provide international banks direct access to information about the financial condition of a firm, and place them in an advantageous position to compete with local banks.

Norman S. Fieleke attempted to test the relationship between superior financial technology and aggressive marketing in an international banking context via foreign bank operation.[11] Basing his theory on the success of U.S. overseas branch banks, he stated that success was primarily motivated by the advantages that these branches have in aggressive marketing and financial technology through detailed knowledge of clients' banking requirements and in pursuit of a policy of profit maximization and risk minimizers. Fieleke found it difficult to provide statistical data to support his study of foreign banking operations and the variability of the rate of return, using techniques he envisaged as the cause and effect of the link.

A different theoretical approach by Ian Giddy, based on the conventional theory of foreign direct investment and product life cycle theory, distinguishes three types of international banking.[12] Arm's length international banking, like the new product stage, is conducted from a home base in an environment free of regulatory barriers. The major function of an international bank is to accept deposits from and make loans to foreign clients and thus hold a correspondence relationship with overseas banks for other banking purposes. The second type of international banking is offshore banking, where the primary function of the bank is to participate in money market activities internationally. The offshore banks, or as Giddy called them, Eurocurrency centers, are primarily involved in the purchase and placement of Eurocurrency funds, Eurocredit activities, and foreign exchange transactions for the bank as well as clients. This stage is similar to the standardized product stage presented by Raymond Vernon in 1966. The bank takes advantage of mass transactions in a low cost country. Finally, the third type, entitled host-country international banking, refers to physical location of banks abroad. In this form, banks may choose to operate representative offices, agencies, or branches, or may operate wholly-owned subsidiaries.

INTERNATIONAL MONEY MARKETS

International money markets are involved in the borrowing and lending of currencies through various money centers. The international money centers are located around key banking cities with trade financing facilities. Prior to 1960, the money centers focused primarily on trade-related financial transactions. Today, they provide worldwide facilities for the free movement of capital and a marketplace for foreign investments. The major contributors and transactors in these centers are international banks of various nationalities who finance trade, provide services to clients, and invest on behalf of their banks for business gains. Two types of money market centers have been defined: external (international) money centers and internal (domestic) money centers. The difference is in the locality and type of people making transactions within the specified market. The international money markets are located outside of the country of origin and are involved in transactions by nonresidents. The best-known are Eurocurrency markets. These markets are basically "wholesale." Their advantage over domestic markets rests in the abundant supply of funds available at a significant cost advantage. Examples of international money markets are London, New York, Paris, Zurich, Tokyo, Geneva, Antwerp, Amsterdam, and Hong Kong. Another form of international money center is known as the "offshore" financial center. These centers provide financial services in limited variety. The best known offshore financial centers are Luxemburg, Cayman Islands, the Bahamas, Bahrain, Panama, and the Netherland Antilles.

Eurocurrency Market

A Eurocurrency market consists of banks that deal in convertible currencies outside the country of origin. These banks, known as "Eurobanks," accept deposits and make loans. They may be foreign banks or overseas branches of international banks. The Eurocurrency market serves two major functions. First, it provides an efficient and convenient time deposit center with a variety of maturities. Second, it serves as a loan-granting institution to corporations and finances trade. The deposit and lending activities are mostly short term in nature, ranging from a few days to a few years. Eurocurrency exists for any convertible currency. For example, the "Euro" form for the dollar is the Eurodollar, for the pound sterling is the Europound, for the Japanese yen is the Euroyen, for the French franc is the Eurofranc, and for the German deutsche mark is the Euromark. The best known of these "Euro" forms is the Eurodollar.

The prefix "Euro" is universal, applied to various world currency centers. The center can be located anywhere in Europe or in Asia or even in the United States. The U.S. facilities for Eurocurrency transactions are called "international banking facilities" (IBF). IBFs, as described in chapter 2, are facilities that offer time deposits and loans to foreign nonresidents, with transactions denominated in different currencies. Information about Eurocurrency market activities is provided by the *Annual Report* of the Bank for International Settlement (BIS) and by the *World Financial Markets* of the Morgan Guaranty Trust Company.

Eurodollar Market. A Eurodollar is a dollar deposited outside the United States. The deposit can be originated by an individual investor, by a corporation, or by a bank from the United States or another country. The Euromarket specializes in accepting short-term deposits and making short-term loans. The funds are used to satisfy liquidity requirements of banks and financial firms, as well as for trade financing and interest arbitrage.

The bulk of the transactions in the Eurocurrency market are in the form of U.S. dollars. Since 1976, an average of 76 percent of the gross Eurocurrency market size has been denominated in U.S. dollars. The United Kingdom, and London in particular, is the most prominent Eurocurrency center. The United States and New York rank second in line, with France in third place. The German deutsche mark is a distant second behind the U.S. dollar in Eurotrading activities. Approximately 60 percent of the Eurodollar funds are deposited in Europe, 20 percent in offshore centers, 10 percent in the United States, and the rest in Canada, Japan, and the rest of the world.[13]

The development and progress of the Eurodollar market can be traced back to a number of factors. Many of these factors were external to direct U.S. influences, others were the result of the U.S. regulatory and internal economic status at the time. The external factors included the U.S. participation in the Marshall Plan, which caused large quantities of dollar transfers to European markets, and the reluctance of Russia to deposit dollars inside U.S. territorial control during the late 1940s and 1950s. The Russian reluctance factor, along with the lack of facilities for foreigners to borrow dollars outside the U.S. market, caused increasing attention toward European banking centers, especially the banks in London, Paris, and Zurich.

Another factor that stimulated the growth of the Eurodollar market was the higher yields in Europe. Individual investors, commercial banks, and businesses shifted their funds abroad to take advantage of the spread between European interest rates and the current U.S. rate. The sterling crisis of 1957 added another dimension to the emergence of the Eurodollar market. The weak pound, and the British government's imposition of tight lending in sterling to nonresidents, elevated the U.S. dollar to become a leading currency. The British banks sought alternatives to the pound sterling and turned to the dollar to maintain their financial position in world markets. The action aided London banks to maintain financial stability and at the same time paved the road for the city of London to become a center for international trading in the U.S. dollar.

Internal factors in the United States also contributed to the strength of the Eurodollar market. The status of the United States as the world's largest creditor, along with the sheer size of world trade in the U.S. dollar during the decades of the 1950s and 1960s, focused world attention on the importance of the dollar in international currency markets. A further push came internally through the U.S. balance-of-payment deficits of the 1960s and U.S. government Regulation Q, the U.S. Interest Equalization Tax of 1963, and the U.S. Foreign Direct Voluntary Act of 1965.

U.S. balance-of-payment deficits led to accumulations of dollars in the hands of nonresidents, paving the way for the 1963 legislation limiting capital outflow from the United States. The U.S. Interest Equalization Tax effectively closed the U.S. capital markets to foreigners, including U.S.-owned foreign affiliates. This act not only limited the short-term flow of money market funds, but also affected medium- and long-term borrowing in U.S. markets. In response, U.S. banks sought alternative courses of action by shifting funds abroad to escape taxation, and also sought the alternative sources of medium- and long-term funds in the newly created Eurobond markets. In 1965, the U.S. government imposed voluntary restrictions on American corporate foreign direct investment. The reluctance of corporations to comply with the ruling compelled the American government to force the issue by mandatory restriction in 1968. The restriction squeezed the U.S. multinational firms' traditional funding channel to that of the affiliates. In seeking a new source, U.S.-based corporations turned to the Eurodollar market for financing their affiliates' financial needs. Finally, Regulation Q, a ceiling on deposits under $100,000, caused the outflow of funds overseas to escape restriction.

During the decade of the 1970s, the energy crises of 1973 and 1979 channelled wealth to OPEC nations. The Arab nations, mistrusting America for political reasons, channelled their accumulated surplus dollars into European markets. This action further strengthened the importance of the Eurocredit market and established the Eurodollar as the major source of credit currency within the existing markets.

Eurocurrency Instruments and Eurodollar Deposits. Prior to 1980, the borrowing rate for Eurodollar loans was tied to the London Interbank Offered Rate (LIBOR). Since mid-1980, the U.S. money market rate is also considered an alternative or supplement to the LIBOR rate. There are two types of Eurocurrency instruments: Eurodeposits and Eurobonds. Eurodeposits have a maturity of less than one year. They may appear in the form of one-day time deposits to three- to six-month certificates of deposit. Normal deposits are $100,000 and over. The interest rates on Eurodollar loans are usually floating rates, especially for the intermediate and long-term maturities. The rate ties to LIBOR, normally quoted at 1.5 percent above that rate. The Eurobond maturity term ranges from 30 days to seven years. The bonds are denominated in $500,000 base, up to $100 million and more, typically in $1 million units.

Approximately 85 to 90 percent of Eurodollar deposits are in the form of straight-term deposits, with the funds placed in the bank for a specific maturity and at a fixed interest rate. More recently, the floating rate has been introduced for "roll-over credits," with a periodically adjustable clause of every three to six months. The other 10 to 15 percent of Eurodollar deposits are in the form of negotiable certificates of deposit (CDs), first offered in 1966 by the London branch of Citicorp. The negotiable CDs have a stated maturity at a fixed or floating rate of interest. There is a secondary market for this type of deposit, to aid the owner to cash funds prior to the stated maturity date. Nearly 120 banks and 25 broker/dealers are currently involved in issues and secondary market activities associated with negotiable CDs.

Three types of CDs are in issue. The "tap" CD is a certificate of deposit of a particular maturity and yield. Normally tap CDs are short-term instruments with maturities of less than one year. They are traded in multiples of $1,000, with a usual minimum purchase amount of $25,000. Often denominations range from $250,000 to $5 million, with possible maturities of 48 hours to five years. The second type of CD is the "tranche" CD, an intermediate-term issue. The tranche CD is often issued in denominations of $10,000 to $25,000, for a total of $10 million to $25 million. Each tranche can be liquidated according to prearranged agreements. The tranche CDs are suitable for small investors as the aggregate is composed of several small tranches, each with the same interest rate, maturity, and payment dates.

The third type of CD is Special Drawing Rights (SDRs) certificates of deposit. This form of CD became operational in London in 1980, based on the basket valuation of five major currencies. The currencies in the SDR are the U.S. dollar, the German deutsche mark, the Japanese yen, the French franc, and the U.K. pound. The market interest rate is the interbank offered rate of the five currencies. Credit Suisse–First Boston maintains the secondary market for SDR certificates of deposit. This type of CD has a minimum denomination of 1 million SDRs in multiple issues.[14] The advantage of SDR or the currency basket valuation is due to the stabilizing effects of diversification and the low volatility of valuation in the system. The idea originated with IMF's basket valuation of their monetary exchange system and has been adopted by international banks in their pursuit of a more stable market lending rate environment. The European community also considered the multicurrency basket valuation in the calculation of their European currency unit (ECU) system.

Asian Currency Market

The Asian Currency Market was created in 1968 by the government of Singapore to facilitate dollar deposits in the same manner as in the European currency market. The permission to draft outside funds was granted to the Singapore branch of the Bank of America, the largest world bank at the time. The motivation, on one hand, was a challenge to Europe's banking community and, on the other hand, a desire to gain access to the Asian foreign exchange reserve funds of neighboring regional countries. The Chinese and Japanese were the major targets, but other Asian countries were also persuaded to participate. One major accomplishment of this market was the act of intermediation between Asian and European money centers. Nevertheless, the Asian market has remained more regional than the Eurocurrency market.

To stimulate deposits, the government of Singapore reduced the tax levies on interest earned from offshore banks from 40 percent to 10 percent, and granted licenses to certain banks in Singapore to issue Asian currency units (ACU). Similar to the European basic LIBOR rate, the Asian basic rate is expressed in Singapore Interbank Offered Rate (SIBOR). Both fixed and floating interest rates are available in a close peg to the LIBOR rate. The market grew very rapidly in its first ten years. By March 1980, 108 financial institutions were licensed to operate ACUs. In order to safeguard outflows of funds from local banks, deposits by Singapore residents were limited to about $2.5 million for corporations and $125,000 for individuals. About 60 percent of ACU assets mature in less than three months and another 18 percent in less than six months. On the liability side, nearly 75 percent mature in three months. The size of the market was estimated to be near $160 billion by the end of 1986.[15]

INTERNATIONAL BOND MARKETS

International bonds are securities sold outside the country of the borrower. The first development of this market can be traced back to the late nineteenth century. The active cities at the time were all European: the major money centers of London, Paris, Antwerp, Amsterdam, and Berlin. In the early twentieth century, New York joined other international bond centers in a dominant position, but soon the crash of 1929 dampened the activities of these international money centers. The temporary halt was reversed in the early 1950s, with New York City once again in the forefront.

There are two types of international bonds: Eurobonds and foreign bonds. The Eurobond issues are sold principally in countries other than the country of the currency. Four types of Eurobonds are in use. "Straight debt" and "convertible notes" are the two fixed rate bonds, with one major difference. The convertible note bondholders have the option to convert their notes into common stock at a predetermined price or conversion ratio during the stipulated period. A "floating rate note" is a straight-debt issue with a variable rate of return. The rate is adjusted at regular intervals of three or six months to reflect changes in the short-term money market rate. The fourth type of Eurobond is known as the "currency option bond." Here the bondholders have an option to purchase the note in one currency, but receive the principal and interest in another currency.[16] This form of investment is a hedge against variation in the price of one currency versus another currency. The key to success with the currency option bond is the accurate forecasting of the foreign exchange market movement, within the time span of the investment.

Foreign bonds are issued by foreign borrowers in the country in which the issue is sold, in denominations of the currency of that country. The distinctions between the two types of international bonds are simply associated with the place of sale, and the base country of the borrowing firm. For example, a bond issued by a U.S. corporation in dollar denominations in Great Britain is a Eurobond. But a similar bond issued by a foreign nationality and sold in the United States by U.S. investment bankers, would be a foreign bond.

The Eurobond market is the larger of the two markets. The issues are in the bearer form with call provision, sinking funds, and may be in the form of multiple currency bonds with floating rates. Two key advantages of the Eurobond market are liquidity and tax flexibility. Liquidity is assured by the existence of the secondary market. Tax flexibility is enhanced by the fact that the country of residence of the issuing owner (borrower) is not a matter of public record, nor is the interest paid on the Eurobond subject to withholding taxes. Most of these issues originate from offshore, tax-haven, international money centers, free of regulation. Often national governments restrict international bond issues at home, but are more relaxed on foreign issues sold in the host market. For this reason, Eurobond issues and sales are growing more rapidly than foreign bonds.

MULTINATIONAL BANKING AND LENDING AGENCIES

A multinational bank and lending agency is a financial institution whose policy is guided by socioeconomic aspirations of the member nations or region, in pursuit of economic development. Because of the inequality among the world nations, circumstances necessitate that more fortunate ones assist the poorer countries. To achieve and promote development, the international lending agencies provide loans and guarantees, directly or through private businesses, for such projects as building roads, dams, and electrical plants, and also for temporary relief to those needy nations who have difficulties in their balance of payments, and those who need hard currencies to complete trade transactions.

Much of the multinational banking and lending activities involve facilitating the transfer of funds to the developing countries through financial loans or technical assistance. Each lending institution is guided by a constitutional charter designed to pursue a specific policy and program. The groups under review in this section are the International Monetary Fund, the International Bank for Reconstruction and Development (World Bank), Inter-American Development Bank, Asian Development Bank, African Development Bank, and European Investment Bank.

International Monetary Fund

The International Monetary Fund (IMF) was established on December 27, 1945, and commenced financial operation on March 1, 1947. The first article of the fund's constitution prescribed six objectives for the organization: (1) to promote international cooperation by consultation and collaboration on international monetary issues; (2) to facilitate the growth of international trade and the development of economic productivity; (3) to promote exchange stability; (4) to seek elimination of exchange restrictions and trade barriers; (5) to provide temporary financial assistance to member countries to correct payment imbalances; and (6) to seek reduction of both the duration and magnitude of payment imbalances.[17]

Agreement on the constitution and functions of the IMF was reached by 44 member nations, participating in the Bretton Woods Conference in New Hampshire in July 1944. Since then, the fund has gone through various reforms. The compensatory financing facilities were established in 1963 to assist members to cope with temporary shortfalls in export receipts. A buffer-stock-financing facility was created in 1969 to enable members to make contributions to approved international buffer stock arrangements. By this mechanism, the fund made financing available to dampen export price fluctuations, thereby reducing the variability of export receipts. In 1974, the fund enlarged quotas with a longer repayment period for assistance under credit tranche policies to countries experiencing balance of payment difficulties due to structural weakness or current account deficits. It also established two temporary oil facilities in 1974 and 1975 to help members, mostly from the non-OPEC Third World, to meet the increased cost of oil imports in those years.

The Jamaica Agreement of January 1976 demonetized gold as an IMF reserve asset. The proceeds of the sale were to be placed in a trust fund to help the poorer nations. Members could also sell their own gold reserves at the market price rather than at the previous par value price. The Second Amendment of the Articles of Agreement, effective April 1, 1978, gave members the right to adopt exchange arrangements of their choice, with the fund's supervision. The official price of gold was abolished and SDRs became the principal reserve asset of the IMF. In May 1981, a policy of enlarged access was adopted to succeed the supplementary financial facilities. IMF quotas increased to $76 billion, and voting rights were adjusted to reflect the new distribution of trade and reserves, pushing OPEC quotas to a total of 10 percent. The special oil facility recommended in the 1976 Jamaica meeting was confirmed for an amount of $9 billion for use by countries with balance of payments problems due to increased oil prices.

Membership, Organization, and Quotas. Membership in the fund is open to any state that is prepared to fulfill the obligations of membership contained in the fund's articles of agreement. The present membership includes all the industrial countries (with the exception of Switzerland), most developing nations, and some centrally planned economies in Africa, Asia, and Europe. The USSR participated in the Bretton Woods Agreement but did not join the fund. Most of the Communist bloc have chosen not to participate, or have withdrawn on the grounds that the association is mainly serving the interests of capitalist nations. Each member of the fund has a quota in SDRs that determines the member's participation, borrowing capability, and voting rights.

The IMF is organized and governed by three boards: the board of governors, the executive board, and the managing director committee. The organizational body is subdivided into five divisions, each serving a specific function. These consist of the regional departments, the functional department, special services, the information statistics liaison, and support services.

World Bank

The International Bank for Reconstruction and Development (IBRD), or World Bank, was created in 1945 under the Bretton Woods Agreement. The major purpose of the organization at the time was to provide financial assistance for postwar reconstruction and development of the war-torn nations. The bank's function and activities have been redirected since 1968 to provide economic and financial support for the advancement of developing nations. The principal emphasis of the World Bank today is to offer or guarantee loans and technical assistance for the productive reconstruction of poor countries. Toward achieving this goal, the bank uses its own capital and also organizes private capital or financing. The organization is an intergovernmental institution structured in the corporate form and owned by member governments. Typically, the projects involved are substantial and are part of the infrastructure of the borrowing nation. All loans require governmental guarantees. The interest charge is based on the bank's borrowing cost, plus a small fee.

In September 1987, the bank, under new leadership, pledged to revitalize the role of the bank in assisting the heavily indebted, middle-income countries to grow out of debt and recession. In fiscal 1988, IBRD, or the main lending body of the institution, increased its lending activity from the previous year by $600 million, to a total of $14.8 billion. Of the total, 43 percent was committed to the highly indebted, middle-income countries.[18]

The World Bank is supported by four institutional affiliates. The International Financial Corporation (IFC) was established to stimulate private investment in developing nations. During fiscal 1988, the IFC approved 92 investments for a total of $1.3 billion. This was an increase of 38 percent over the previous year and 83 percent since 1985. A large proportion of this investment was in Latin America, reflecting the presence of good investment opportunities. The International Development Agency (IDA) was created for making soft loans to developing countries. The principal beneficiaries of the IDA program are countries that need supplemental sources of capital, but because they have weak balances of payment are unable to finance their developmental projects with conventional terms. The corporation recorded $4.5 billion in contributions, a 30 percent or $1 billion increase over the previous year. About half of the total went to countries of sub-Saharan Africa to reduce their high indebtedness. The third affiliated organization is the International Centre for Settlement of Investment Disputes (ICSID). The center provides facilities for conciliation and arbitration of investment disputes between contracting states and nationals of other contracting states. As of June 30, 1988, the contracting states included 89 members of the World Bank and Switzerland. In 1988, there were nine disputes pending before the center. The fourth and newest affiliate of the World Bank is the Multilateral Investment Guarantee Agency (MIGA). This agency was created in 1988 to provide insurance to cover noncommercial risk and to encourage the flow of investment for productive purposes among member countries, in particular to developing nations. MIGA's authorization reached $1.08 billion in capital by the end of 1988.[19]

Inter-American Development Bank

The Inter-American Development Bank (IADB) was established in 1959 and commenced operations in 1960. The general purpose of this bank is to provide technical assistance and to direct financing to regional member countries. Originally, the IADB consisted of 19 Latin American countries and the United States. Today, it has 43 member countries, 25 from the region, plus the United States and Canada. Other members include the United Kingdom, France, Germany, Japan, and Switzerland. Usually the financing is limited to 50 percent of the cost of the project, subject to the capability of the borrower to finance the remaining cost of the project. Other considerations include socioeconomic impacts, along with the likelihood of the project becoming self-sufficient once it has been implemented.

The term and interest charge vary depending on the type of project and the level of poverty of the borrowing country. The length of the amortization period is between 15 and 25 years, with a grace period of 4 years. The interest charge ranges from 5 to 10 percent, depending on the type of currency used. If the loan is in local currency, the rate is normally 5 percent and under. For loans disbursed in a foreign currency, the rate of interest is almost doubled. Similar charges are applied to the supervision fee of 1 percent and credit commission of 1.25 percent for the total loan. There is no credit commission for loans disbursed in local currency. During 1987, the IADB provided $2.36 billion in lending support to foster Latin America's economic and social development. Historically, the major beneficiaries of the organization have been Argentina, Brazil, Colombia, and Mexico. Together they have borrowed 50.1 percent of the bank's cumulative lending of $39.7 billion from 1961 to 1987.[20]

The Inter-American Development Bank's governing body consists of three units. The policy-decision body of the organization is run by the board of governors. The operation of the bank is delegated to the board of executive directors. The managing directors are the president and the chairman of the board of executive directors. The main source of capital funds originates from member countries, with the U.S. contribution amounting to 51 percent of the capital, and Venezuela in second place with 15 percent.[21] Additional funds are obtained through borrowing in capital markets via bond financing and by commercial terms offered by banks and financial institutions. The permission of the government of the country in which the project would be implemented is required before any funds can be authorized to the borrower. The types of projects include agricultural, industrial, energy, mining, transportation, education, health, tourism, and science.

IADB's growth indicators show that loans from 1961 to 1987 were allocated toward energy (28 percent), agriculture and fisheries (21 percent), industry and mining (16 percent), and transportation and communication (13 percent). The remaining sectors, environment and public health, education, science and technology, urban development, and others, received only 22 percent of the cumulative lending during the past 16 years.[22]

Asian Development Bank

The Asian Development Bank (ADB) was founded in 1966 for the purpose of promoting economic and social advancement in the Asian and Pacific region. It has 45 member countries, 31 from Asia and 14 from Europe and North America. Among the participating members, the Japanese and U.S. share of capital amounted to 32 percent, with Australia, Canada, Germany, and the United Kingdom together holding another 18 percent. The organization is headquartered in Manila, Philippines, and is governed by a board of governors, a board of directors, and a president. The ADB engages in two general types of activities, loans and technical assistance (grants).[23]

The general lending operations include ordinary loans and special fund loans to the governments of member countries, their agencies, and public and private enterprises. The ADB finances projects that pursue the socio-economic development of the region. Two conditions must be met prior to the allocation of funds. First, the borrower should provide evidence confirming that the project is essential and is needed for the development of the country or region. Second, the borrower must demonstrate its inability to finance this project commercially. Normally this condition is met if the borrower has already applied for and has been turned down by a commercial bank prior to completing an application with ADB. Technical assistance is in the form of a grant for specific programs with a focus on agricultural and energy sectors. The institution provides advisory services, consultants, and cooperative sessions with experts from other institutions.

ADB lending operations, on average, range from $1.5 billion to $2 billion per year, with an average loan size of $30 million. A large percentage of borrowing is in Japanese yen, due to the favorable terms prevailing in the Japanese market. The interest charge on loans varies based on the market conditions, the types of loans, and the financial condition of the borrowing nations. The ADB requires a commission fee and a guarantee fee. Agriculture, agroindustry, energy, and social infrastructure projects rank one to four among the bank's lending priorities. The institution also provides the appropriate foreign currency for financing specific projects.[24]

African Development Bank

The African Development Bank (AFDB) was established in 1963 to promote private and public investment for developmental purposes among the member countries in the region. In addition to financial loans, the bank also provides technical assistance in support of projects aimed at national or regional infrastructural development. Financial loans are in the form of direct loans, investments in equity capital, or guarantees to third-party financial commitments. Like other regional banks, the AFDB provides assistance to individual firms, governments, and cooperative regional institutions, including multinationals concerned with the development of Africa.

The main governing body of the African Development Bank is the board of governors. The board sets guidelines for credit policy and delegates authority to the board of directors. The directors are in charge of the operation and execution of policy decisions under the leadership of the president and chairperson of the board. The president is the legal representative of the bank and supervises the daily activities and operations of the institution. At present, the bank has 51 active members, most from the region.

The average term of a loan is 15 years, but longer maturities are possible, with a maximum grace period of 5 years. The interest charge varies, subject to the cost of borrowed funds to the bank, but below the current market interest rate. From 1981 to 1986, the bank charged an average interest rate of 7 percent, a commission fee of 1 percent, and a guarantee fee of less than 1 percent. Funds are, in part, raised internally on the financial market of the member countries, or through the issue of capital stock by the bank. The external sources are derived from financial support by industrial nations and by financial institutions who receive guarantees of repayment from the AFDB prior to the commitment. The recipients should provide a plan to demonstrate the urgent needs for projects relating to the social and economic development of the borrower's institution, country, or region. They also should demonstrate the capability to repay the loan within the time frame assigned by the terms of the contract.

European Investment Bank

The European Investment Bank (EIB) was created in 1958 to assist the Common Market community in the pursuit of development and modernization of its economic well-being. The organization is a by-product of the Rome Treaty signed in 1957 and the European Economic Community (EEC) Treaty of 1958. The goal of the EIB was to provide financial and technical assistance for developmental projects in less developed areas, modernization of existing projects, and the projects that require substantial amounts of capital expenditures to benefit several member states. The bank is structured on a nonprofit basis, and is governed by the board of governors, the board of directors, the management committee of the president and chief executive officers, and the auditing committee.[25]

The original members of the EIB were the 6 original members of the EEC. Today it has grown to 12 members, reflecting the growth of the EEC. The bank's activities are not limited to the EEC's member countries; the program has gradually increased over time to cover nearly 70 countries outside the community. Three types of projects receive priority in allocation of loans and grants. The projects related to infrastructure, energy, and industrial development have received the major proportion of the allocations. The regional developmental projects also are given priority over other types of plans.[26]

The original capital of the European Investment Bank was funded by the member countries, and additional capital has been raised through sales of bonds on the international capital market. The terms of loans range from 7 to 20 years, based on the type of project. The infrastructural projects are given longer time for completion. EIB financing covers only 50 percent of the cost of the fixed assets. The interest rate charges are varied, and determined by the cost of capital carried out through private and public bond financing. But in certain cases, an interest subsidy rate of 3 percent from EEC budgetary funds may be allocated to lower the net cost of loans to specific borrowers. There is no predetermined minimum loan level stated in the charter of the association, but the institution refuses to become involved in very high cost projects.[27]

NOTES

1. David K. Eiteman and Arthur I. Stonehill, *Multinational Business Finance*, Addison-Wesley Publishing Company, Reading, Mass., 1986, pp. 246–254.

2. Stephen Hymer, "The International Operations of National Firms: A Study of Direct Foreign Investment," doctoral dissertation, Massachusetts Institute of Technology, 1960; and Charles P. Kindleberger, *American Business Abroad: Six Lectures on Direct Investment*, Yale University Press, New Haven, 1969.

3. Raymond Vernon, "International Investment and International Trade in the Product Cycle," *Quarterly Journal of Economics*, May 1966, pp. 190–207.

4. Richard E. Caves, "International Corporations: The Industrial Economics of Foreign Investment," *Economica*, February 1971, pp. 1–27.

5. Eiteman and Stonehill, pp. 255–256.

6. Robert Aliber, "A Theory of Foreign Direct Investment," in Charles P. Kindleberger (ed.), *The International Corporation*, MIT Press, Cambridge, Mass., 1970, pp. 17–34.

7. Robert Aliber, "Toward a Theory of International Banking," Federal Reserve Bank of San Francisco, *Economic Review*, Spring 1976, pp. 5–8.

8. Yoon S. Park and Jack Zwick, *International Banking in Theory and Practice*, Addison-Wesley Publishing Company, Reading, Mass., 1985, pp. 21–22.

9. Organization for Economic Cooperation and Development, "Costs and Margins in Banking — An International Survey," *Financial Market Trends*, June 1980, pp. 93–108.

10. Herbert Grubel, "A Theory of Multinational Banking," *Quarterly Review*, Banca Nazionale del Lavoro, December 1977, pp. 349–363.

11. Norman S. Fieleke, "The Growth of U.S. Banking Abroad: An Analytical Survey," *Key Issues in International Banking*, Federal Reserve Bank of Boston, Conference Proceedings in International Banking, October 1977, pp. 9–40.

12. Ian H. Giddy, "The Theory and Industrial Organization of International Banking," in Robert G. Hawkins, et al. (eds.), *The Internationalization of Financial Markets and National Economic Policy*, JAI Press, Vol. 3, 1983, pp. 195–243.

13. Morgan Guarantee Trust Company, *World Financial Markets*, New York, various issues, 1983–87.

14. Eiteman and Stonehill, pp. 400–401.

15. Monetary Authority of Singapore, *Annual Report*, 1984–86.

16. Dara M. Khambata, *The Practice of Multinational Banking*, Quorum Books, New York, 1984, pp. 60–61.

17. A. W. Hooke, *The International Monetary Fund: Its Evolution, Organization, and Activities*, IMF Pamphlet Series No. 37, 2nd ed., Washington, D.C., 1982, p. 2.

18. The World Bank, *Annual Report*, 1988, p. 31.

19. Ibid., pp. 31 and 79–81.

20. Inter-American Development Bank, *Annual Report*, 1987, pp. 7–9.

21. Khambata, pp. 215–218.

22. Inter-American Development Bank, p. 11.

23. Asian Development Bank, various brochures and publications, 1981–85.

24. Asian Development Bank, *Annual Report*, 1985 and 1987.

25. Commission of the European Communities, European Communities–Information Publications, 1987; and "Steps to European Unity," European Documentation Series, 1985.

26. Khambata, pp. 221–223; and EEC Publications, 1987.

27. Khambata, p. 222; and EEC Publications, 1987.

5 U.S. International Lending Institutions

Lending and borrowing outside a country of origin has been taking place for centuries through international banks and money centers in key market areas. At the same time, exporting countries promote trade and development to take advantage of international opportunities wherever such markets exist, in pursuit of better economic and trade relationships. As a result, the two forces of trade and lending interact to reinforce the flow of funds and the movement of goods and services.

In the twentieth century, the industrialized countries went one step further to stimulate small business exports and provide financial assistance for developing nations who seek basic technology and equipment for daily operation. They established a number of specialized lending institutions to foster these goals. Meanwhile, the economic reality of the time forced commercial banks to retreat from the massive infusion of funds worldwide, and the balance-of-payment deficits and economic deterioration of Third World countries prevented those nations from advancement in international purchasing due to their inability to secure loans of a large magnitude. Thus, intergovernmental and international lending agencies were created to promote economic development and to facilitate the transfer of funds to developing nations. This action, in turn, boosted exports from industrialized countries, especially in their respective minority and small business sectors, since they could not export to overseas and neighboring nations without governmental support.

This chapter reviews the key U.S. international banking and financial institutions that facilitate exports to developing nations through financial programs, guarantees, and technical supports. The institutions involved are the Export-Import Bank of the United States (Eximbank), the Private Export Funding Corporation, the Foreign Credit Insurance Association, the Overseas Private Investment Corporation, and the Agency for International Development.

THE EXPORT-IMPORT BANK OF THE UNITED STATES

Eximbank was created in 1934 and became an independent U.S. government agency in 1945. Basically, Eximbank's purpose is to encourage and supplement the private sector financing of U.S. exports sales by encouraging small- and medium-sized businesses to sell their products and services abroad. Although there is a direct loan program, the main function of Eximbank is not to lend to exporters directly. Instead, it encourages commercial banks and other lenders to make loans by guaranteeing reimbursement to the lender, in part or whole, should an exporter default on its obligation.

At first, the bank was directed by congressional statutes (1) to offer financing to U.S. exporters that was competitive with financing provided by foreign export credit agencies; (2) to determine and engage in transactions that provided a reasonable assurance of repayment; (3) to supplement but not compete with private sources of export financing; and (4) to take into account the effect of its activities on small business, the domestic economy, and U.S. employment. Since its inception, Eximbank has supported more than $190 billion in U.S. export sales to 140 countries, and its operations have resulted in more than $1 billion in dividends to the U.S. Treasury.[1]

Loan Programs

Eximbank has developed a number of programs to aid the financing of exports. These programs cover a wide array of products from mining and construction equipment to raw materials, commodities, and spare parts. Eximbank does not provide commercially available financing, overseas investment support, product guarantees, foreign aid, or foreign exchange risk protection. Table 5.1 outlines the basic features of Eximbank's programs.

The Working Capital Guarantee Program. This program provides exporters with access to working capital loans that would not be provided without Eximbank's assistance and without which the country would not be able to export. Most of the working capital loans guaranteed by Eximbank (in accordance with the Export Trading Company Act of 1982) are expected ultimately to support exports from small- to medium-sized minority and/or agricultural exporters, especially new-to-market producers. Eximbank's guarantee is based on its assessment that the exporter is credit worthy, and has already been turned down by commercial lenders. The guarantee is applied to revolving lines of credit and loans for specific transactions. The coverage is 90 percent, requiring 110 percent security for the outstanding

Table 5.1
Eximbank Program Summary

Terms	Appropriate Programs
Short-Term (up to 180 days)	1. Export Credit Insurance Program 2. Working Capital Guarantee Program
Medium-Term (181 days to 5 years)	1. Export Credit Insurance Program 2. Commercial Bank Guarantee Program 3. Small Business Credit Program 4. Medium-Term Credit Program 5. Working Capital Guarantee Program
Long-Term (5 years and longer)	1. Direct Loan Program 2. Financial Guarantee Program

Major Affiliate Agencies

Foreign Credit Insurance Association (FCIA)
Private Export Funding Corporation (PEFCO)

Source: Export-Import Bank of the United States, "Eximbank Program Summary," The Office of Public Affairs, 1984.

balance. The term of the contract is 12 months and may be extended. For loans up to 180 days, the fee is 1 percent; for the loans with longer maturities, 0.5 percent is added for each additional month or portion thereof.[2]

Commercial Bank Guarantee Program. Eximbank offers guarantees against nonpayment of foreign purchases on medium-term export loans extended by U.S. commercial banks. The coverage is currently available for more than 140 countries, with repayment terms not exceeding five years. The commercial bank guarantee program requires a 15 percent down payment by the borrower. The coverage for commercial risk is 90 percent, with the lending bank's participation of 5 percent of the loan. However, if the lending bank uses its discretionary authority to commit the loan to the borrower first, and then to Eximbank, it must assume 15 percent of the commercial risk. The exporter's participation is also 5 percent for commercial risk. For political risk, the insurance and guarantee coverage is 100 percent.[3]

Small Business Credit Program. The Small Business Credit Program enables U.S. banks to offer medium-term fixed rate export loans to finance sales of small U.S. companies' products and services. Interest rates are fixed at the lowest rates permitted under the export credit guidelines of the Organization for Economic Cooperation and Development (OECD). The interest rate is reviewed and adjusted every six months. Eximbank's loan commitment covers up to 85 percent of the contract price of an export sale financed by the U.S. bank on terms ranging from one to five years. Eximbank will either commit to make a loan to the bank, or it will commit to purchase the foreign debt obligation from the U.S. bank. Eximbank's rate is 1 percent below the minimum interest rate allowed under the OECD International Arrangement on Export Credits. The U.S. commercial bank is required to add 1 percent to Eximbank's rate so that the rate on the export loan is equal to the OECD arrangement rate as determined by the country category. Eximbank limits aggregate loan commitments per buyer to $10 million per year, and $2.5 million per transaction. The application fee is $0.65 per $100 of the loan amount for five-year obligations.[4]

Direct Loans and Financial Guarantees. Direct loans and financial guarantees provide financing assistance for U.S. exports of heavy capital equipment and large-scale installations for a term of more than five years. The bank's long-term financing takes the form of either a direct credit to the public or private overseas credit. This private credit may be denominated in either U.S. dollars or a foreign currency acceptable to Eximbank. The maximum loan limit is $10 million, with repayment guarantees by a financial organization (central bank) in the buyer's country. The coverage is 85 percent, with a 15 percent down payment by the buyer. The commitment fee is 0.5 percent per year on the undisbursed amount of each direct loan. The authorization fee is 2 percent of the loan value, applicable one time during the life of the loan.[5]

Export Credit Insurance. Export Credit Insurance (ECI) was created in 1961 to provide protection against the risk that the foreign purchaser would not pay its obligation for commercial or political reasons. ECI policies are sold and serviced by the Foreign Credit Insurance Association (FCIA), a group of U.S. insurance companies acting as agents for Eximbank. Policies offered are many and varied. ECI offers four types of coverage: (1) single-buyer policies for medium-term sales, (2) multi-buyer policies that cover numerous short-term transactions during a 12-month policy period, (3) master policies that cover short- and medium-term sales, and (4) special new policies for companies that had export sales of less than $750,000 a year in the last two years and that have not previously used Eximbank or FCIA programs. The ECI policy covers two types of risk: commercial defaults and political risks. Examples of commercial defaults are: economic deterioration in the buyer's market area, fluctuation in demand and unanticipated competition, shifts in tariffs, technological changes, operating cost inflation in the buyer's market, and national disasters. Examples of political risks are revolution and insurrection, confiscation of the buyer's assets, revocation of export-import licenses, detention of shipments, and growing balance-of-payment problems.[6]

Eximbank's Interest Charge and Country Categories

Under Eximbank's Direct Credit Loan Program, the Medium Term Credit Program, and the Small Business Credit Program, the interest rate charged will vary with the category of the country to which the exports will be shipped and with the repayment period of the loan. Table 5.2 exhibits the annual interest rate charged and country categories.

Financial Contribution and International Exposure

Eximbank has apparently been successful in accomplishing some of its objectives. As mentioned previously, the bank supported $190 billion in export sales during its first 50 years of operation. Eximbank has supplied a measure of encouragement, through its financing programs, for small- to mid-sized firms to enter the export market. The financial supports sustained American jobs and contributed to the benefits that international trade brings to both buyer and seller markets. Table 5.3 gives a summary of the authorizations and international financial exposure of Eximbank for the years 1982 to 1987.

In 1987, Eximbank programs were used by U.S. exporters in 38 states, the District of Columbia, Puerto Rico, and the Virgin Islands. The volume of exports supported by Eximbank rose by 45 percent in 1987 over 1986, to $9.3 billion. One major policy change that helped the organization was the shift in Eximbank authorization programs, from loan authorizations to guarantee and insurance authorizations. The loan authorization allocation was reduced from $3.5 billion in 1982 to $599 million in 1987. This policy change should help improve Eximbank loan losses, as banks and insurance companies become more involved in evaluating country risk factors. However, despite this improvement, Eximbank recorded $460.9 million in losses during the year. Table 5.4 provides a detailed authorization summary of allocations of loans, guarantees, and export credit insurance for 1987.

Recent Policy Changes

Over the past decade, Eximbank's financial condition has deteriorated. For the six years 1982–87, cumulative losses totaled $1.9 billion. John A. Bohn, Jr., president and chairman of the board of directors of the bank, assigns the principal cause of losses to the differential between the bank's borrowing and lending rates in response to competition from foreign credit

Table 5.2
OECD Annual Interest Rate and Country Categories

Annual Interest Rate: July 15, 1989 - January 15, 1990

Country Classification	5 years or less	Over 5 years
I. Relatively Rich	CIRR[a]	CIRR[a]
II. Intermediate	9.15	9.65
III. Relatively Poor	8.30	8.30

Country Categories for OECD Export Credits Arrangement

I. GNP per capita of $4,000 or more, as of 1979 IBRD figures.

II. GNP per capita of $680 - $3,999; not eligible for IDA or mixture of IDA and IBRD financing.

III. GNP per capita below $680; eligible for IDA or IBRD and IDA financing.

Source: Export-Import Bank of the United States, "Medium- and Long-Term Export Loans and Guarantees," August 1988.
[a] Commercial Interest Reference Rate.

agencies in the 1970s. At the end of September 1986, Eximbank's weighted average interest receivable rate was 8.51 percent, which was 3.19 percent under its weighted average interest expense rate of 11.7 percent.[7] The trend continued with minor improvement in 1987–88.

In order to control this costly practice of export credit subsidies, Eximbank negotiated with the principal trading nations of the OECD to forge a closer linkage between costs of funds and officially supported export credit interest rates. Furthermore, Eximbank reorganized in 1986 to fulfill the objectives Congress intended in creating the agency, which were to supplement and engage in transactions that provide a reasonable assurance of repayment. The continuous decline in the bank's reserves and changes in the competitive nature of international trade signaled the bank's management that it could not continue business as usual. The management responded with the following reorganization, published in the bank's 1986 annual report: (1) reorganized the bank into geographical divisions to simplify access

Table 5.3
Loan and Export Sales Authorization
(Billions of U.S. Dollars)

	FY82	FY83	FY84	FY85	FY86	FY87
Loan Authorization	3.5	0.8	1.5	0.7	0.6	0.6
Guarantee Authorizations	0.7	1.7	1.3	1.3	1.1	1.5
Insurance Authorizations	5.1	6.8	5.8	6.5	4.4	6.4
Total Authorizations	9.3	9.4	8.6	8.5	6.1	8.5
Export Sales Supported	12.2	10.4	10.4	9.3	6.4	9.3
Loans Receivable	16.6	16.9	17.5	15.9	14.3	11.2
Borrowings Payable	14.1	14.7	15.7	15.4	14.3	12.5
Capital & Reserves	3.0	2.8	2.5	2.1	1.8	1.3
Gross Revenue	1.4	1.4	1.6	1.6	1.5	1.3
Net Loss	0.2	0.2	0.3	0.3	0.3	0.5
Worldwide Exposure	38.2	38.2	38.2	35.0	32.2	29.9

Source: Export-Import Bank of the United States, **Annual Reports**, 1983-87.
 Note: Eximbank's fiscal year is from October 1 to September 30.

to Eximbank's loan and guarantee program; (2) established a separate division of economists and analysts to improve the country risk assessment capability; (3) increased direct credit coverage up to 85 percent of report value; (4) initiated a pilot program offering medium-term lines of credit in key markets where similar lines were extended by foreign governments to their exporters; (5) pursued an aggressive targeted program to combat foreign-tied aid credits; (6) introduced the new multi-buyer insurance coverage through FCIA, featuring equalized coverage against political and commercial risks and reduced reporting requirements and waiting periods; and (7) introduced coverage for lease transactions, including protection against expropriation, under both financial guarantee and FCIA insurance programs.

The bank's management also proposed two other solutions: first, a one-time direct appropriation to Eximbank; second, a waiver of prepayment penalties for the Federal Financing Bank, which would enable the bank to

Table 5.4
Authorization Summary for 1987
(Millions of U.S. Dollars)

	Number of Authorizations	Amount Authorized	Export Value
Direct Loans	19	331.6	427.8
Intermediate Loans	72	39.5	46.6
Medium-Term Credits	176	215.4	96.3
Small Business Credits	45	12.4	10.4
Financial Guarantees	19	1,019.6	1,674.9
Bank Guarantees	86	385.7	454.1
Working Capital	23	18.6	20.7
Other Guarantees	30	81.6	76.8
Export Credit Insurance	1,094	6,444.0	6,457.5

Source: Export-Import Bank of the United States,
 Annual Report, 1987.

refund its outstanding high rate borrowing at today's more favorable rates. Neither of these two remedies is expected to turn around Eximbank's financial deficit in the near term. However, it is a step to slow down deterioration and make the work more manageable.

On March 31, 1987, Chairman Bohn, speaking before the bank's Annual Exporters' Conference in Washington, D.C., announced further steps to reflect the realities of today's international economy and the need for expanding American exports and for recapitalizing Eximbank resources.[8] These steps include improving both the quality and quantity of credit risk protection; qualifying in advance the amount of principal and interest guaranteed; exploring new approaches to risk protection, such as lease financing and asset-based financing, to minimize country risk; adopting a new system of risk-related fees; being open in more countries, and providing equal access to all Eximbank programs to any responsible party; simplifying documentation for greater efficiency; and reorganizing the Working Capital Guarantee Program to include simplified documentation, reduced commercial risk retention on commitments made under delegated authority, and an improved system for the payment of fees on guarantees of revolving lines so that the fees reflect actual usage of the credit amount.

Despite these actions, it is generally believed that the bank will soon move to a negative reserve position, possibly in the early 1990s. The short-term remedies may not help the bank's continuous losses, and a turnaround is not expected until the mid-1990s or later. From an early report on the 1988 performance record and a 1987 statistical financial ratio analysis, it appears that the Eximbank ratio of reserves to total assets were further depleted to nearly 2 percent from the 12 percent ratio in 1982. The ratios of net income to operating income and to assets are in the negative column, and the delinquent loans to total loans ratio is at a record high of 40 percent. This would seem to indicate that Eximbank has not been able to adequately control the quality of its loans.

PRIVATE EXPORT FUNDING CORPORATION

The Private Export Funding Corporation (PEFCO) of New York is an affiliate organizational member of the Export-Import Bank of the United States. It was set up in 1970 to finance medium- and long-term export transactions. The organization is composed of commercial banks, industrial firms, and one investment banking firm. As an affiliate of Eximbank, the corporation deals only with those countries with whom Eximbank can deal, and those who comply overall with Eximbank programs. PEFCO helps U.S. lenders by providing guarantees of the repayment of principal and interest if buyers fail to comply with their obligations in repayment of the financed debt.

FOREIGN CREDIT INSURANCE ASSOCIATION

The Foreign Credit Insurance Association (FCIA), an independent U.S. government agency, is an association of leading insurance companies, operating in cooperation with and as an agent of Eximbank. It offers insurance policies protecting U.S. exporters against the risk of nonpayment by foreign debtors. The association consists of 50 property and casualty insurance companies that provide insurance against political and commercial default. The commercial risks may result from economic deterioration in the buyer's market, unanticipated competition, shifts in tariffs, technological changes, or fluctuations in demand. The political default may arise as a result of war, revolution and insurrection, or asset expropriation, license revocation, and shipment detention.

Types of Insurance Policies

FCIA provides exporters policies tailored to their needs. The credit insurance gives exporting companies fundamental protection on the riskiest part of their asset portfolio, foreign receivables. It also protects the exporter against the buyer's failure to pay its dollar obligation for commercial and political reasons, and encourages the exporter to offer competitive credit terms to prospective buyers. Overall, five types of insurance policies are in force, each designed to provide coverage for a special type of exporter for specific periods of time.

Short-Term Single-Buyer. This policy enables exporters to cover single or multiple shipments to one buyer under a sales contract. The coverage protects against export credit risks, both political and commercial. The major advantage of this policy is that the exporters have opportunities to selectively insure transactions with or without linking them to bank financing. The short-term coverage applies to credit sales to a foreign buyer or export letters of credit opened by a foreign issuing bank. For consumer items, parts, and raw materials, the term of credit is up to 180 days. For agricultural commodities, capital equipment, and quasi-capital equipment, the insurance term can be extended to 360 days. Products that are less than 50 percent U.S. content and certain defense products are not eligible for this type of coverage. FCIA can also issue a policy for up to 12 months to accommodate multiple shipments under a sales contract.

The foreign credit insurance policy requires that the premium be paid on the total principal insured volume. There is also a preshipment coverage added to the premium rate. The final invoice rate is based per $100 value. The minimum premium ranges from $2,500 for sovereign buyers and political coverage to $10,000 for private buyers. The percentage of coverage is equalized for both commercial and political risks. There is 100 percent coverage for sovereign obligors, 90 percent for the private sector and other nonsovereign obligors, 95 percent for letter of credit transactions, and 98 percent for agricultural transactions. A claim may be filed with the FCIA office 90 days but not exceeding 240 days after the due date. The association pays 60 days after the claim and documents are submitted. Upon payment, the insurer releases and transfers payment on the debt obligation to FCIA and notifies the buyer to make future payments to the association.[9]

Multi-Buyer. The Multi-Buyer Export Policy covers shipments during a one-year period against political and commercial risks. This policy insures short-term sales with repayment terms generally up to 180 days and medium-term sales with repayment up to five years. For short-term Multi-Buyer Policies, the exporter may choose to cover 90 percent of commercial risks and 100 percent of political risks. The coverage for short-term transactions normally applies to the gross invoice amount. Medium-term sales require 15 percent cash payment by the buyer on or before the due date of the first installment; therefore, the coverage applies to the balance.

The FCIA's Multi-Buyer coverage applies to credit sales for any goods produced and shipped from the United States during the policy period. Products that are less than 50 percent U.S. content for short-term sales and less than 90 percent U.S. content for medium-term sales are not eligible for this coverage. Two options are available to exporters under this policy. Option A, or split coverage with deductibility, provides 100 percent of loss due to commercial events. Option B, or equalized coverage with deductibility, insures against 95 percent of loss on short-term sales and 90 percent of loss on medium-term sales, either political or commercial. Receivables from sovereign obligors are 100 percent insured, without deductibility. The claim process is similar to the short-term Single-Buyer Policy.[10]

New-to-Export. New and occasional exporting companies can insure their sales of U.S. products against loss by acquiring commercial risk protection for the first two years of the policy's life. This opportunity includes 95 percent commercial coverage and 100 percent political coverage and no deductible. Thereafter, the exporter's coverage reverts to FCIA's standard policy, with deductibility, up to the total of five years. The commercial loss deductibility is $2,500 in the third year, $5,000 in the fourth year, and $7,500 in the fifth and last year. Similar to the other FCIA policies, products with less than 50 percent U.S. content and certain defense products are not eligible for coverage. Short-term sales involve repayments of up to 180 days; and for capital goods and certain consumer durables, repayment terms may be extended to 360 days. The policy is generally written for one year but may be cancelled by either party 30 days after written notice.[11]

Because the New-to-Export Policy is a special program designed for small and new exporters, there are several additional restrictions on the qualifications. First, the export and affiliate agent's average annual export credit sales during the preceding two years should not exceed $750,000. If the firm is new and has only one year of recorded sales, then the firm's first year of export sales may not have exceeded $1 million. Second, there should be no prior FCIA coverage during the last two years, either directly or through an affiliated entity. As soon as the exporter's eligible shipments exceed $1 million during any of the five years of coverage, the applicant no longer will be qualified under the New-To-Export Policy and must apply under a Multi-Buyer Policy.[12]

There are two types of insured credit limits under the New-To-Export Policy. The Discretionary Credit Limit (DCL) allows an exporter to exercise credit authority for creditworthy buyers up to a specific limit, without seeking prior approval from FCIA. Most new policyholders will not have a DCL. The second type of limit is the Special Buyer Credit Limit (SBCL), which, in fact, is two policies in one, requiring that the FCIA policy be in full force and the insured also submit an SBCL application for coverage on each eligible buyer. The premium rates are determined by the length of the credit terms and the type of buyer. The minimum premium is $500.

Bank Letter of Credit. The FCIA Bank Letter of Credit Policy applies to irrevocable letters of credit that conform with the Uniform Customs and Practices for Documentary Credits (UCP), 1983 Version, Publication Number 400 of the International Chamber of Commerce. The coverage applies to sales of any goods produced and shipped from the United States during the policy period, and for services performed by U.S. personnel in a host country. The products exported should contain at least 50 percent U.S. content to be eligible under this policy.[13]

For consumer items, parts, and raw materials, the Bank Letter of Credit Policy provides coverage up to 180 days. In regard to agricultural commodities, capital equipment, and quasi-captial equipment, the application may be insured for terms of up to 360 days. The insurance coverage against different categories of risk includes commercial losses caused by insolvency of the foreign bank, foreign exchange inconvertibility, cancellation of import or export licenses, expropriation, revolution, and war. On the U.S. dollar denomination letter of credit, the policyholder has an option to select coverage limits on interest of a floating prime rate minus 0.5 percent, based on the *Wall Street Journal*'s daily published report. Claims may be filed 60 days after the insured has made formal written demand on the issuing bank, and within 120 days of the due date. Upon settlement, the insured is required to release and transfer the right to default to the FCIA.[14]

Political Risks. This policy covers sales of U.S. goods and foreign receivables against losses due to political reasons on a short-term credit basis. The term involves repayment ranging from delivery to 180 days, in accordance with the Short-Term Political Risks Policy offered by the Eximbank. FCIA is the agent of Eximbank in administering the Political Risks Policy. The coverage is available for transfer risk as well as other forms of political risks, to include the cancellation or nonrenewal of an import or export license, restrictions on exports of products, restrictions on importation of the products into the buyer's market, revolution, civil war, and other political occurrences. Eximbank compensates exports for 100 percent on a political risk.[15]

The Political Risks Policy establishes a $5 million per country limitation of liability and requires a minimum annual premium of $500. The policy is normally written for one year, with a 30-day cancellation clause on written notice by either party. On overdues and claims, exporters must report on a monthly basis all the amounts that are 90 days past due. Upon settlement of the claim, the exporter transfers the unpaid portion of the contract and all future payments to the insurer.

Operating and Financing Lease. The Operating and Financing Lease Policy insures and protects exporters against loss of lease payments and the fair market value of lease products, both in commercial and political cases. The coverage is available for a cross-border lease as well as an international lease. In the first case, the lessor and lessee are in two different countries. In the second case, both the lessor and lessee are in the same country, other than the United States. Overall, the policy covers defaulted lease payments and government prevention of repossession. The policy is available to any financially responsible leasing company, bank and trust, manufacturer, or even partnership of various nationalities that participates in the financing of U.S. export leases. The coverage for sovereign leases is 100 percent and for all other types 90 percent.[16]

OVERSEAS PRIVATE INVESTMENT CORPORATION

The Overseas Private Investment Corporation (OPIC) was created by the Foreign Assistance Act of 1969, and became operational in 1971. OPIC is a self-sustained U.S. government agency whose purpose is to promote economic growth in developing countries by encouraging U.S. private investment in those nations. The corporation presents two principal programs: (1) the insurance of investment against political risk and (2) the financing of enterprises through direct loans and loan guarantees. At present, OPIC operates in 100 developing countries.

The concept of political risk insurance coverage dates back to 1948 and the Marshall Plan. At the time, insurance was offered against the risk of currency inconvertibility in order to generate capital formation for rebuilding war-torn Europe. Later on these resources were restructured to supplement direct aid programs to the world's developing nations. In 1961, the insurance program was shifted to the newly formed Agency for International Development (AID), and was broadened to include insurance coverage for revolution and insurrection as well as loan guarantees. However, since AID's primary purpose was the administration of government assistance, Congress decided in 1969 to establish OPIC for the insurance of private business and private capital.[17]

Insurance Program

OPIC insures U.S. investments against the political risks of inconvertibility, expropriation, and political violence. The inconvertibility coverage protects investors against the inability to convert into U.S. dollars the local currency received as profits, earnings, or return of capital on an investment. This includes protection against adverse discriminatory exchange rates but not devaluation of a country's currency. The expropriation coverage protects an investor against loss of investment due to expropriation, or confiscation by actions of a foreign government. Expropriatory actions provoked or instigated by the investor are not covered. The compensation by OPIC in the event of expropriatory action is based on the book value of the incurred equity investment or the principal and the accrued interest.

The political violence coverage protects investors against losses due to war, revolution, insurrection, and civil strife (terrorism and sabotage). Two types of coverage are offered for losses due to political violence. The Business Income Coverage (BIC) extends over income losses resulting from damage to the insured's assets caused by political violence. Compensation is based on expected net income plus continuing operating expenses. The Assets Coverage shields the tangible property and losses caused by political violence. The basis of compensation is the extent of the basic fair market value of the asset, or the cost of repair or replacement.

The premiums for OPIC's insurance coverages are based on the nature of the investor's undertaking and the project's risk portfolio. The insurance premium fee is paid annually and in advance. The base rates for most manufacturing and service projects are 30 cents per $100 of coverage for inconvertibility, 60 cents per $100 of coverage for expropriation, and 45 cents to 60 cents per $100 of coverage for political violence, depending on the type of loss, business income or assets.[18]

Finance Program

The finance program presents direct loan and loan guarantee techniques that provide medium- to long-term funding to ventures involving significant equity and management participation by U.S. businesses. All the projects considered for financing must be commercial and financially sound, and host-government approval is required for a guaranteed loan prior to OPIC commitment. Eligible enterprises include agriculture, energy, fishing, forestry, manufacturing, mining, production, storage and processing, and certain service industries such as tourist facilities, commercial hotels, leasing companies, and distributorship facilities. The key to OPIC commitment is that the funded projects must not have a significant adverse impact on the U.S. economy and employment situation.

Direct loan financing ranges from $100,000 to $6 million for ventures involving U.S. small businesses or corporations. In 1988, small businesses were defined as industrial companies with annual sales of less than $130 million and nonindustrial companies with stockholders' equity of less than $47 million. The interest charge is parallel to the commercial rate but varies according to the projects. Corporations that are not eligible for direct loans may participate in OPIC's loan guarantee program. Under this program, which is available to all businesses regardless of size, OPIC will issue guarantees covering both commercial and political risks in obtaining funds through a variety of U.S. financial institutions. The loan guarantees range from $5 million to a maximum of $50 million. The maturities generally range from 5 to 12 years, with repayment made in equal, semiannual payments following the grace period.[19]

Performance Report

In fiscal year 1987, OPIC recorded new highs and significant gains in many areas. The corporation supported a total of 165 projects in 41 countries, the highest level in 15 years. Significantly, 62 percent of these projects were in the poorest developing nations. The finance commitment reached $225.8 million for a record 31 investment projects in 20 countries. The insurance volume covered 144 projects, for a total of $1.8 billion. The capital and reserves amounted to $1.2 billion, an increase of 11 percent over the previous year, with net income of $102 million, the highest in corporate history. The OPIC chairman claims that its activities created 15,000 new host-country jobs, an aggregate total investment of $2.3 billion for developing nations, approximately $2 billion in new U.S. exports, and a positive U.S. net trade effect of $1.7 billion over the first five years of project operations.[20]

AGENCY FOR INTERNATIONAL DEVELOPMENT

The U.S. Agency for International Development (AID) was established in 1947 to carry out economic assistance programs to help the people of developing countries. The main purpose of this program is to improve the quality of human life, increase economic resources and productive capacities, and promote economic and political stability in friendly countries. During the Marshall Plan, U.S. AID activities were concentrated in Europe, but the emphasis now is on the developing nations in affiliation with the International Development Cooperation Agency (IDCA).

The Foreign Assistance Act of 1961 authorized the president of the United States to exercise international development aid under an agency. Executive Order 12163 of September 29, 1979, delegated the authority to the director of IDCA as set forth in the Foreign Assistance Act of 1961. The act authorized AID to administer two kinds of foreign assistance: economic support funds and development assistance. In addition, the agency, in cooperation with the Departments of Agriculture and State, carries out activities that include the sale of agricultural commodities on concessional terms, the donation of agricultural commodities, and the provision of food under the Food for Development Program. Other activities include humanitarian relief assistance in incidents such as earthquakes, famine, flood, and drought.[21]

Policies and Organization

The agency emphasizes four major thrusts to achieve successful economic development. These are the use of market force to stimulate growth, policy dialogue to adopt rational economic policies, institutional building of infrastructure, and technology transfer to enable countries to produce their own resources. The Development Assistance Program concentrates on agriculture, rural development, nutrition, health, population planning, education and human resources, energy, and development of private enterprises. The Economic Support Fund provides resources to address basic development needs in improving infrastructure and to sustain economic progress to restore equilibrium. The aim here is also to help friends and allies in dealing with threats to their security and independence. An example of some of the special programs supported by AID are the long-term program for the development of the Sahelian region of West Africa to promote regional food self-reliance, American schools and hospitals abroad, housing guarantee programs for lower-income families in developing countries, the Food for Peace Program for combating hunger and malnutrition, and investment in transfer of science and technology to developing countries to explore the potential use of technology for development.

The organization of AID consists of a central headquarters in Washington, D.C., including the Office of the Administrator, the Office of the Executive Secretary, the Board for International Food and Agricultural Development Support, six regional offices, three geographic bureaus, and a number of overseas missions and offices. The Bureau for Program and Policy Coordination is responsible for the agency's overall program policy formation, planning, coordination, resource allocation, and evaluations. The geographic bureaus service Africa, Latin America and the Caribbean, and Asia and the Near East.

The 1987 foreign aid program totals were less than 1 percent of the overall budget or about $6 billion. The funds supported over 1,500 development assistance programs in 70 countries.[22] Of the total budget of $7.2 billion for AID and P.L. 480 programs in 1987, 23 percent was allocated to Development Assistance, 54.5 percent to the Economic Support Fund, 20.4 percent to P.L. 480 — Food for Peace, and the remaining 2.1 percent to the Housing Guaranty Program.[23]

Program Coverage

Like other U.S. lending agencies, AID provides soft loans with a repayment schedule and financing guarantees against noncommercial risk, risk of currency inconvertibility, and expropriation, if the financing involves private enterprises in the economic development of less developed areas. The first program, known as "investment guarantee," protects direct investment abroad against noncommercial risks. This program is limited to certain losses on investments related to confiscation, expropriation, war, and other related cases. The second program, "convertibility guaranty" contracts, protects investors against the risk of inconvertibility of local currency into U.S. dollars. This program neither guarantees nor covers depreciation in currency values. The third program mainly covers expropriation with compensations. This is known as "expropriation guarantee," which mainly covers the principal but not the interest value added income of future earnings.[24]

The U.S. AID's goal of building stronger economies in less developed countries is also an aim to generate new markets for U.S. commodities. The agency believes that helping America's friends in the Third World to meet short-term needs is a way to create demand for U.S. exports. Thus, the investment in development of the Third World is a two-way street, because it promises trade expansion opportunities for U.S. businesses at home. For example, when the Morrison-Knudsen engineering firm of Idaho, with the help of the U.S. Trade and Development Program (an affiliate of AID), was selected in 1986 by the government of Nepal to conduct a feasibility study on a major hydropower facility, the firm was pleased with the $650,000 contract but did not plan on additional business. However, during the course of this contract, the Idaho firm was able to impress a Chinese firm also involved in the study and was invited to examine and conduct a similar study in China. At final count, Morrison-Knudsen obtained $20 million in additional business. Similar developments have caused increases in U.S. exports to AID-assisted Caribbean countries from $3.9 billion in 1984 to $4.9 billion in 1987, and nontraditional exports from that region to the U.S. from $913 million in 1983 to $1.96 billion in 1987. The bottom line is that the developing world is a promising market for U.S. exports. In the first ten months of 1987, from the total of $144 billion exports from the United States, $65 billion or 45 percent went to developing and newly industrialized countries. Europe's share was $57 billion or 39.6 percent, and Japan received the remaining $22 billion or 15.4 percent.[25]

NOTES

1. Frederick D. Wolf, "Recapitalizing the Export-Import Bank of the U.S.: Why It Is Necessary; How It Can Be Accomplished," testimony before the Subcommittee on International Finance, Trade, and Monetary Policy, House of Representatives, February 25, 1988, Enclosure 1, p. 7.

2. Export-Import Bank of the United States, "Eximbank Programs and Small Business," and "Working Capital Guarantee Programs: The Basics," Washington, D.C., 1984, p. 2.

3. William M. Arnold, Export-Import Bank of the United States, excerpt from the presentation and handout to the International Bank Lending Seminar, University of Virginia, October 1984.

4. Export-Import Bank of the United States, "Eximbank Programs Summary," The Office of Public Affairs, Washington, D.C., 1984, pp. 5-7.

5. Ibid., pp. 2-3.

6. Export-Import Bank of the United States, "Eximbank Programs and Small Business," pp. 2-3.

7. Export-Import Bank of the United States, *Annual Report*, 1986, p. 1.

8. Export-Import Bank of the United States, "Exim News," The Office of Public Affairs, Washington, D.C., March 31, 1987, pp. 1-2.

9. Foreign Credit Insurance Association, "Your Competitive Edge in Selling Overseas," New York, May 1988, pp. 6-7; and "The FCIA Short-Term Single Buyer Export Credit Insurance Policy," New York, November 1986.

10. Foreign Credit Insurance Association, "The FCIA Multi-Buyer Export Credit Insurance Policy," New York, May 1987; and "Your Competitive Edge in Selling Overseas," May 1988, New York, pp. 8-9.

11. Foreign Credit Insurance Association, "The FCIA New-to-Export Policy," New York, December 1987.

12. Ibid.

13. Foreign Credit Insurance Association, "The FCIA Bank Letter of Credit Policy," New York, August 1987.

14. Ibid.

15. Foreign Credit Insurance Association, "The Political Risks Policy," New York, June 1987.

16. Foreign Credit Insurance Association, "The FCIA Operating and Financing Lease Policies," New York, September 1988.

17. Overseas Private Investment Corporation, *Programs and Services*, Publication 0688, Washington, D.C., 1988, pp. 1-2.

18. Overseas Private Investment Corporation, *Investment Insurance Handbook*, Publication 0588, Washington, D.C., 1988, pp. 6-7.

19. Overseas Private Investment Corporation, *Investment Finance Handbook*, Publication 1187, Washington, D.C., 1988, pp. 3-5; and Publication 0688, 1988, p. 5.

20. Overseas Private Investment Corporation, *Annual Report*, 1987, pp. 2-4 and 14-17.

21. "AID Statement of Organization, Functions, and Procedures," *AID Handbook 17*, Trans. Memo No. 17:402, August 26, 1987, pp. 1-5.

22. United States Agency for International Development, *The AID Challenge*, Washington, D.C., November 1988, pp. 12-13.

23. United States International Development Cooperation Agency, *Development Issues 1988*, the 1988 Annual Report of the Chairman of the Development Coordination Committee, Washington, D.C., 1988, p. 90.

24. Nicholas L. Deak and JoAnne C. Celusak, *International Banking*, New York Institute of Finance, Prentice-Hall, Inc., New York, 1984, pp. 268-69.

25. United States Agency for International Development, *Highlights*, Vol. 5, No. 3, Summer 1988, p. 1.

6   Motivation and Area of Specialization

Christopher Columbus discovered America in 1492; Foreign bankers discovered it in the 1970s.

One of the more interesting structural developments in the world's banking industry in the past two decades has been the rapid rise to prominence of multinational banks. Historically, banks of various nationalities participated in international transactions via affiliates or branches in several countries. Multinational banks from major industrial countries went one step further by acquiring interests in the subsidiary form of organization, thus promoting a more permanent desire for presence in international money market centers. U.S. banks have been the forerunners in this development. During the 1960s, major U.S. banks set up offices abroad to conduct their international banking activities. These banks opened branches or acquired ownership interest in one or several foreign financial institutions, mainly in Europe.

The U.S. international banking expansionary movement of the 1960s was followed by foreign banks' penetration into U.S. money and capital markets. European, Canadian, and Japanese banks swarmed in to enjoy the positive and regulation-free environment of the 1970s. At the beginning several of these banks were regionally oriented and became allied with U.S. or other foreign banks to establish the so-called consortia banks. While the early penetration was pioneered by multinational banks, soon their presence was accompanied by medium- and even some small-sized banks. This expansionary move brought into effect a change in banking and, as a result, a new competitive environment.

The questions often arising are: Why are foreign banks interested in acquiring U.S. banks? What was the economic environment that invited such a strong presence? What motivated foreign banks to come to the United States? Did regulatory authorities welcome foreign banks' presence? The answers to these questions, as well as scrutiny of other major financial developments of the 1960s and 1970s, will provide clarification of the purpose of foreign banks' rapid expansion in the U.S. market. The motivation and areas of specialization employed by foreign banks should shed light on these bold moves.

MOTIVATION BEHIND INTERNATIONAL BANKING

One primary factor separating multinational banks from domestic banks is their ability to scan the world for investment opportunities and to have access to money and capital markets in all the continents. Multinational banks can draw funds from or invest excess funds across nations in a manner that permits diversification at the lowest possible marginal cost. Their ability to raise funds is not subject to specific local laws or domestic economies. Instead, they are privileged to a wide array of opportunities, some with favorable regulations, e.g., shell bank centers. This dimension has an impact on the marginal cost of funds, as the efficient frontier opportunity curve provides multinational banks lower marginal costs in comparison with a similar sized local bank involved in domestic activities. Thus, a multinational bank, due to its ability to diversify internationally, can behave differently from a domestic bank. This behavior would contribute to higher profitability and better access to more efficient forms of distribution of regional funds.

A bank may establish a foreign presence for a variety of reasons and in a variety of forms. The type of office selected represents the banks' risk management preferences, in accordance with their financial strength and the degree of regulatory freedom permitted by the laws of host nations. International banking presence can be achieved via correspondent banking or the establishment of an actual organizational concern in a foreign country. The dynamics of expansion may fall into five categories: to finance trade, to serve clients, to participate in the money market and retail banking, to escape restrictions, and to invest abroad. A summary of the various factors responsible for international banking expansion and its components are presented here. Many of these variables interact to motivate banks to enter foreign markets.

Trade Financing

Trade financing is the oldest motive and instrument behind international banking. Historians have written about the international banking and trade scenes of ancient Egypt, the Middle Ages, and the Renaissance. Trade is a

Table 6.1
Motivation Behind International Banking
(A Summary)

Trade Financing

Finance international movement of merchandise

Finance trade logistics and distribution

Provision of financial trade instruments

Service to Clients

Corporate clients: domestic and international

Individual clients: domestic and international

Establishment of close contact with individual
and institutional investors

Investment advisory and related services

Money Market and Retail Banking

Foreign exchange trading

Participation in retail banking and
deposit-taking activities

Participation in money market instruments

Tapping funds from other international money
markets

(continued)

two-way transaction, involving finance, distribution, and logistical support
on both ends of the trading location, thus requiring a bank on each side of
the transaction to facilitate movement of goods, services, and capital. This
interaction between a bank and international trade may occur in various
forms. The starting point is the financing of international movements of
merchandise and services. To accomplish the task, an international bank
must advance funds for distribution and logistics, including financing of
packaging, shipping, storage, and leasing. Instruments used in trade financing are bills of exchange, letters of credit, drafts and bankers' acceptances,
and provision of foreign exchange services.

Table 6.1
(continued)

Regulation Circumvention

Avoid regulations at home

Take advantage of favorable tax climate

Seek investment in politically stable nations

Avoid interest rate control regulations

Investment

Diversification and reduction of risk

Higher profits

Participate in asset management abroad

Take advantage of opportunities for the
profitable placement of funds

Answer forces of competition

Participate in growing market in a stable
investment environment

Establish links with security markets and
long-term investment funds

Service to Clients

Service to corporate clients is the strongest desire of international institutions. As trade financing is the oldest motive, service to corporate clients is the most progressive one in the recent years. The relationships between a multinational bank and corporate clients are mostly wholesale in nature, consisting of on-the-spot loans, foreign exchange transactions, credit, and eco-political environmental reports. The representative offices of multinational banks provide valuable information concerning the status of economic variables in the host country and credit market data and information, as well as introduce the corporation's representatives to local businesses. The desire of foreign banks to provide global services is often initiated and reinforced by pressure from local corporate customers in need of financial services, or by forces of competition, or desire for participation in a growing market to serve new clients.

The services to individual clients receive secondary or even tertiary importance, except when a bank desires a retail operation, because these services are normally small in nature and volume, generate low profit, and necessitate a large operating cost. The types of services to individual customers are limited to short-term loans, foreign exchange transactions, and related, routine, daily banking services. A major limitation of the services to clients is the limited capacity of many foreign banking offices in the host countries. The limitation is due to the regulatory environment of host countries and the types of offices multinational banks select to operate. For example, with the exception of a subsidiary form of office, other types of banking offices are not fully equipped to provide full banking services. Some forms of offices are not in a position to offer short-term credits or payroll services. Others deal only in trade financing or lending of a wholesale nature. A limited number elect to operate retail banking. As a result, their global banking operations are somewhat restricted.

Money Market and Retail Banking

The money market operations of an international bank with offices abroad consist of participation in foreign exchange markets on behalf of clients or the bank itself, tapping funds from other international money centers and participating in the purchase or sale of money market instruments. The foreign banking offices have long been active in federal funds, and the issuance and trade of negotiable certificates of deposit. Participation in Eurocurrency and Eurobond markets is common and, in a way, contributes to the efficient flow of capital. The retail banking operation is a new phenomenon, which grew rapidly in recent years, but is limited to industrial nations' territorial activities. The retail services consist of a wide range of domestic and international financial services, including deposit taking (both demand and time deposits), lending, provision of certificates of deposit, and other banking services. Retail banking is sought when banks have exhausted other avenues or when investment in local financing is desired. The operation is normally conducted via a subsidiary form of office.

Regulation Circumvention

One motive for a bank to expand its activities outside of the home market by establishing an office or an affiliated organization is to avoid regulatory restrictions or taxes at home. A bank may seek to take advantage of a favorable tax climate abroad, avoid the interest rate control provision of a federal regulation, or take advantage of other favorable banking laws of host nations. The United States provided such an environment prior to the IBA of 1978. Foreign banks were not subject to the regulatory environment of the Federal Reserve System in regard to the reserve requirement ratio and interstate banking and bank holding companies' restrictions; nor were they considered subject to the antitrust law provision of banking acquisitions. In the area of taxation, the United States provided the lowest business tax rate of any industrial nation. The other financial centers of Singapore, Hong Kong, and the Caribbean Islands also provided a favorable atmosphere by offering tax incentives and a favorable regulatory climate. It is also fair to consider some countries' political and economic stability for investment as a force behind foreign banks' international expansion.

Investment

One major consideration in the movement of banks to internationalize their activities has been their desire to take advantage of investment abroad. Components of this motive are diversification, reduction of risk, and possibly higher profit. Three areas of investment banking activities are participating in asset management investment services, establishing links with security markets, and taking advantage of opportunities for the profitable placement of funds. These considerations are reinforced by the desire of banks to be a part of a growing market in a stable investment environment. Competition from other multinational banks, and banks' own desires to preserve or expand their market share in accordance with their long-term investment policies, are also factors that contribute to the further desire for international investment.

Surveys of chief executive officers of multinational banks, as well as other multinational corporations, point to the desire for higher profit as the key motivation behind foreign investments. Saturated home markets, such as the present status of the stock and money markets in Japan, present another reason for financial institutions to enter foreign markets. Participation in asset management investment activities on behalf of clients or for the banks' investment portfolio demands entrance into new territories in order to participate in the growing markets of other nations and to tap long-term investment funds. In recent years, stock market participation by various nations has received tremendous attention. While U.S. banking laws prohibit banks' direct participation in underwriting, distribution, and trade of securities, European and Japanese banking laws do not separate banking from commerce, thus permitting banks to participate in security transactions. However, U.S. laws do not prohibit foreign banks from acquiring brokerage houses.

RECENT MAJOR DEVELOPMENTS

Five key developments during the past 25 years have spurred the expansion of international banking and opened a new dimension in the world of financial markets. These events were: (1) the emergence and growth of

Eurocurrency markets, (2) the rapid economic growth of Europe and Japan, (3) the oil energy crisis of the 1970s, (4) increased internationalization of businesses and interdependence among nations, and (5) the current economic environment of the United States compounded with budget and trade deficits and slow economic growth.

The Eurocurrency market is primarily a means of transferring short-term funds across national boundaries and a mechanism for shifting funds among banks, corporations, and other money-center institutions. From 1950 to 1970, European and Japanese industrialization reached maturity with low inflation and rapid expansion. Demand for funds increased internationally, necessitating global borrowing and transferences of funds. The energy crisis of 1973, the increase in the price of OPEC oil in 1979, and Arab nations' reluctance to deposit surpluses in the United States further boosted activities of international banking and opened a new dimension in world financial affairs. The circumstances changed even further with continuous U.S. balance of trade and budget deficits of the 1980s, and the increased U.S. dependence on an inflow of international funds.

The emergence of financial interdependence and progress in international banking developed two new dimensions in international lending and investment activities. Syndicated loans and investment banking progressed to a new phase, and increased to an all-time high by the end of the 1970s. In February 1981, a report by the World Bank and *Euromoney* put the 1980 share of volume of the top 20 managers, by 17 participating multinational banks, at 89 percent of the total capacity of leading syndicated loan managers.[1] Another development was the broadening of the size of banks as they evolved to participate in international activities. International financial activities, once the monopoly of very large-sized banks, were now conducted by most medium-sized banks and even some small-sized agricultural banks.

MOTIVES FOR FOREIGN BANKING EXPANSION IN THE UNITED STATES

Prior to World War II, foreign banking offices in the United States had been established in conjunction with trade between the United States and the parent country, mainly from Canada, England, France, Germany, and Japan. After World War II, the dollar became the internationally preferred currency and the United States a major financial center, with New York City the headquarters for an increasing number of multinational corporations. Soon, the three states of New York, California, and Illinois liberalized state laws, permitting foreign banks to open offices. This was the first step toward expansion of foreign banking. The most common motives for entering the United States were to finance trade and to maintain and expand existing business-client relationships. Investment in banking was first conducted by foreign financial institutions, but soon individuals and nonbank organizations joined the banking group to expand by establishing new institutions or acquiring existing ones. Eight general motives have been identified for foreign banking expansion in the United States. The motive and type of expansionary activities reflect the parent bank's overall U.S. or worldwide strategy. The strategy consists of a continuation of present activities, such as trade financing; or following corporate clients abroad; or expanding into new areas, such as retail banking, asset management, and investment advisory services; or taking advantage of new opportunities.

Public Relationships and Services

Foreign banks have been able to better serve their home-country customers by expanding their international operations, especially to the largest economy in the world. The key motivation here is to finance trade and to sustain and expand corporate clients' relationships. This motive may derive from sustaining and expanding the corporate relationships that were originally established in the home country, serving U.S. corporate clients with businesses in the bank's home market, or obtaining third-country clients. Often these services are initiated by corporate customers in need of financial services in the United States or by individual investors seeking opportunities outside the home market. Not to be overlooked, competition and fear of losing the market to other banks motivated bankers to seek expansion into the diversified U.S. market. In discussion with executive officers of corporations from Canada, Denmark, Japan, and Singapore in Atlanta in 1986, this author gathered that America has a special place in the minds of foreign corporate executives and a unique place in their investment strategy decisions. One compared the United States to the sun, shining over other market countries. Another one compared it to a red apple, with other countries as seeds, coexisting and growing via opportunities initiated here in the United States. This view was reaffirmed by Michel Fraisse, Adjoint Director General of Societe Lyonnaise de Banque, in a presentation to the conference on the EEC market in June 1987, in Lyon, France.[2] While Mr. Fraisse was quite forceful in emphasizing the interdependency among the world financial markets and suggested that more cooperative effort is needed among multinational banks, he also prudently pointed out the importance of the U.S. market to European banks and admired the diversity and strength of the U.S. financial market.

The second factor that contributes to the desire of foreign banks to expand into the U.S. banking market is to establish close contact with individual and institutional investors, and to gain access to the general public's hard-core deposits. From 1945 to 1960, Europe and Japan were in need of hard-core currency to rebuild their infrastructure of economy after the war. This financial need opened an opportunity for U.S. banks to expand branching operations overseas, and also necessitated foreign banking pres-

Table 6.2
Motives Behind Foreign Banking Expansion in the United States

---

Public Relationships and Services

To sustain and expand the corporate clients'
relationships.

To gain access to the general public's hard-core
deposits and to participate in retail banking.

To establish close contact with individual and
institutional investors.

To offer asset management, and investment-advisory
and related services.

Regulations

To take advantage of the favorable regulatory and
political climate in the United States.

Currency and Financial Markets

To take advantage of the dominant role of the dollar
in international finance and trade.

To participate in diversified U.S. money and capital
markets and have better access to the largest economy
in the world.

To take advantage of opportunities for profitable
placement of excess funds in a low-risk and stable
investment environment.

---

ence here in the United States to tap funding for consumption at home.
Later on, as Europe's and Japan's economic strengths were reinforced, and
as home-country, multinational corporations began to emulate the expansion of U.S. markets, retail banking and money market activities extensively
increased. Major expansion began by the mid-1960s and intensified in the
1970s. Foreign direct investment doubled from $5.6 billion in 1965 to $11.3
billion in 1971, as European companies favored the United States' industrial
markets.[3] In the 1970s, foreign banks also entered to offer asset management and investment advisory and related services. The U.S. money and
capital markets provided an opportunity for foreigners to channel their

trade surpluses with the United States into an investment, thus demanding that their banks provide these extended services in a dollar-based market.

In the early stages, foreign U.S.-based banks confined their banking operations to wholesale banking. These banks focused mainly on offering a wide range of domestic and international services to major corporate clients. The complete range of retail banking services intensified in the second half of the 1970s with increased expansion in the subsidiary form of banking offices and with the Japanese entrance into the California banking market to serve the large Japanese and South and East Asian communities in Los Angeles and San Francisco.

One reason for foreign banks' slow progress in the U.S. retail banking industry is the high front-office cost of establishing a new entity and operation. Retail banking requires high commitment in capital and fixed assets, which results in low returns. A wholesale operation is low in cost compared with a retail operation. To overcome this deficiency, foreign banks elect to acquire existing institutions instead of starting new ones. Acquisition of a U.S. bank is a shortcut to foreign bank expansion and provides easy access to U.S. markets, without the additional cost of start-up and marketing required for a foreign bank to attract customers. Furthermore, the depressed stock price of U.S. banks in the 1970s encouraged acquisition of existing banks over de novo banking establishments.

Regulations

To take advantage of the absence of U.S. federal guidelines and examinations of foreign banking practices was one of the intrinsic motivations behind foreign banking expansion in the United States. Prior to the IBA of 1978, foreign banks were exempt from the reserve requirements and FDIC insurance, and were permitted to conduct interstate banking activities and participate in security transactions. Widely publicized concerns expressed by American bankers, legislators and private citizens pivoted upon the point that U.S. institutions do not have equivalent opportunities abroad, and these foreign banking institutions have benefited from the lack of appropriate regulations. In July 1966, the Congressional Joint Economic Committee published a research report recommending that foreign banking activities should be included under the supervisory domain of the national banking authorities—namely the comptroller of the currency and the Federal Reserve System. In 1973 the House of Representatives introduced H.R. 11440, urging national policy changes to include foreign banking entities. This recommendation was reinforced by the National Bank Act of 1975 and the FINE Commission Report. The warning of the fact that sooner or later a legislative ruling would be in effect forced foreign banks to accelerate their course of expansion to take advantage of the relaxed legal environment. This inducement benefited a large number of these foreign banks as their activities were grandfathered in part by the passage of the IBA in 1978.

The regulatory motivation reinforced the action. From 1930 to 1960, only 37 new foreign banks entered the United States, an average of 1.2 banks per year. The number of new entrances increased to 36, or an average of 3.6 banks per year, from 1961 to 1970. The fear of regulation quadrupled the newly established banks during the decade of 1970s, as the number of new banks increased to 164, for an all-time record of 16.4 banks per year. The total number of foreign banking offices, excluding representative offices, increased from 105 in 1972 to 295 in 1978, the year of international banking regulation. While the number of foreign banking offices continued to increase to a record high of 674 by the end of 1988, the recent increase cannot be attributed to the regulatory obsession. Other factors, such as the continuous decline in the value of the dollar and the U.S. budget and trade deficits, have presented ample opportunities for surplus nations to channel their surplus dollars for distribution and investment in the U.S. market.

Some critics also blame the preference of U.S. banking authorities to sell the weak and troubled banks to foreigners as a key regulatory motive behind foreign acquisition of the American banks in recent years. Examples often mentioned are the National Bank of North America, New York, La Salle National Bank of Chicago, and First Western Bank and Trust Company of California. U.S. regulatory authorities deny the accusation, clarifying their position by referring to the limitations set by antitrust laws, the banking regulatory provisions that prohibit U.S. bank branching across state lines, and the BHC Act that prevents acquisition of a bank in any state in which it has its principal operations.

Currency and Financial Markets

Bank marketers point to the role of market strategy as the key motivation behind the foreign banks' acquisitions and involvement in special activities. The motives behind special tactical market activities are the desire to take advantage of the dominant role of the dollar in international finance and trade, and the strong desire of foreign investors to participate in diversified U.S. money and capital markets. The acquisition of a well-established, reputable U.S. bank gives foreign investors a cost advantage and easy access to the U.S. money market. Furthermore, access to the largest economy in the world presents another dimension to the collective preferences of foreign banking in the Americanization of their banking activities.

After World War II, as the United States moved toward becoming the world's largest trader and creditor, with the dollar as the most demanded currency in the world financial markets, the importance of banking in the domestic U.S. foreign exchange and money markets became more appealing than ever. At first, the international bankers were compelled to take advantage of large sums of short-term funds in major national and international money centers, employing these funds for interest rate arbitrage in other money and loan markets. The dollar base provided this opportunity for profitable placement of funds domestically and internationally. Later on, the foreign exchange market was used as a vehicle to channel excess dollars back into the United States to take advantage of the favorable exchange rates, as the U.S. dollar lost ground in value in the world currency markets.

In addition, the differences in time zones enabled foreign banks to adjust their exchange position at any time, day or night, and to offer their corporate customers and individual investors around-the-clock, foreign exchange trading services. This flexibility also aided the banks in improving their capacity to invest in the spot- and future-currency markets during the course of business transactions. The dollar-based activity further improved multinational banks' activities in Eurodollar and Eurocurrency markets as the U.S. money market played as a source of liquidity during the period of tightly squeezed demand for hard currencies.

The nation's large and diversified money and capital markets, with their wide range of negotiable, short- and long-term obligations attracted foreign banks and those interested in interest rate arbitrage. The bankers' acceptances, CDs, commercial paper, and federal fund sector of the money market, as well as the relatively low stock price of U.S. corporations, aroused the interest of foreign banks to invest their holdings of U.S. dollar balances, or to refinance their foreign loans. During the past 20 years, foreign banks have established over two dozen brokerage securities firms, with controlling shares in four of the ten largest security dealerships in the U.S. markets. The aim of the move was to enter into the business of underwriting and trading of domestic and foreign securities in the major capital center of the world — New York City.

There were three reasons for the surge of interest in the U.S. security market. First, for the major European and Japanese banks, home-country laws do not separate banking from commerce. For a century, these banks have been involved in the underwriting, trading, and investment advising services. As a result, they have accumulated a large portfolio of funds to be invested on behalf of their clients. The stable, low-risk economic environment of the United States provided them with the desired opportunity for implementation of their long-term policy. In fact, many of these banks and individual clients have held a large sum of investments in the U.S. blue-chip and technology stocks during the past three decades. The need to more easily manage and also to be involved in further acquisitions required presence and closer market exposure. Second, the U.S. market offered a wider and more diverse range of stock trading than any other market. Third, the two devaluations of the U.S. dollar in the 1970s and the continuous decline in the value of the dollar in the 1980s provided a favorable foreign exchange price trend for investment in U.S. markets. And finally, the depth, size, and prestige of the New York Stock Exchange and the desire for active participation in the international securities markets inflamed considerable desire for foreign banks to establish a foothold in the American capital market.

Competition and Location

The fear of losing customers and a share of the market to competition was a factor in foreign banks' decisions to expand their presence in the United States. This factor, combined with the saturated market at home and the desire to set up a foreign exchange operation in the prestigious New York market, generated a force behind the policy decision to enter U.S. financial markets. It was the general belief among foreign investors and business executives that the American economic, banking, and financial markets were still young and growing. Therefore, it was appropriate, in setting long-term marketing strategy, to be prepared to be present in this large, diversified, growth-potential market. The countries of England, Germany, France, Hong Kong, and the Netherlands historically benefited from this market participation in financial and industrial areas. The new generation of exporters such as Japan, South Korea, Taiwan, and Thailand recently accumulated surpluses in their balance of payments with the United States and have looked for a safe market with a friendly political environment in which to invest their excess funds. In 1988, Japan accumulated a trade surplus of $96 billion, nearly 58 percent of which was with the United States. The United States had another $25 billion in trade deficits with the Southeast Asian countries of Singapore, South Korea, Thailand, Taiwan, and the Philippines, creating the need for a large market for redistribution. Japan invested an average of $7 billion per month in U.S. Treasury and other securities in the first quarter of 1987, and poured over $40 billion into the bond market in the past few years. This recent development and surge in Japanese interest in the U.S. stock, bond, and real estate markets was welcomed by market analysts as a positive move in the recycling of the U.S. dollar.

In reality, a combination of factors have contributed to the decision of foreign investors and banking concerns to enter the U.S. market. However, the lack of legislation and foreign banking regulations in the 1970s, along with the deterioration in the value of the U.S. dollar and the budget and trade deficits, have accelerated the movement of these institutions and intensified acquisitions of U.S. banks. In the future, the expansion will continue at a slower pace, unless progress is made to improve U.S. trade deficits and reinstate the real value of the dollar. These two factors are the keys in determining the future expansion of foreign banking in the United States.

AREA OF SPECIALIZATION

It is generally believed that the primary banking activities of foreign banks' U.S. offices are related to providing banking services to home customers operating in or trading with a U.S. firm, and the limitations of their own respective domestic markets, compared with the realistic size, diversity, and wealth of the U.S. economy. However, from general information, it is not very clear whether or not foreign banks' activities are predominantly with their home customers operating in the United States, but there is strong evidence that the regulatory opportunities of the 1970s and size of the U.S. market have a lot to do with foreign banks' strong showing in the U.S. market. Accurate inside information is hard to obtain because most banks feel that their bank-customer relationship is confidential and should not be a matter of public domain.

A survey of selected major European, South and East Asian, and Japanese banks conducted in 1986 reveals that the foreign banks' U.S.-office banking activities are concentrated in the five major types of banking services. These consist of corporate financing, money market activities, trade financing, foreign exchange trading, and retail banking. Corporate banking and trade financing rank high because foreign banks follow the customers abroad and expand corporate relationships that were originally established in the home country. Their emphasis on money market activities is due to the dominant role of the dollar in international finance and an abundant surplus of dollars at home. Furthermore, locations in the United States, primarily New York, enable foreign banks to become involved in the prestigious, international, multinational corporate business environment, as well as to diversify their operations and assets among the dollar-based international capital markets.

Banks usually engage in foreign exchange trading on behalf of their customers and for their own accounts, in order to balance their foreign exchange position. Retail banking prevails as an area of interest because of the relatively sound and stable economic and political environment in the United States, which provides diversification in terms of a hedge against potentially more volatile domestic conditions, such as high inflation, slow growth, and even political and economic uncertainty. In addition, the regulatory opportunities of the 1970s and, in some respects, the bank failures of the 1980s provided an unprecedented favorable environment for foreign banks to engage in retail banking in the United States.

Overall, foreign banking activities consist of 24 types of services. The selection is subject to the bank's size, dimension, and long-term policy objectives. Table 6.3 presents the list of services provided by the major foreign banks. These activities are divided into the five areas of general banking services, money market activities, loans and leasing, management, and investment services.

Table 6.3
Areas of Services of Foreign Banks in the United States

GENERAL BANKING	LOANS AND LEASING
Correspondent banking	Corporate financing
Private banking	Trade financing
Credit services	Loan syndicate and leasing
	Energy and project financing
MANAGEMENT SERVICES	
Investment management	Real estate financing
Country advisory report	Mergers and acquisitions
Document safekeeping and services	Factoring
	MONEY MARKET
	Foreign exchange dealing
INVESTMENT SERVICES	Currency note dealing
Security underwriting	CD services
Security trading	Forfeiting
Venture capital	Promissory note discounting
Financial commodity dealing	Issuance and trading of letters of credit and bills of lading
	Import-export drafts

Banks with longer historical presence in the United States and greater strength in assets size are engaged in more areas of banking activities than other banks. Similarly, countries with a greater trading relationship with the United States, such as Canada, Japan, the United Kingdom, Italy, France, and Germany, engage in a greater variety of banking services than those that are involved in limited trading transactions. Table 6.4 reveals the result. Both Western and Asian groups ranked corporate banking as the most preferred

Table 6.4
Areas of Specialization of Selected European and Asian Bank Groups, by Rank

	Corporate Banking	Money Market Activities	Trade Financing	Foreign Exchange Trading	Retail Banking	Other Activities
Preference:						
W. European	1	2	3	4	5	6
Asian	1	3	2	5	3	6
In practice:						
W. European	1	2	3	4	5	5
Asian	2	2	1	3	4	5

Areas of Specialization and Form of Organization
(By Rank)

	Corporate Banking	Money Market Activities	Trade Financing	Foreign Exchange Trading	Retail Banking	Other Activities
Branch	1	1	1	1	1	1
Agency	2	2	2	2	3	2
Subsidiary	3	3	3	2	2	2
Others	4	4	4	4	3	4

Number of Specialties (Average)

European Group		Asian Group	
France	5	Hong Kong	6
Italy	5	Indonesia	4
Netherlands	5	Japan	6
Switzerland	5	South Korea	4
United Kingdom	6	Taiwan	4
West Germany	5	Thailand	4

activity; but in practice, they differ. Banks from developing countries are more inclined toward trade financing than corporate banking. The average number of specialized services is also indicative of their banks' market participation, but not necessarily their desired activities. These bank activities are limited by nature, due to the size and strength of their assets. In fact, economy of scale of large size exists when one considers dimension of services in relation to rank in assets.

Branches, agencies, and subsidiaries rank one to three in all areas of activities with one exception. The subsidiary commercial banks are more active in retail banking, while agencies are more active in money market activities. The reason is simply the nature of agencies, which do not accept deposits; subsidiaries, in turn, are heavily oriented toward the domestic market and retail banking. Overall, banks with a branch or agency form of organization tend to involve themselves with a wider scope of specialization than those with other forms. Naturally, those with more highly specialized activities control a larger number of related offices. When consideration is given to the comparison of the Japanese and Hong Kong banks versus major Western European banks, no major differences are observed. Among them, the Japanese are more inclined toward retail banking, while the French and West Germans are least interested. Hong Kong, Japan, and the United Kingdom scored high in all major specialization areas, with Japan and the United Kingdom each recording 22 types of services provided and with Hong Kong participating in 18 active services. All major countries' banks uniformly provide the following ten services:

- Corporate financing
- Correspondent banking
- Money market activities
- Trade financing
- Loan syndication
- Foreign exchange activities
- Credit management services
- Real estate financing
- Private banking
- Investment management

One major difference between small- and large-sized foreign banks is their expansion of international banking networks and their areas of activities. Larger-sized banks are involved in more areas of activities and demonstrate a more expansionary desire to move toward newer services. Smaller banks' activities concentrate on serving home-market clients, trade financing, correspondent banking, and limited activities in the areas of money market and foreign exchange investments. Most small banks avoid venture capital financing, factoring security underwriting, and merger and acquisition activities. Retail banking is mentioned by banks of all sizes and nationalities as a growth area that needs further exploration. As other areas of activities are saturated due to their limitations and competition, retail banking receives special attention. This is where future expansion is expected to occur.

NOTES

1. Dwight B. Crane and Samuel L. Hayes III, "The Evolution of International Banking Competition and Its Implications for Regulation," *Journal of Bank Research*, Spring 1983, p. 46.

2. The EEC conference was sponsored by the Cooperative Internationale of the Ecole Superieure de Commerce of Lyon, France, for American faculty, in June–July 1987.

3. Fred H. Klopstock, "Foreign Banks in the United States: Scope and Growth of Operations," *Monthly Review*, June 1973, p. 143.

7 Market Structure and Activities of Foreign Banks

During the past several years, international banking has entered a new competitive stage and climate in international financial markets. The attractiveness of establishing a banking facility in the United States is enhanced by the role of the dollar as a transaction currency in world trade and investment. A large number of foreign banks initially entered the United States to serve the U.S. activities of their home-base corporate clients. Later, with the contacts and expertise developed through their U.S. presence, these U.S.-based foreign banks started to finance transactions between the United States and their home countries and compete for the domestic business.

As leaders in modern international banking, U.S. banks often performed central roles in international financial transactions and in pioneering world trade and investment activities. Foreign banks, particularly European and Japanese, have practiced international banking for centuries, but with a limited base in the United States. They sought to capitalize on growing international trade and lending opportunities developed during the 1960s and 1970s, as the United States consolidated its economic power, investment, and lending to clearly dominate world trade. The resulting effect was an increase in foreign banks' U.S. market share and the acquisitions that generated much political debate in the 1970s. Some important contributions of these institutions were their participation in the smooth recycling of petrodollars from oil-exporting countries to the rest of the world, in development of internationally syndicated loans, and in loans to finance balance-of-payments deficits and other governmental projects.

FOREIGN PARTICIPATION IN U.S. BANKING MARKETS

At the end of 1988, 460 foreign banks from 60 countries participated in financial activities in the United States ranging from corporate banking and trade financing to foreign exchange trading, retail banking, and other financial concerns. As revealed in tables 2.1 and 2.2 in chapter 2, the number of foreign banking offices tripled during the 1970s, with an average increase of 32.7 offices per year. The peak year was 1978, in response to the expected passage of the IBA, as foreign banks' expansion accelerated to take advantage of the grandfathering provision of the international banking law of 1978. A similar trend was observed in assets expansion. The assets of foreign banks increased from $26.1 billion in 1972 to $127.6 billion in 1979, an average growth of $20.3 billion per year. During the 1980s, the expansionary movement further accelerated, as the number of offices reached an all-time high of 674 with $653 billion in assets. The key factors contributing to this development were the U.S. budget and trade deficits, the large number of U.S. bank failures, and large accumulated dollar surpluses of some major industrial countries as they searched for a means of investment and recycling in a stable market environment.

Meanwhile, branches and subsidiaries grew at the expense of agencies. The decline in the importance of agencies can be traced to two specific factors: (1) the relatively slow growth in the activities of the Canadian agencies that were the pioneers in establishing this form of office; and (2) the rapid growth of branches and subsidiaries of European banks in the 1970s on the East Coast, and Japanese banks in the 1980s on the West Coast. Two reasons have been advanced for this development. First, the European banks from the major industrial countries—all well-known, large institutions—attempted to develop retail-oriented businesses in the United States, often through acquisitions, to expand their deposit-taking activities from both domestic and foreign sources, and to offer reciprocal treatment to American banks active in deposit taking at home and abroad. The second reason is due to the shift in organizational preferences of Japanese banks in the areas of retail banking and money market activities. Their growth through acquisition in retail banking, particularly in California, and their desire to have branches in New York State forced a shift from the agency form of offices to branches in the late 1970s and the 1980s. This desire was compounded by the Japanese improvement in their capital position, in part from appreciation of the yen, and in part from their desire to participate in money market CDs and other deposit sources in the United States.

Geographical Location

The U.S. geographical location of foreign banks has followed a pattern of international trade and money market opportunities. In 1988, the ten cities with the most foreign banking offices jointly shared 90 percent of all U.S.

offices of foreign banks (see table 7.1). The overwhelming majority of foreign banks can be found in the three states of New York, California, and Illinois. The three cities of New York, Chicago, and Los Angeles jointly held 72 percent of the top ten cities' foreign banking offices and 65 percent of all foreign banks' offices in the United States. New York City ranked number one with a total of 461 offices, equivalent to 44 percent of all foreign banking and representative offices in the United States. Many foreign banks have located in New York City because it remains the financial center of the world's largest economy and because the state has chosen to accommodate more IBFs, authorized by the Federal Reserve. The state has exempted IBFs from local and state taxes to enable them to more easily conduct their international banking business.

Due to the concentration of foreign banks in a few money-center cities, the major responsibility of their supervision and control falls on four Federal Reserve districts. Nearly 93 percent of all foreign bank offices are located in the Federal Reserve districts of New York, Atlanta, Chicago, and San Francisco. The New York district is home to 47 percent of these offices, San Francisco to 26 percent, and Atlanta and Chicago each to approximately 10 percent of the total number of foreign banking offices.[1]

Assets, Deposits, and Loans Composition

The dramatic growth of foreign banks in the United States has resulted in a substantial increase in their assets, deposits, and business loans. Since 1981, U.S.-based foreign banks' assets, deposits, and commercial and business loans increased by an average rate of 13.7 percent, 15.2 percent, and 13.3 percent, respectively. In comparison with U.S.-owned U.S. banks, this growth was dramatic. The U.S. banks grew an average of 6.5 percent, 6.4 percent, and 6.8 percent in assets, deposits, and commercial and industrial loans, respectively, during the same period (see table 7.2). Their performance reflects the economic reality of the early 1980s, during which an initially high interest rate in the United States gave way to high unemployment, large trade and budget deficits, and the weakening of the U.S. dollar. While foreign banks were able to use the prevailing economic condition in their favor, American banks struggled to survive. From the beginning of 1981 to the end of 1988, the FDIC reported 821 bank failures, nearly half of which were subject to reorganization, merger, or sell-out. At the same time, over 200 savings and loan associations collapsed as a result of bad loans and shortages of funds. A good proportion of these troubled banks and some others were acquired by foreign investors, as banking authorities reluctantly favored foreign acquisitions to reduce concentration of power and reinforce competition.

The heavy concentration of commercial and industrial loans in the portfolios of foreign banks is indicative of their wholesale business orientation.

Table 7.1
Ten Cities with the Most Foreign Banking Offices
(as of December 31, 1988)

Cities	Agencies	Branches	Commercial Bank Subsidiaries	Edge Act Banks	Invest- ment Companies	Represen- tative Offices	Total
New York	33	224	36	7	10	151	461
Los Angeles	65	25	12	0	0	24	126
Chicago	0	54	2	2	0	26	84
Houston	13	0	0	6	0	56	75
San Francisco	29	8	6	2	0	18	63
Miami	36	0	4	9	0	8	57
Atlanta	14	0	0	0	0	10	24
Dallas	1	0	0	0	0	14	15
Washington, D.C.	0	3	0	1	0	11	15
Seattle	0	9	0	0	0	3	12
Ten largest	191	323	60	27	10	321	932
All U.S. Offices of Foreign Banks	206	346	84	28	10	362	1036
Ten Largest as a Percentage of All Foreign Bank Offices	93	93	71	96	100	89	90

Source: Calculated from Board of Governors of the Federal Reserve System, **Structural Data for U.S. Offices of Foreign Banks**, December 31, 1988. Data about representative offices are from **American Banker**, March 6, 1989, p. 4A.

Table 7.2
Growth in Assets, Deposits, C&I Loans of U.S. Banks from June 30, 1981 to June 30, 1988 (Billions of U.S. Dollars)

Year	Assets	% Chg.	Deposits	% Chg.	C&I Loans	% Chg.
			Foreign Banks in the United States			
1981	261.6	–	126.0	–	69.2	–
1982	285.4	9.1	148.6	17.9	83.0	19.9
1983	321.6	12.7	179.0	20.5	84.9	2.3
1984	380.9	18.4	228.2	27.5	92.9	9.4
1985	423.8	11.3	259.5	13.8	105.7	13.8
1986	461.0	8.7	255.3	(1.6)	114.2	8.0
1987	571.9	24.1	314.0	23.0	138.5	21.3
1988	638.3	11.6	331.2	5.5	164.3	18.6
			U.S.-Owned U.S. Banks			
1981	1,474.9	–	1,110.7	–	276.3	–
1982	1,569.3	6.4	1,177.2	6.0	303.7	9.9
1983	1,681.4	7.1	1,264.8	7.4	311.0	2.4
1984	1,734.6	3.2	1,304.7	3.2	360.0	15.8
1985	1,883.3	8.6	1,400.3	7.3	378.0	5.2
1986	2,050.7	8.9	1,540.8	10.0	402.0	6.2
1987	2,158.5	5.3	1,609.4	4.5	419.5	4.4
1988	2,289.2	6.1	1,711.3	6.3	433.9	3.4

Source: **American Banker**, March 6, 1989, p. 3A.
Reproduced with permission.
Note: Foreign bank office data exclude representative offices. Data for 1985 were not adjusted for the sale of Crocker National Bank, San Francisco, by Midland Bank PLC, London, to Wells Fargo Bank NA, San Francisco. Thus 1986 growth is understated for foreign-owned U.S. banks and overstated for U.S.-owned U.S. banks.

During the decade of the 1980s, commercial and industrial loans amounted to an average of 24 percent of foreign banks' assets in comparison with an average of 10 percent for retail-oriented banking. By contrast, U.S. banks contributed 30 percent of their assets to retail banking operations, and an average of only 19 percent to commercial and industrial loan activities.[2] On the deposit side, a larger proportion of foreign banks' deposits were generated externally, mostly from major corporate and individual clients abroad.

U.S. banks, on the other hand, accumulated a large percentage of their deposits domestically, from small depositors, corporations, and institutional investors. The distinction between the two groups is clear. U.S. banks serve retail businesses, while foreign banks are in wholesale businesses in the United States.

Business Activities of Foreign Offices

The dramatic growth of foreign banks is not limited to the growth in the number of foreign banking offices or their assets size, but also reflects their deposit-taking services and business loans. The data in table 7.3 illustrate the across-the-board increase in portfolio assets and liabilities of foreign banks, as of June 30, 1988. The growth in the number of offices and assets demonstrates the desire of foreign banks to further expand their role in the U.S. market. The growth in deposits and business loans reveals, in part, their success in generating additional business and attracting new customers. Agencies, branches, and subsidiaries, the major beneficiaries of the expansion, have grown largely in double digits in their progress toward development of a new market environment. The most progress has been made by branch offices, at the expense of agencies. Subsidiaries grew steadily over time, in response to the nature of their activities, which were limited in part by their retail banking operations.

A comparison of U.S. offices of foreign banks with all U.S. banks reveals that foreign banks grew in all categories by a ratio of 3 to 1. Since 1981, foreign offices as a percentage of all U.S. banks increased from 2.8 percent to 4.7 percent. At the same time, their assets and deposits increased from 15.2 percent and 10.2 percent to 21.8 percent and 16.2 percent, respectively. More dramatic was the growth of commercial and industrial loans, as today foreign banking offices grant one out of every four commercial and industrial loans in this country.

Commercial and Industrial Loans. From the top ten countries granting commercial and industrial loans held by banks' U.S. offices in 1988, six were from Western Europe (United Kingdom, Italy, France, Switzerland, Germany, and the Netherlands), three from Asia (Japan, Hong Kong, and Israel), and one from North America (Canada). The top ten control 42 percent of all foreign family banks, 58 percent of all foreign banks' U.S. offices, 90.5 percent of all commercial and industrial loans, and 89 percent of all assets and deposits (see table 7.4).

Among the group, Japan dominated the banking activities and showed the most progress. In regard to the number of family banks, Japan was followed distantly by France and West Germany, but received closer competition from Canada and the United Kingdom in the number of U.S. offices. More dramatic was the financial strength and daily business activities of

Table 7.3

Assets, Deposits, and C&I Loans of U.S. Offices of Foreign Banks, as of June 30, 1988 (Billions of U.S. Dollars)

Types of Offices	Number of Offices	Assets	Deposits	C&I Loans
Agencies	194	$ 86.1	$ 17.1	$ 25.2
percentage change	6	10.4	17.1	11.0
Branches	349	$ 393.5	$ 198.9	$ 93.3
percentage change	16	12.1	4.0	23.6
Subsidiary Banks	85	$ 152.0	$ 112.9	$ 43.9
percentage change	-1	11.5	6.3	15.2
Edge Act Banks	28	$ 2.4	$ 1.9	$ 0.3
percentage change	-2	4.3	11.8	4.3
Investment Companies	10	$ 4.2	$ 0.3	$ 1.7
percentage change	-1	-6.7	-25.0	-19.0
Totals for U.S. Offices of Foreign Banks	666	$ 638.3	$ 331.2	$164.5
percentage change	18	11.6	5.5	18.6
Totals for All U.S. Banks	14,064*	$2,927.5	$2,042.5	$598.2
percentage change	-4	7.2	6.2	7.2

Ratio of Foreign to All U.S. Banks	- Percentage		
1981	2.8	15.2	10.2	20.3
1982	3.2	15.5	11.2	21.7
1983	3.6	16.0	12.4	21.4
1984	3.6	17.7	14.9	20.5
1985	4.1	18.6	15.6	21.8
1986	4.3	18.4	14.2	22.1
1987	4.4	20.9	16.3	24.8
1988	4.7	21.8	16.2	27.5

Source: **American Banker**, March 6, 1989, p. 3A.
   Note: Percentage changes are over the previous year. Data are
         from June 30th of one year to June 30th of the next year;
         due to this date selection and assumptions, the number of
         offices and assets used here do not exactly match similar
         data provided previously in other sections.
   * Includes domestic and foreign banks.

Table 7.4
Top Ten Countries in C&I Loans Booked by Banks' U.S. Offices, 1988[a]
(Billions of U.S. Dollars)

Countries	No. of Family Banks	No. of U.S. Offices	C & I Loans	Ratios (C&I)	Deposits	Assets
Japan	33	116	$ 83.1	50.6%	$162.1	$328.7
	3	17	34.9%		8.4%	19.4%
United Kingdom	11	46	$ 15.1	9.2%	$ 30.0	$ 45.4
	-1	-1	8.6%		4.5%	10.7%
Canada	6	46	$ 13.1	8.0%	$ 21.9	$ 46.3
	*	-5	-0.8%		-1.8%	0.7%
Italy	12	25	$ 9.1	5.5%	$ 13.5	$ 37.8
	*	*	13.8%		-14.0%	0.3%
Hong Kong	10	32	$ 7.2	4.4%	$ 19.8	$ 27.5
	-1	*	-5.3%		-1.5%	5.0%
Switzerland	6	17	$ 7.2	4.4%	$ 11.8	$ 22.6
	-1	1	30.9%		22.9%	-6.6%
France	14	41	$ 5.0	3.0%	$ 15.1	$ 27.3
	-1	*	-15.3%		-1.3%	5.0%
Israel	4	26	$ 3.2	1.9%	$ 9.2	$ 10.6
	*	4	3.2%		8.5%	6.0%

Netherlands	4	17	$ 3.0	1.8%	$ 4.4	$ 10.1
	*	*	25.0%		*	21.7%
Germany	13	22	$ 2.7	1.6%	$ 6.9	$ 13.5
	*	*	8.0%		*	16.4%
Top Ten	113	388	$148.7	90.5%	$294.7	$569.8
	-1	16	20.2%		4.8%	12.5%
All Foreign Banks in U.S.	266	666	$164.3	100.0%	$331.2	$644.5
	*	2	18.6%		5.5%	11.6%

Source: **American Banker**, March 6, 1989, p. ■A.
Note: The second line for each country shows the changes over the
  previous year; an asterisk (*) represents no change. Foreign
  bank offices exclude representative offices. The ratio of C&I
  loans column is the ratio of the country's banks to all offices
  of foreign banks in the United States.
  ■ June 30, 1988

135

these foreign banking institutions. Japan held 50.6 percent of all commercial and industrial loans, 49 percent of all deposits, and 51 percent of assets of foreign banking offices in the United States.

Among the top 38 foreign banks with more than $1 billion in business loans outstanding in the United States, 18 are chartered by Japanese entities, 5 by Canada, 4 by the United Kingdom, 2 by Italy, and the rest by other nationalities. The most active bank in commercial and industrial loans is the Bank of Tokyo with $9.0 billion in loans outstanding. The second and third in rank are the Sumitomo Bank of Osaka, Japan, and the Mitsubishi Bank of Tokyo, each with approximately $8.1 billion in loans outstanding. Overall, Japanese banks held the largest pool of over $1 billion in commercial and industrial loans, an amount equal to $72.9 billion or 61 percent of all loans in this category. The second and third in rank are British banks with total commercial and industrial loans of $14.0 billion or 11.7 percent of the total, and Canadian banks with an allocation of $12.8 billion or 10.7 percent of the loans outstanding.[3]

Assets and Liabilities Structure of Agencies and Branches

Assets Structure. The growth of foreign banks' assets has resulted in a doubling or tripling in the size of various categories of assets of these institutions. Two major components of the foreign banks' assets (use of funds) are loans and securities. The loan category is the most important asset item for these institutions, consisting of $227.6 billion or 47 percent of the agencies' and branches' banking assets in 1988. This item more than doubled in the decade of the 1980s, with commercial and industrial loans to depository institutions as major beneficiaries. The loans to depository institutions have been nearly evenly divided between commercial banks in the United States and banks in foreign countries. Interest in real estate loans exploded in 1986 and 1987 as foreign banking offices increased their allocations to this account from an average of $5 billion in 1982 to an all-time high of $17.6 billion in 1988. The reason for this upsurge is twofold: first, alternative investments were saturated and their returns declined; and second, non-Western foreign banking entities became more accustomed to real estate loans and reacted more favorably to the high market demand of recent years. The bulk of this investment went to large apartment house projects, minimalls, and building complexes.

As table 7.5 reveals, nearly 81 percent of total commercial and industrial loans in 1988 was acquired by businesses in the United States. The other 19 percent was borrowed by foreign entities. This trend is contrary to the norm during the 1970s, when the larger proportion of commercial and industrial loans went to foreign borrowers. The loans to foreign governments and official institutions grew steadily, amounting to 3.7 percent of the total assets of agencies and branches. Loans for purchasing or carrying securities,

Table 7.5
Assests and Liabilities of U.S. Agencies and Branches of Foreign Banks
(Billions of U.S. Dollars)

Item	1982	1985	1987	1988[a]
Total Assets	207.7	311.6	460.8	478.4
Securities	6.0	18.7	33.0	34.9
U.S. Treasury	3.6	4.5	5.7	6.6
U.S. government agencies and corporations	0.5	1.0	3.6	4.1
Bonds, notes, and corporate stocks	1.8	13.2	23.7	24.2
Federal funds sold and securities purchased under agreement to resell	6.9	9.7	18.1	16.2
Loans (net)	127.0	163.4	219.8	227.6
Real estate loans	5.0	5.7	14.3	17.6
Loans to depository institutions	50.1	55.8	67.3	62.2
Commercial banks in U.S.	26.9	30.6	34.8	32.5
Banks in foreign countries	26.9	25.1	32.4	29.3
Commercial and industrial loans	57.0	73.0	108.6	118.1
U.S. addresses	33.3	49.9	85.7	95.9
Non-U.S. addresses	23.6	23.1	22.9	22.1
Loans to foreign governments and official institutions	12.6	15.9	17.6	17.9
Loans for purchasing or carrying securities	–	5.6	3.0	3.0
Total Liabilities	207.7	311.6	460.8	478.4
Total deposits and credit balances	91.4	149.9	224.9	215.0
Demand deposits and credit balances	4.0	4.4	5.9	6.6
Time deposits	87.4[b]	38.7	54.1	54.0
IBF Deposit liabilities	–	106.8	164.8	154.4
Federal funds purchased and securities sold under agreement to repurchase	18.9	33.4	37.2	54.2
Other borrowed money	49.8	59.4	96.3	99.1
All other liabilities	17.2	28.1	43.4	45.1
Net due to related depository institutions	30.4	40.7	59.1	64.9

Source: Calculated from the **Federal Reserve Bulletin**, Table 73,
pp. 179-183, December 1982; Table 68, pp. 158-162, December
1985; Table 4.30, pp. A76-A78, June 1988; and Table 4.30,
pp. A78-A81, January 1989. The numbers do not add up to the
total, due to rounding, and selection of specific items.
[a] As of June 30, 1988
[b] Includes international banking facilities

by security dealers for margin trading and other uses, were negligible, accounting for less than 1 percent of the assets per year.

During the 1970s, foreign banks' participation in security transactions was limited to less than 3 percent of their investment assets portfolio. The situation changed in the 1980s, as allocations increased to $34.9 billion or 7 percent of the active assets. From this total, 69 percent was invested in bonds, notes, debentures, and corporate stocks, including state and local securities. The investments in U.S. Treasury securities were very small, ranging from $3.6 billion to $6.6 billion during 1982 to 1988, despite strong indication of Japanese desire to purchase this form of risk-free securities. The obligation of U.S. government agencies' securities received some attention only since 1987, when the alternative forms of investment failed to provide expected high returns. Overall, the foreign banks' investments were very conservative in nature, wholesale oriented, and mostly allocated to the high-return, low-risk forms of activities.

Liability Structure. On the liability side, the bulk of funds originate from liabilities to nonrelated parties. This fund group consists of demand and time deposits and credit balances, international banking facilities' deposit liabilities, federal funds purchased and securities sold under agreement to repurchase, and other borrowed money and liabilities. The second subgroup contains the net due to related depository institutions, from the foreign head office and other U.S. and foreign branches and agencies of the bank, the bank's parent holding company, and majority-owned banking subsidiaries owned both directly and indirectly.

Agencies are barred from accepting deposits from the public in the host nation; instead they keep credit balances that consist of receipts from transactions and undisbursed loan balances for the same purpose as short-term transaction accounts. Thus, in a way they present a form of deposit account. The total demand and time deposits, IBF deposit liabilities, and credit balances amounted to $215 billion or 45 percent of all the liabilities of foreign banks' agencies and branches in 1988. Of this total, 72 percent or $154.4 billion were deposits with IBFs, and the rest with other forms of offices within the system. Of all types of deposits, time deposits held an edge of 10 to 1 in ratio to demand deposits, with substantial growth in recent years. Federal funds purchased and securities sold under agreement to repurchase, historically, together represented 5 to 10 percent of the liabilities, on average, reaching its peak of 11.3 percent of the total liabilities in 1988.[4] Other forms of borrowing and liabilities ranged from 25 to 30 percent of the liability accounts of agencies and branches. The contributions by head offices, banks' parent holding companies, and their subsidiaries were, on average, 15 percent. This is a quite smaller percentage than one would expect from these institutions, nearly one-third of whose activities are initiated or connected with parent or affiliated banks.

Because of their status as nonlocal banks, agencies and branches of foreign banks have a markedly different liability structure than domestic banks. Deposits from nonbanks play a relatively minor role in the funding of U.S. offices of foreign banks. Out of the total deposits and credit balance of $215 billion in 1988, only $60 billion originated from individuals, partnerships, and corporations. From this $60 billion, $35.7 billion was deposited by domestic residents and the rest from foreign countries.[5] On the other hand, the deposits by banks from foreign countries amounted to $81.5 billion or 38 percent of the total deposits. Approximately 90 percent of this deposit account was held by foreign origin; only 10 percent was deposited by foreign branches of U.S. banks. Interestingly, the deposit contributions by commercial banks reached $61 billion in 1988, with 80 percent held by U.S. branches and agencies of other foreign banks. Only 20 percent of this total came from other commercial banks in the United States. Collectively, the interbank deposits amounted to $142.5 billion in 1988, 60 percent of which were from banks of foreign countries and 40 percent from commercial banks in the United States.[6]

Finally, the share of foreign governments and official institutions, including foreign central banks, amounted to $11.3 billion in deposits or 5 percent of total deposits. This is an indication that the foreign government officials dealt with the Federal Reserve and U.S. banking offices, and not with an affiliated member. Overall, the analysis of the foreign banking offices' assets and liabilities structure demonstrates three distinct characteristics. First, the deposits from nonbanks compose only a small portion of their sources of funds; the bulk of these deposits originate via interbanks with a good proportion from foreign countries. Second, as with U.S. banks, the loan category is the most important asset item for these institutions, with commercial and industrial loans to businesses in the United States as the major beneficiaries. Third, these offices' investments in securities, including U.S. Treasury securities, are relatively very small; furthermore, their contributions to the liability account of parent banks and their subsidiaries are primitive and have not developed as one might expect.

A Comparison with U.S.-Insured Commercial Banks. The major difference between the U.S.-insured commercial banks' assets and liabilities structure and that of foreign bank offices is mainly associated with the size and dimension of their banking activities. The assets and liabilities of U.S.-insured commercial banks are five times larger than their foreign, U.S.-based counterparts.[7] The U.S. banks are more domestic-oriented than foreign bank offices. In 1988, from the $1.8 trillion in gross loans, one-third was allocated to real estate and one-third to C&I loans. The same allocations for foreign bank offices were 9 percent and 51.3 percent, respectively. Loans to individuals for the purchase of household goods, family, and other personal expenditures, and loans to finance agricultural production and loans to farmers by U.S. banking institutions accounted for 20.5 percent of the gross loans by domestic banks. Foreign banks contributed a negligible

Net Loans (U.S. Banks)[8]	$1822.7 billion
Real estate loans	612.8
Loans to depository institutions	64.4
Commercial and industrial loans	594.2
Loans to individuals for household	346.2
Obligations of state and local governments	50.9
Loans to finance agricultural production and to farmers	28.5
Other loans	125.7

amount to the same category. These data demonstrate the retail-oriented desire of U.S. banks versus wholesale-oriented preferences of foreign offices. The loans from foreign banks' U.S.-based offices to their related foreign governments and official institutions consisted of 8 percent of the gross loans, more than two and one-half times those of U.S. domestic banks. On the other hand, the U.S. banks' obligation to state and local governments amounted to $51 billion; no such contribution was recorded by foreign bank offices. The U.S. foreign banks' only connection with state and local governments is via the purchase of a small amount of securities issued by these institutions to finance local and regional needs.

From the security account point of view, there are wide differences in the uses of funds. In 1988, the securities purchased by insured, U.S. commercial banks amounted to $519 billion or 17.3 percent of total assets, with nearly 60 percent invested in U.S. Treasury securities and government agency obligations. Another 22 percent was used to purchase securities issued by state and local governments. On the other hand, agencies and branches of foreign banks in the United States invested only 17.3 percent of their securities funds for the purchase of U.S. Treasury securities and 13.9 percent in the obligations of U.S. government agencies and corporations. The bulk of foreign banks' investment in securities was in stocks and bonds of corporations. A total of $23.3 billion or 68.6 percent of the allocation of funds for securities was in this area.

Total Securities (U.S. banks)[9]	$519.1 billion
U.S. Treasury and government agencies' obligations	313.3
State and local governments' securities	115.5
Other securities	90.3

On the liability side, the key differences are in the sources of funds. Total deposits consist of 82 percent of U.S. domestic bank liabilities and sources of funds. Of this total, three-fourths is generated through time deposits, money market deposit accounts, and certificates of deposit. The other one-fourth is generated from demand deposits. Foreign bank offices, in contrast, raise only 47 percent of their source of funds from deposit accounts, mostly from their international banking facility offices. The large proportion of this fund originates from wholesale deposits and large certificates of deposit, not from large numbers of small deposits by the general public. This policy trend reaffirms the wholesale nature of foreign banks' U.S.-based offices versus the retail orientation of U.S. domestic banking offices.

Total Liabilities (U.S. banks)[10]	$2818.5 billion
Total deposits	2305.0
Federal funds purchased and sold under agreement	252.1
Other borrowed money and liabilities	261.4

THE WORLD'S LARGEST BANKING CONCERNS

The number of U.S. banks ranked among the world's largest banks, based on assets and deposits, has declined substantially since 1955, giving rise to concerns that U.S. banks' competitive position in the international marketplace may be weakening. In 1956, based on deposits, 25 U.S. banks ranked among the world's top 50; the number dropped to 18 by 1962, and steadily fell further, to 13 by 1970 and to 6 by year-end 1978. In contrast, the number of Japanese and German banks increased to a rank of one and two, at the expense of American banks during the same period. (See table 7.6.) However, in absolute terms, the American banks have grown steadily since 1956.

This decline in ranking of U.S. banks is the result of significant economic growth in Japan and Western Europe in the 1960s and 1970s, and the continuously sluggish economy of the United States in the early 1980s. In addition, two other factors significantly contributed to the U.S. banks' loss of global standing. One was government policies regarding domestic bank operations and expansionary opportunities, and the other is the role of exchange rates in explaining the mechanical reranking of the world's top banks. Laws and regulations may restrict or motivate the scope of banking activities, as previously discussed in chapters 3 and 6. The continuous decline in the value of the dollar in the 1980s automatically upgraded the status of foreign banks with respect to the United States, and does not necessarily reflect what was actually accomplished by these world class institutions. A comparison of published data indicates that the U.S. world ranking status is continuing to decline as foreign institutions gain in world financial strength. In 1983, based on assets, the United States ranked second among countries with 8 of the world's 50 largest banks. Japan held the first rank with 17 banks, followed by France, Germany, and Great Britain, each with 5 banks. Table 7.7 presents the world status of U.S. banks in 1983 compared with 1986 and 1988.

In 1986, U.S. banks relinquished their second ranking to Germany with the loss of 4 banks from the list of the 50 largest banks. Other rankings had minor changes, with one exception: Canada's status was reduced to eighth,

Table 7.6
Nationalities of the World's Largest Banks, Number of Banks in the Top 50, by Deposit Size

Country	1956	1962	1970	1978	Rank 1956	Rank 1978
Japan	3	9	11	16	4	1
Germany	–	4	4	8	–	2
United States	25	18	13	6	1	3
Italy	3	5	4	2	4	9
United Kingdom	7	5	4	4	2	4
Canada	6	5	5	3	3	6
France	3	3	3	4	4	4
Netherlands	–	–	1	3	–	6
Switzerland	–	–	3	3	–	6
Belgium	–	–	–	1	–	10
Australia	1	–	1	–	7	–
Other*	2	1	1	–	7	–

Source: C. Steward Goddin and Steven J. Weiss, "U.S.
Banks' Loss of Global Standing," The Office
of the Comptroller of the Currency,
June 1980, p. 2.
* None of which had more than one bank in the
top 50 in any year covered.

having only 1 bank in the top 50 companies. In 1987 and 1988, more than ever, the fluctuation of foreign exchange rates influenced the country rankings of the world's banks. In 1988, the decline in rank continued for U.S. banks to fourth, despite the holding of its position with 4 banks among the world's 50 largest banks. More disturbing was the assets position of the banks among the 50 largest banks. By the end of 1983, Citicorp and Bank of America ranked first and second, with Chase Manhattan at number 14. Other U.S. banks ranked numbers 24, 29, 38, 43, and 46. However, by 1988, Citicorp ranked number 8, Chase Manhattan number 33, Bank of America number 37, and Chemical Bank number 48. In contrast, Japan was home to the world's 7 largest banks, and 18 of the 30 largest banks.[11]

By the late 1970s and early 1980s concern was expressed about the decline in U.S. banks' preeminence among the world's largest banks. Aside from national pride in ranking, it is a general belief, accepted by banking authorities and experts, that the innovative capacities of U.S. banks will remain intact and in the forefront of the industry. Furthermore, none of the U.S. banks should be blamed for the decline in rankings. The key concern here is the overall decline in the relative worldwide strength of the U.S. economy, extended well beyond the field of banking. To recapture the glorious status of the 1950s and 1960s, the U.S. economy should improve and sustain growth to the historical rate of 5 percent real growth in GNP and the real value of the dollar should be reestablished. This accomplishment is beyond the present expectation for the U.S. economy, and should not be anticipated before the year 1995 or soon thereafter.

U.S. BANKING ABROAD

During the second half of the twentieth century, U.S. banks, as leaders in modern international banking, often performed central roles in the development of world banking and in recycling the surplus funds among International money-center markets. Accordingly, they influenced and were greatly affected by change in world market events. Their activities can be divided into three phases. First came the period of rapid growth during the 1960s, as the U.S. banks branched out internationally to capitalize on growing world trade and to increase the lending portfolios of their corporate clients. The second phase started with the recycling of petrodollars, and the growth in the amount of syndicate loans disbursed in the 1970s. The third phase started in the early 1980s, when banks began exploring new opportunities

Table 7.7
World's 50 Largest Banking Companies, Ranked by Assets

Country	1983 No. of Banks	1983 Rank	1986 No. of Banks	1986 Rank	1988 No. of Banks	1988 Rank
Japan	17	1	22	1	20	1
United States	8	2	4	3	4	4
West Germany	5	3	6	2	8	2
United Kingdom	5	3	4	4	4	4
France	5	3	4	4	5	3
Netherlands	1	8	3	6	3	6
Switzerland	2	7	3	6	3	6
Hong Kong	1	8	1	8	1	8
Canada	4	6	1	8	1	8
Brazil	1	8	1	8	-	-
Italy	1	8	1	8	1	8
China	-	-	-	-	1	8

Source: **Fortune**, June 11 and August 20, 1984, and June 6 and August 1, 1988; and **American Banker**, July 31, 1987, for the year 1986.

and focused on earnings, with the application of financial innovation and technology in response to the world competition in strengthening market links around the world. Table 7.8 presents the foreign branches of the U.S. member banks for the period 1955 through 1987.

U.S. Foreign Branches

The number and assets of U.S. foreign branches increased continuously from 1955 to 1985, and thereafter declined marginally. This growth varied significantly by region. At first, the major countries of Europe had the largest and most accessible financial markets. Because of these markets and the strong trading ties of these countries with the United States, the assets of European branches of U.S. banks easily dominated those of U.S. bank branches in other regions of the world — ranging from 60 to 80 percent of the total share during the period 1960 to 1980. Today these represent 43 percent of the world's U.S. foreign banking share in assets.[12]

In Latin America, the number of U.S. branches at year-end 1986 was 216. Attaching a significance to this number may be misleading, because the size of assets of U.S. branches remained relatively small, at $12 billion, and a large percentage of these offices and assets were controlled by a very few large U.S. banks. On other hand, U.S. banks steadily increased their presence in Asia, especially in Hong Kong and Singapore, due to the emergence of this region in growing trade relationships, and as an offshore banking center. Since 1965, the number of U.S. branches in Asia more than quadrupled, but their assets remained relatively low; in fact, they declined from $65.2 billion in 1984 to $59.2 billion in 1986.

The U.S. branch banking interest in the Caribbean islands began in the late 1960s and steadily increased to a peak of 206 branches with $118.6 billion in assets in 1983. Today, there are 180 Caribbean offices with $100.2 billion in assets. These offices enable parent banks to enter the Eurodollar market to provide foreign loans, and to tap outside funds without being subject to the restrictions imposed by U.S. foreign credit laws or other regulations imposed by the Federal Reserve's control on capital funds. The branch banking activities of U.S. banks in Africa and the Middle East account for only 4 percent of the total number of offices and 2 percent of the total assets. The countries of Canada, Australia, and Mexico have almost no U.S. foreign branches, because until very recently all prohibited foreign bank branching. Citicorp's branches in Mexico have been grandfathered, because they were in operation before Mexico's banking revolution in the 1930s. Australia and Canada also relaxed their branching prohibitions, now permitting branching through local subsidiary banks. The following are the selected major U.S. branch sites by country for the year 1986.[13]

Country	Number of Branches	Assets ($B)
Argentina	64	$ 1.6
Bahamas	70	67.2
Cayman Islands	85	32.7
United Kingdom	64	99.9
Hong Kong	75	12.3
Japan	29	19.3
Singapore	27	14.3

Table 7.8
Foreign Branches of U.S. Member Banks, 1955–87

Year	No. of Banks with Foreign Branches	No. of Foreign Branches	Total Assets ($B)
1955	7	115	2.0
1960	8	131	3.5
1965	13	211	9.1
1970	79	532	52.6
1975	126	762	162.7
1980	159	787	343.5
1985	162	916	329.2
1986	151	899	331.5
1987	153	902	350.0

Region – 1986			
Europe	–	194	143.9
Latin America	–	216	11.7
Caribbean	–	180	100.2
Africa	–	18	3.0
Asia	–	218	59.2
Middle East	–	21	3.8
U.S. Territories	–	52	9.6

Source: Federal Financial Institutional Examination Council, **Annual Branch Reports of Condition**, FFIEC 030; and James V. Houpt, "International Trends for U.S. Banks and Banking Markets," Study No. 156, May 1988, pp. 7, 46–47.

Note: The total assets represent gross assets. During the 1980s, nearly $30 billion to $50 billion of these assets were claims on other branches of own bank. Thus, net or adjusted assets is equal to gross assets minus claims. The total assets for 1987 are estimated.

U.S. Foreign Subsidiaries

As shown in table 7.9, subsidiaries represent a smaller component of the international activities of U.S. banks than do foreign branches, but they are growing steadily. A subsidiary may be organized via a bank holding company or through an Edge corporation, subject to Section 23A of the Federal Reserve Act. Major development of the subsidiary form of organization started in the mid-1960s and climbed rapidly in the 1970s.

The activities of subsidiaries reflect the local banking and tax laws of host nations. From the total of 860 subsidiary offices of U.S. banks abroad, 67 percent or 578 offices are located in Europe, Asia, and Latin America. Europe is home to 32 percent of all U.S. banking subsidiary offices and 52

Table 7.9
Foreign Subsidiaries of U.S. Banking Organizations

Region	Offices		Assets ($B)	
	Number	Percent	Amount	Percent
Europe	279	32.4	68.9	52.0
Latin America	153	17.8	5.2	3.9
Asia	146	17.0	12.6	9.6
Africa	52	6.0	1.0	0.8
Middle East	4	0.5	5.3	4.0
Canada	33	3.8	8.2	6.2
Australia and New Zealand	49	5.7	8.7	6.5
Offshore centers[a]	84	9.8	14.6	11.0
United States[b]	60	7.0	7.9	6.0
Total	860	100.0	132.2	100.0

Source: Board of Governors of the Federal Reserve
System, Annual FR 2314 Reports; and
James V. Houpt, "International Trends for
U.S. Banks and Banking Markets," Staff Study,
No. 156, May 1988, p. 11. Data are for 1986.
  [a] The Bahamas, Cayman Islands, Channel
Islands, and Netherland Antilles.
  [b] These are mostly holding companies for
foreign investments (not Edge corporations)
and leasing companies that are treated as
foreign subsidiaries under Regulation K.

Table 7.10
Principal Activities of Foreign Subsidiaries of U.S. Banks

Activity	No. of Companies	Assets ($B) Amount	Percent
Commercial Banking	85	63.4	52.6
Investment/Merchant Banking	49	27.1	22.5
Consumer Finance	17	8.3	6.9
Securities Brokering and Dealing	3	7.5	6.2
Leasing	13	3.7	3.1
Trust Activities	6	3.1	2.5
Consumer Finance	12	2.7	2.2
Other Financial Activities	17	4.9	4.1
Total	202	127.7	100.0

Source: Board of Governors of the Federal Reserve
System, FR 2068 and FR 2314 Reports; and
James V. Houpt, "International Trends for
U.S. Banks and Banking Markets," Study
No. 156, May 1988, p. 12.

percent of all the subsidiaries' total assets, collectively. Among the European U.S. subsidiaries, 44 percent of the offices are located in the United Kingdom, controlling 43 percent of U.S.-European subsidiary assets and 22.2 percent of all the U.S. foreign subsidiaries' assets. Other countries with large U.S. banking investments are West Germany with 9.3 percent of the total assets and 2.4 percent of the number of offices, Canada with 6.2 percent of the total assets and 3.8 percent of the offices, and Hong Kong with 5 percent of the total assets and 9 percent of the offices. The U.S. share of the Japanese market is very small, consisting of 2 percent of all the subsidiaries' offices but only 0.6 percent of their total assets.[14]

One feature of the U.S. banking subsidiaries abroad is their diversity and the types of activities pursued in the daily conduct of their business activities. For example, in the United Kingdom, U.S. subsidiaries conduct merchant or investment banking with retail mortgage lending operations. In West Germany, these offices concentrate on wholesale banking with an emphasis on consumer banking. In Australia, Hong Kong, and Singapore, the activities are mainly merchant banking and commercial financing, with a touch of retail operations. Overall, the activities are dominated by commercial banking and investment/merchant banking services. Other types of activities are segmented to a specific market to serve special local needs.

NOTES

1. Board of Governors of the Federal Reserve System, *Structural Data for U.S. Offices of Foreign Banks*, December 31, 1988, Part 3, pp. 1–41.

2. Ibid., *Federal Reserve Bulletin*, various issues, tables about assets and liabilities of U.S. branches and agencies of foreign banks, and domestic and foreign offices, insured commercial banks' assets and liabilities.

3. "Foreign Banks in the United States," *American Banker*, Vol. 154, No. 44, March 6, 1989, p. 2A.

4. The net contribution for this account in 1988 was $38 billion, with the liability account exceeding the asset account. As a result, the foreign bank offices were net sellers of this obligation, using this account as a means of raising funds.

5. Board of Governors of the Federal Reserve System, *Federal Reserve Bulletin*, Vol. 75, No. 1, January 1988, Table 4.30, pp. A78–A81.

6. Ibid., p. A79.

7. The assets of the U.S.-insured commercial banks, domestic and foreign offices, as of December 31, 1988, are $3039.1 billion. Similar data for the foreign bank offices in the United States are $653.2 billion, with agencies' and branches' share reaching $513.7 billion. All the data and information in this section were derived from the *Federal Reserve Bulletin*, June 1989, tables 4.20 and 4.30, pages A72–A73 and A90–A93.

8. Ibid., pp. A70–A73.

9. Ibid.

10. Ibid. pp. A90–93.

11. *Fortune*, June 11 and August 20, 1984, June 6 and August 1, 1988; and *American Banker*, Vol. 152, No. 149, July 31, 1987, p. 28, for the year 1986.

12. James V. Houpt, "International Trends for U.S. Banks and Banking Markets," Staff Study No. 156, Board of Governors of the Federal Reserve System, May 1988, pp. 7–9 and 46–47.

13. Ibid., pp. 9 and 46–47.

14. Ibid., table 3, p. 11.

8   Major Foreign Banking Concerns in the United States

The health of a nation reflects the characteristics of the economy that the system serves. The success of an economy is measured by its financial strength and business conduct. One barometer of this success is the degree of net exports of a country; another one is the continuous flow of funds across its borders. Since the early 1960s, the volume of world trade has grown rapidly, and banks have expanded abroad to keep pace. Communication and modern technology became major components of banking and finance. Today, banks and businesses finance their activities internationally to ensure the most efficient participation in emerging markets. While international banking has provided substantial opportunities and rewards to bankers, it has also presented substantial risks.

To operate in this environment, a bank needs to be equipped with three weapons. It needs, first, to be financially strong and internationally active wherever the market demand calls for it; second, to be sophisticated and equipped with modern computers and proficient in the applications of technology; and third, to be managerially prudent and technically confident to participate around the world in less familiar environments. The first and second rules require financial strength with large assets and deposits. The third factor necessitates employment of experienced technicians with geocentric attitudes.

Foreign banks in the United States are composed of two different groups. One group consists of multinational banks from industrial countries with worldwide exposures, and the second group represents developing nations with limited financial activities. The multinational banks have three major characteristics: (1) most are large with assets in the billions of dollars; (2) they consist of a very few dominant banks with a large network of worldwide offices; and (3) they are very active in international investment activities. The majority of these banks have been involved for centuries in financing international trade and foreign exchange transactions. They have operated efficiently by using "shell" banking centers like Hong Kong, Singapore, and other international facilities to channel their funds across borders, in a prudent and fashionable manner, with the use of computers and other modern technological equipment. The developing countries' banks, on the other hand, are simply agents of their governments, providing basic trade financing and intergovernmental transactions. The scope and dimension of these banking activities are limited and historically they have shown little interest to expand in the vast financial market of the United States.

Unlike the American multinational banks, which are newcomers to the scene, European multinational banks have accumulated a portfolio for accomplishments in both friendly and hostile environments, through years of operations with colonies. Therefore, it was not uncharacteristic of them to envisage the opportunities in the United States during the late 1960s and early 1970s, and to plan expansion in the years following.

BANKING EXPANSION BY COUNTRY AND REGION

The presence of foreign banks and investors in the U.S. markets is neither new nor inappropriate. Foreign multinational banks have been involved in U.S. banking, trade, and economic activities since colonial times. These institutions provided the U.S. economy substantial financial support, and initiated the transfer of banking technology to local banks. In the mid-1700s, British merchant banks pioneered in the establishment of banking in the United States to finance trade transactions.[1] A more formal and diverse form of foreign banking became operational shortly after the Civil War, with the establishment of the first agency in New York. By 1880, the foreign banking sector held an estimated 15 percent share of the California banking market and owned the state's third and fourth largest banks.[2] The efforts and capital of foreign banks were especially helpful in financing the growth of the U.S. railroads and the foundation of early light industries.

Expansion by Country

In evaluating the activities and market shares of foreign banks, one must recognize that the foreign banks in the United States are principally engaged in wholesale banking and interbank transactions. The retail banking activities are in the primitive stage, and have not reached takeoff level. Table 8.1 presents the total investments of U.S. banking institutions owned by foreign banks, by country. The aggregate assets of these U.S. banking offices give foreign banks a very strong presence in the U.S. banking system. As shown in this table, Japan owns by far the greatest share of the U.S. banking

Table 8.1
Total Assets of U.S. Banking Institutions Owned by Foreign Banks, by Country (Millions of U.S. Dollars)

Country	1980 Assets	1980 Rank	1985 Assets	1985 Rank	1988 Assets	1988 Rank
Argentina	2,538	14	1,547	19	864	32
Australia	833	17	2,641	17	3,931	16
Austria	-	-	378	38	1,198	25
Bahrain	74	35	528	33	1,028	27
Belgium	388	20	2,285	18	3,131	17
Bermuda	-	-	5	57	138	50
Brazil	4,427	9	4,002	13	4,282	15
Canada	15,718	3	39,509	3	39,252	3
Cayman Is.	-	-	-	-	130	52
Chile	-	-	44	54	86	54
China	-	-	490	35	964	29
Colombia	250	25	532	32	825	33
Denmark	158	30	716	29	2,048	21
Dominican Rep.	-	-	-	-	29	57
Egypt	-	-	288	45	175	49
Ecuador	-	-	75	51	188	48
El Salvador	-	-	-	-	1	59
Finland	-	-	63	52	1,420	22
France	12,926	4	20,580	6	29,255	5
Greece	632	18	793	27	1,225	23
Hong Kong	11,921	5	23,284	5	25,732	6
India	188	28	435	36	750	36
Indonesia	-	-	1,507	20	2,666	19
Iran	186	29	45	53	17	58
Ireland	257	24	4,480	12	6,425	11
Israel	4,097	10	7,813	9	9,249	10
Italy	9,217	7	29,090	4	39,859	2
Japan	72,484	1	178,631	1	360,854	1
Jordan	-	-	144	50	316	44
Kuwait	-	-	1,118	22	993	28

(continued)

system, more than any other country or region. Italy ranks second with Canada and the United Kingdom at third and fourth places. Canada and Italy outranked the United Kingdom in 1986 and 1987 as British banking investments nose-dived from $57 billion in 1980 to $33 billion in 1988.

While the reason for the decline of British banking interest is unclear, one may attribute it in part to the sudden variation in the exchange rate between British pounds and U.S. dollars. In fact, the same circumstances are true in regard to our currency relationship with the German deutsche mark and Japanese yen. But the key differences that separate these two countries from

Table 8.1
(continued)

Country	1980 Assets	Rank	1985 Assets	Rank	1988 Assets	Rank
Luxemburg	–	–	729	28	756	35
Malaysia	62	36	295	44	525	41
Mexico	3,894	12	3,935	15	4,431	14
Netherlands	3,668	13	7,118	10	10,126	9
New Zealand	104	32	609	30	892	31
Norway	–	–	297	43	1,153	26
Pakistan	282	23	595	31	669	38
Panama	–	–	196	46	136	51
Peru	–	–	25	56	31	56
Philippines	109	31	325	40	321	43
Portugal	467	19	314	41	658	39
Qatar	–	–	41	55	117	53
Saudi Arabia	–	–	407	37	744	37
Singapore	96	34	333	39	380	42
South Africa	–	–	169	47	78	55
South Korea	2,200	15	3,259	16	4,617	13
Spain	2,166	16	3,947	14	6,086	12
Sweden	–	–	929	25	1,210	24
Switzerland	11,312	6	18,338	7	23,879	7
Taiwan	289	22	1,307	21	2,745	18
Thailand	213	27	820	26	824	34
Turkey	–	–	157	49	310	45
U.A.E.	–	–	308	42	258	46
U.K.	25,136	2	57,028	2	32,708	4
Uruguay	–	–	159	48	214	47
Venezuela	345	21	1,085	23	2,603	20
West Germany	7,253	8	8,801	8	13,025	8
Yugoslavia	101	33	526	34	655	40
Other W. Eur.	3,898	11	6,392	11	5,045	13
Mult. Countries	221	26	1,055	24	936	30

Source: Board of Governors of the Federal Reserve
System, **Structural Data for U.S. Offices of
Foreign Banks**, 1980-88.
Note: All numbers have been rounded to the nearest
number.

other major European countries are that West Germany and Japan have
accumulated larger trade surpluses with the United States and are the largest
net creditors in the world. In 1988, Japan accumulated $96 billion in trade
surpluses, nearly 58 percent with the United States. Similarly, West Germany's world trade surpluses in the same year were $74 billion, 20 percent of
which was with the United States. At the same time, the United Kingdom
recorded $21 billion in deficits, and its surplus trade with the United States

was relatively small. Other major European countries also recorded deficits in their balances of trade, despite their positive trade accounts with the United States.

The table also sheds light on a few other factors. First, most foreign banks from the Third World countries are newcomers to the U.S. market. These banks are all small, with average U.S. banking assets under $400 million, and are mainly engaging in limited activities to finance trade and banking transactions between the United States and their home countries. Very few of these offices are involved in retail banking and other global investment activities. Second, there have been minor changes in the ranking among countries, with two exceptions. Italy improved its position in rank from number 7 before 1980 to number 2 in 1988, with assets increasing from $9 billion to $39 billion. The OPEC countries, once the major source of dollar funds in the late 1970s, scored very low in rank, ranging from 20 and lower.

Expansion by Region

The expansion of major U.S. banking institutions owned by foreign banks, by country and region, can be measured in two ways. One is a comparison by assets; the second is a comparison of the type of offices they select to hold. The significance of evaluating countries' activities within a region is to demonstrate the economic and financial strength of the country within a specific region versus the strength of the countries and the region as a whole. The best example of the difference in practice is the Western European region in comparison with the Asian region. One presents uniformity in norm, the other one shows the case of domination by one or two countries within the region. Table 8.2 illustrates this point.

Western European and Canadian banking presence dates back to the mid-nineteenth century. Japanese banks, on the other hand, appeared on the American scene in the twentieth century and became dominant in the 1970s. Other countries within the region, with the exception of Hong Kong, are newcomers, with limited experience in the U.S. market. Nevertheless, economic and financial strength and a country's ability to participate in world trade are the key determinants in successful transmission of resources, not the country's historical presence. The following analysis supports this comment.

Asset Comparison by Region. On the surface, the Asian and Middle Eastern region is the strongest region. The strength of the region is mainly carried by the two countries of Japan and Hong Kong. The region, by itself, controls 63 percent of all the assets of the foreign banking institutions, with the two dominant countries of Hong Kong and Japan carrying the major share. The banking institutions from these two nations own 43 percent of the family banks in the region with Japan owning one-third of all. More severe segmentation exists in regard to assets ownership. The two giants in

Table 8.2
Total Assets of U.S. Banking Institutions Owned by Foreign Banks, by Type of Offices, 1988
(Millions of U.S. Dollars)

Country/Region	No. of Family Banks	Agencies	Branches	Subsidiaries	Investment Companies	Edge Corp.
Western Europe						
Austria	3	–	1,198	–	–	–
Belgium	3	–	3,107	–	25	–
Denmark	5	136	1,636	275	–	–
Finland	2	–	1,420	–	–	–
France	12	2,535	22,714	1,683	2,259	64
Germany	13	2,011	11,014	–	–	–
Greece	1	–	126	1,099	–	–
Ireland	2	–	424	6,001	–	–
Italy	12	4,339	34,659	861	–	–
Luxemburg	1	756	–	–	–	–
Netherlands	5	882	7,721	1,495	–	28
Norway	5	–	535	–	618	–
Portugal	4	401	257	–	–	–
Spain	8	1,207	2,879	1,336	128	536
Sweden	4	92	277	–	841	–
Switzerland	6	1,165	22,708	–	6	–
Turkey	1	–	310	–	–	–
U.K.	11	1,881	13,577	16,928	–	323
Yugoslavia	3	–	537	119	–	–
Others	2	–	–	4,725	320	–

Latin America					
Argentina	3	485	380	–	–	–
Brazil	16	1,750	2,102	419	–	11
Chile	1	–	86	–	–	–
Colombia	5	147	52	417	–	209
Dominican Rep.	1	–	–	29	–	–
Ecuador	2	44	–	144	–	–
El Salvador	1	1	–	–	–	–
Mexico	6	3,701	–	730	–	–
Panama	2	136	*	–	–	–
Peru	1	–	31	–	–	–
Uruguay	1	–	214	–	–	–
Venezuela	7	1,134	315	305	–	849
Asia & Middle East					
Bahrain	3	78	950	–	–	–
China	1	–	964	–	–	–
Hong Kong	10	355	2,405	22,696	–	275
India	3	140	583	22	–	–
Indonesia	7	651	2,015	–	–	–
Iran	3	17	–	–	–	–
Israel	4	684	2,802	5,763	–	–
Japan	35	47,596	259,116	53,949	16	249
Jordan	2	–	194	–	–	122
S. Korea	6	1,275	2,839	503	–	–
Kuwait	2	–	993	–	–	–
Malaysia	2	41	484	–	–	–
Pakistan	3	–	669	–	–	–
Philippines	6	17	166	139	–	–
Qatar	1	–	117	–	–	–

Table 8.2
(continued)

Country/Region	No. of Family Banks	Agencies	Branches	Subsidiaries	Investment Companies	Edge Corp.
Saudi Arabia	2	–	744	–	–	–
Singapore	5	246	134	–	–	–
Taiwan	1	2,101	148	496	–	–
Thailand	5	210	614	–	–	–
U.A.E.	3	–	208	–	–	50
Other Countries						
Australia	7	847	3,084	–	–	–
Bermuda	1	–	–	–	–	138
Canada	7	6,274	21,628	11,276	–	74
Cayman Islands	1	130	–	–	–	–
Egypt	1	–	175	–	–	–
Mult. Countries	1	–	–	936	–	–
New Zealand	1	134	758	–	–	–
South Africa	1	–	78	–	–	–
Western Europe	103	15,405	125,099	34,522	4,197	951
Latin America	46	7,398	3,180	2,044	–	1,069
Asia & Middle East	104	53,411	276,151	83,568	16	696
Other Countries	20	7,385	25,723	12,212	–	212
Total	273	83,600	430,154	132,348	4,213	2,928

Source: Calculated from Board of Governors of the Federal Reserve System,
Structural Data for U.S. Offices of Foreign Banks, 1980–88.

* Less than $1 million.

the group control 93 percent of all assets, with Japan's share of the total reaching 87 percent of the region's assets.

Other notable, second-ranked members of this group are the banks from Israel, South Korea, and Taiwan. Israel ranks number 3 in the region and number 10 among all the foreign banks in the United States. The South Korean expansion began in the 1970s with its invasion of U.S. industrial markets, but did not progress as expected, due to the strong competition from the Japanese and also due to its inexperience in the banking industry. In fact, over time its rank deteriorated from number 15 in 1980 to 18 in 1986 and 16 in 1988, as other foreign banks improved their assets position more rapidly. South Korea's success depends strongly on its ability to capture a large share of the U.S. import market and its innovative approach to bank marketing. Like South Korea, Taiwan's banking presence is primitive but growing. The banking establishments from this country conduct their financial activities via the agency form of offices, with a recent surge of interest in the subsidiary form of organization.

Historically, OPEC nations' banking entities have demonstrated no strong interest in having a presence in the competitive and complex banking market of the United States, in large part due to political reasons. European money centers have benefited from this situation, as the OPEC nations have generously contributed to the development of Eurodollar and Eurocurrency markets.

The most organized, historically active region of all is the Western European region, with substantial financial power and expertise in all areas of financial activities. It accounts for 28 percent of all banking investments and 38 percent of all family banks. Its major difference from the Asian group is the relative uniformity in overall contributions of the countries within the region. No truly dominant country exists among the group, despite Italy's superiority in overall ranking. The largest within the group are Italy, the United Kingdom, France, and Switzerland. Italy owns 12 percent of the region's family banks and controls 22 percent of the region's total assets. The United Kingdom owns 11 percent of the region's family banks and controls 17 percent of all the banking investment portfolio. They are followed by France and Switzerland, with 16 and 13 percent of the total assets, respectively.

One surprising nation among the Western Europeans is West Germany. Despite West Germany's economic, industrial, and banking domination in Europe, its concentration of power in U.S. financial markets is secondary. The Germans have never felt comfortable operating financial institutions in the United States, despite their export market success in the areas of automobiles and other industrial goods. Their share of Western European banking investments in the United States consists of only 7 percent of the total European banking assets. However, overall, Germany ranks number 8 among all countries, with 84 percent of their investment allocation devoted to the branch banking form of offices.

Among the Latin American countries, Mexico and Brazil provide the major contributions. Together they control 64 percent of the Latin American banking assets, and own 48 percent of the region's family banks. But their domination is far from what has been presented by the Asian countries of Hong Kong and Japan. No single country in this group controls more than 32 percent of the assets allocation. Their group activities are very limited in nature and, to a very large degree, related to the trade between the United States and their home countries. No aggressive expansionary behavior has been observed among the group; in fact, their ranking status has remained almost unchanged or, for some, deteriorated.

In regard to the status of the other countries category, Canada provides the real challenge. As the largest trading partner with the United States, Canada participates in all forms of activities and types of banking offices, except investment companies. Overall, it ranks number 3 among the nations with $39 billion in assets at the end of 1988. Australia's banking relationship with the United States was not historically strong, due to the fact that in the past, Australia prohibited branch banking by foreign, nonalliance nations. Consequently, various states in the United States retaliated by barring Australia from branching here, thus limiting its presence and activities. In 1987, Australia relaxed its banking law to accommodate foreign participation. As a result, it is expected that its banking activities in the United States will increase in the years to come.

Office Comparison by Region. International banking presence in the United States in the early stages was in the form of agencies. The reasons for this development are twofold. One was that most banks were merchant banks and banking activities were limited to financing international trade and providing foreign exchange services for home-country clients. The second reason was that some state regulatory limitations discouraged branching facilities. For example, the New York State banking laws adopted the reciprocity rule, preventing foreign bank branching if the applicant bank's country prohibited U.S. branching. Similarly, a California state law prohibited foreign banks from participating in deposit-taking activities without FDIC insurance. As a result, the agency form of offices prevailed as the most desirable form of office organization.

By the end of the 1960s, as international banking advanced into the takeoff stage, the limitations of the agency form of organization started to negatively affect those banks that desired more flexible types of services; therefore branching received considerable attention. Nevertheless, the selection of a form of office is largely determined by the long-term policy goal of the participating banks and the type of activities pursued in relationship to the size of the market they serve at a given time. Overall, following the branches in rank are agencies and subsidiaries. Subsidiaries have received special attention in recent years due to the preference of foreign banks to expand their activities into retail banking operations. However, based on asset allocation, the choices are not uniform among the countries and regions.

Among the Western European countries the choice is clear. Based on assets, banks from Western Europe rank branches, agencies, and subsidiaries as their first, second, and third choices, respectively. On the other hand, Latin American countries' preferences are with agencies over branches and subsidiaries. But variation exists within the group, without a clear norm. For example, while Mexico and Venezuela choose the agency form of organization as first preference, Brazil selects the branch banking formation. Others have demonstrated no uniform pattern. One clear distinction is that the countries with stronger export markets are more inclined toward branch banking than any other form of office. This trend is apparent, with some exceptions, among all the countries in the regions.

For the Asian and Middle Eastern region, with the exception of Singapore, Taiwan, and Iran, the preference is with branch banking. This form of banking office received over half of the total asset allocations of this region. The two prominent members of the group, Hong Kong and Israel, traditionally prefer the subsidiary form of organization due to their desire to participate in retail banking. Japanese banks are also moving in that direction as their subsidiaries gain at the expense of agencies. Among the other countries category, Canadian banks have followed in Japan's footsteps, whereas others have historically remained unchanged. Canadian banks, at the beginning, started with agency facilities, but soon switched to branch and subsidiary forms of organization for the conduct of their banking operations. Australian and New Zealand banking activities historically have not been strong in the United States, exclusively choosing branches and agencies for their banking services.

FOREIGN BANKS' CURRENT STATUS REPORT

This section deals with select characteristics and practices of foreign banks in the United States in recent years. The report is subdivided into four sections, addressing a variety of issues, from the introduction of the foreign banks with the most assets, the most new offices opened and offices closed, and profitability of foreign banks' U.S. subsidiaries, to review of standby letters of credit booked by U.S. branches and agencies of foreign banks by home region and country. As a bank's commitment to international business grows, the bank offers its customers a broader range of services, but also exposes itself to wider and different forms of risk that may appear on the balance sheet in the form of increases or decreases in assets, or on the income statement in the form of profits or losses.

Major Foreign Banks

The 25 largest foreign banks in the United States at year-end 1988 had total assets of $420.9 billion or 64 percent of the assets of all foreign banks. These banks represented seven countries from three regions (see table 8.3). From the Asian region, Japan had 16 banks and Hong Kong had 1 bank. The rest of the 8 banks were from Western Europe and Canada — with 6 and 2 banks, respectively. Among Western Europeans, the United Kingdom and Italy each had 2 banks, and France and Switzerland each had 1 bank. From

Table 8.3
Top 25 Foreign Banks with the Most Assets in the United States, December 31, 1988

U.S. Rank	Bank	Home Country	Assets ($B)	No. U.S. Offices
1	Bank of Tokyo	Japan	42.7	11
2	Mitsubishi Bank	Japan	31.6	8
3	Dai-Ichi Kangyo Bank	Japan	30.6	6
4	Fuji Bank Limited	Japan	30.4	7
5	Industrial Bank of Japan	Japan	28.1	7
6	Sanwa Bank	Japan	28.0	8
7	Hong Kong & Shanghai Bank	Hong Kong	24.9	18
8	Sumitomo Bank	Japan	22.2	7
9	Bank of Montreal	Canada	16.6	16
10	National Westminster Bank	U.K.	16.2	6
11	Tokai Bank	Japan	14.3	5
12	Swiss Bank Corporation	Switz.	14.2	7
13	Mitsubishi Tr. & Bkg. Corp.	Japan	13.6	3
14	Mitsui Tr. & Bkg. Corp.	Japan	11.2	4
15	Mitsui Bank	Japan	10.5	5
16	Daiwa Bank	Japan	9.8	4
17	Banque Nationale de Paris	France	9.5	9
18	Long Term Credit, Japan	Japan	9.2	4
19	Banco di Roma	Italy	9.1	3
20	Bank of Nova Scotia	Canada	8.7	6
21	Sumitomo Tr. & Bkg. Corp.	Japan	8.6	3
22	Banca Nazionale Del Lavoro	Italy	8.0	5
23	Barclays Group	U.K.	7.8	13
24	Taiyo Kobe Bank	Japan	7.6	5
25	Yasuda Tr. & Bkg. Co.	Japan	7.5	3
	TOTAL		420.9	174

Source: Board of Governors of the Federal Reserve System, **Structural Data for U.S. Offices of Foreign Banks**, 1988.

the 8 largest Asian banks, 7 were from Japan. The Japanese banks collectively controlled 73 percent of the assets of the 25 largest banks and 55 percent of the assets of foreign banks in the United States.

Overall, 15 foreign banks have assets exceeding $10 billion each, of which 8 have assets exceeding $20 billion each, all of these from Asia, with 7 from Japan. The top 25 foreign banks in the United States are also among the 100 largest banks in the world; 6 out of 8 top Japanese banks are in this group, and represent the world's 6 largest banks. The result shows the strength of the Japanese banks not only in this group but also internationally, with ownership of 20 of the world's 50 largest banks.

New Banking Offices Opened and Closed

Between June 30, 1987, and June 30, 1988, 38 foreign banking offices opened in the United States and 13 closed their doors. Of the newly created banking offices, there were 11 agencies, 21 branches, 5 subsidiaries, and 1 investment company. The collective assets of de novo offices were $19.5 billion, with 6 having above $1 billion in original assets. The largest carried assets equal to $3.5 billion. The nationality composition consisted of 15 from Japan, 3 from the United Kingdom, 3 from France, and 2 each from Switzerland and Israel. Most of the rest were from Western Europe and Latin America, each opening 1 banking office. New York State was the major beneficiary, attracting 20 of these new banking offices, followed by California with 6, Illinois with 4, Georgia with 3, Texas with 2, and New Jersey, Massachusetts, and Florida each with 1 office.[3]

Of the 13 foreign banking offices closed during 1987–88 from ten nations, there were 5 branches, 4 agencies, 2 investment companies, 1 subsidiary commercial bank, and 1 Edge bank. The closed offices carried assets equal to $2.2 billion, with one holding assets above $1 billion. Of the others, four held assets above $100 million and the rest had assets under $100 million. Collectively, these offices provided C&I loans in the range of $700 million during 1987–88. Seven of the closed offices were in New York, four in California, and the other two were in Florida and Texas. The nationality composition of this group was mixed, with no clear loser. The United Kingdom, France, and Sweden each closed its doors to two offices, and the remaining countries one.[4] At the outset and in balance, the new offices outperformed the closed ones in every category.

Profitability of Foreign Banks' U.S. Subsidiaries

One concern expressed during the heated debates of the 1970s and early 1980s, regarding superiority of foreign banks in the United States over domestic counterparts, was that U.S. banking laws favored foreign banks over local banks in the acquisition of troubled banks, and in providing them with a more flexible working environment than its own banks. This flexibility supposedly provided foreign banking entities with a healthier business environment than U.S. banks, thus indirectly affecting their higher profitability in comparison with other banks serving the same markets.

A review of general characteristics of acquired banks and the prices paid to acquire these institutions indicates that the claim is not totally true. Prior to acquisition, the banks had four general characteristics: (1) with a few notable exceptions, the acquired banks were mainly small- to medium-sized, with most having assets below $100 million; (2) they were located primarily in New York and California; (3) they either had low profitability, experienced losses, or were in receivership; and (4) they generally had lower liquidity, higher proportions of loans to total assets, and greater reliance on money markets for their funding than did other banks in their peer groups.[5]

A review of the price/earnings ratio of U.S. bank stock during the 1970s, a period of accelerating rates of acquisitions, reveals that the P/E ratio dropped from 1.2 in 1972 to 9.6 in 1976 and to 5.0 in 1980. This indicates that prices outperformed earnings, causing profits to deteriorate, given prevailing economic conditions. At the same time, a comparison of domestic and foreign banks that paid a price–book value ratio for acquired banks shows that foreign banks paid a higher price than domestic banks. From 1974 to 1978, foreign-owned U.S. banks paid, on average, a price–book value ratio of 2.22 versus 1.44 by domestic counterparts when they acquired or merged with a U.S. bank.[6]

Following acquisition, earnings generally improved, though not completely to peer group levels, while equity ratios attained peer levels as a result of infusions of capital by their new owners. Furthermore, the business orientations of the acquired banks did not change materially. As a result of greater diversification of the lending portfolio, somewhat less emphasis was placed on retail lending as a proportion of the total. Within the total group, the greater improvement in earnings and the largest increase in capital took place at banks acquired by foreign individuals.[7]

On the profitability side, a review of the first half of 1987 and 1988 return on assets reveals that U.S. subsidiaries of foreign banks, on average, gained 0.35 and 0.45 percent, respectively. The median return was much higher, 0.61 and 0.68 percent, indicating that a very few large losses distorted the actual higher return of the majority of these banks. The record indicates that 74 banks recorded gains while 10 recorded losses during 1988. The return was quite a bit better in 1986, when these banks recorded an average return of 0.54 percent, with gainers outperforming losers by 79 to 7.[8] Similar data for U.S.-insured commercial banks showed a gain of 0.62 percent on assets in 1986 and 0.12 percent in 1987. The low return of 1987, in part, is the result of the $15 billion loss of major U.S. multinational banks on their international operations. In reality, the overall profits on the domestic business rose by $3 billion in 1987, to 0.64 percent of assets. The profitability of banks without foreign offices rose four basis points, to 0.74 percent; the turnaround in farm lending, in part, contributed to this improvement.[9]

One should not conclude here that foreign banks are disadvantageous, nor that the U.S. banks provide a better competitive return on overall performance. Generalization may not present the most accurate picture. What is more proper is to compare various sizes and types of offices within their designated categories. A comparison of the U.S. and foreign banks with assets above $5 billion provides quite different conclusions. U.S.-insured commercial banks recorded a loss of 0.86 percent in 1987 versus a positive net gain by foreign banks in the same asset size category. Similarly, the low return by foreign banking subsidiaries due to their high front-office costs should not be associated with the agency or branch office asset-income performances. Unfortunately, detailed data for comparison are not available; thus, generalization is often used as a means of interpretation.

Standby Letters of Credit

Traditionally off-balance-sheet activities have been very important sources of income for banks. Today, more than ever, banks use these activities to improve profitability without increasing assets. One example of these activities is the issuance of standby letters of credit. A standby letter of credit is a guarantee that if the borrower fails to honor its obligation, the issuing bank will provide full support of the document. It is a paper transaction that requires no internal adjustment within the bank's balance-sheet system. Most of these letters of credit support debt raised by other institutions, such as borrowing in the commercial paper or bond markets, but also can be used by a parent bank helping to finance a branch office to obtain local loans.

For example, a parent or a subsidiary bank may use its prestige and credit to help foreign affiliates of a U.S. customer find short-term funds within a foreign country. The U.S. subsidiary or parent bank may then arrange for an irrevocable letter of credit in favor of a local bank in the foreign affiliate of the U.S. customer's country. The letter of credit authorizes the local bank to draw sight drafts on the U.S. bank for a certain amount of credit, to be drawn and honored only if the affiliate customer does not repay its loan. This standby letter of credit does not involve the issuing bank (U.S. subsidiary), except if the borrower defaults on its obligation. By this arrangement, the local or foreign bank makes a loan to the affiliate with a guarantee for payment, but no exchange or transaction is required and no risk is incurred.[10]

In recent years, foreign branch offices have been very active in using this technique, especially in regard to the issues of U.S. states and municipalities. From 1980 to 1987, the standby letters of credit booked at U.S. branches and agencies of foreign banks increased from $3.5 billion to $103.1 billion, nearly half of which were originated by Japanese banks. The breakdown of the activities indicates that Western European countries and Japan together issued nearly 87 percent of all the standby letters of credit, with the combined share of the five countries of Japan, the United Kingdom, Switzerland, France, and Canada reaching 74 percent in 1987. Table 8.4 shows the standby letters of credit booked at U.S. branches and agencies of foreign banks, by home region and by major participating countries.

A COMPARISON OF THE MARKET STRUCTURE AND ACTIVITIES BY WORLD REGION

Previously we have examined the institutional composition of the foreign banks in the United States on the macro level. This section is devoted to the regional comparison on the micro levels, to establish benchmark differences among countries and regions. There are three major criteria to study: first, the strength of each region, based on the number of offices in each assets size; second, the market participation of each region in regard to the type of office and concentration of banking activities by cities; and finally, the chartering provision, entity establishment, grandfathering provision, and FDIC membership status of these institutions. This section is divided into four regions, each designated with its unique characteristics and market

Table 8.4
Standby Letters of Credit of U.S. Agencies and Branches of Foreign Banks
(Billions of U.S. Dollars)

Region and Country	1980	1982	1984	1986	1987
Western Europe	2.1	7.7	11.1	26.8	37.8
Latin America	0.1	0.3	0.2	0.2	0.3
Asia and Middle East	1.0	3.3	8.4	38.3	52.5
Other Countries	0.2	1.6	2.4	9.9	12.5
Total	3.5	13.3	23.5	75.8	103.1
Major Countries:					
Japan	1.0	3.3	8.4	38.2	51.8
United Kingdom	0.6	2.9	4.6	8.5	11.4
Switzerland	0.2	1.2	2.6	8.4	10.3
France	0.6	1.5	1.7	3.9	7.0
Canada	0.2	1.6	2.4	5.6	6.2

Source: James V. Houpt, "International Trends for U.S. Banks and Banking Markets," Study No. 156, May 1988, p. 34.

approach. The outcome will shed light on the peculiarities of the regions and their respective dominant countries, as may be perceived through their expansionary moves.

Western Europe

Western Europe is a progressive wing of the foreign banking industry, advancing constantly over time, to conduct a wide range of business-financial services. As shown in table 8.5, by 1988 there were 103 family banks with 245 offices controlling $180 billion in assets. About 27 percent of these offices were small, with assets of less than $100 million. Their primary activities were in international trade financing and in serving home-country clients. On the other hand, 17 percent of Western European banking offices had assets exceeding $1 billion, representing a wide variety of activities, including retail banking, foreign exchange trading, security financing, and other related banking services. The trend indicates that the larger banks, based on assets, are growing much faster than the smaller ones. The number of banks with assets of $250 million and above nearly doubled during the 1980s, with offices in the assets range of $500 million to $1 billion recording the major growth. The National Westminster Bank, the largest bank in the group, carried assets equal to $13 billion in 1988. Some 83 percent of Western European banking offices were state chartered with 13 percent carrying FDIC insurance. Half have been established as international banking facilities and 39 percent were grandfathered under the International Banking Act of 1978.

Western European banks are traditionally inclined toward agency and branch forms of organization, but recently have shown interest in establishing subsidiary commercial banks (see table 8.6). Nine out of ten foreign investment companies in the United States have been set up by Western European banks. New York City has 115 offices or 47 percent of all Western European offices. Aside from New York City, the other offices of these institutions are spread throughout the major money centers of Chicago, Los Angeles, Miami, and San Francisco. Atlanta and Houston have shown the fastest growth in offices of Western European banks among the secondary-tier cities in recent years.

Latin America

Unlike Western Europe, the Latin American region is not represented by economically strong and financially rich nations. More than 70 percent of the region's total assets are controlled by the three nations of Argentina, Brazil, and Mexico. While these three countries are all industrialized in their own way, none is on the competitive level of financially strong nations like West Germany, Great Britain, or France. The most industrialized country in

Table 8.5
Total Assets and Number of U.S. Banking Institutions Owned by Western European Entities

Year	Number of Family Banks	Number of Bank Offices	Total Assets ($M)	Number of Offices in Assets Size ($M)					Not Reported
				<100	100-250	250-500	500-1000	>1000	
1980	58	141	77,580	46	29	21	11	25	9
1981	70	167	107,271	63	40	14	17	29	4
1982	76	192	122,521	69	41	25	16	35	6
1983	84	211	129,674	72	52	28	19	33	7
1984	90	227	138,891	80	50	26	19	34	18
1985	90	220	162,962	66	48	34	19	42	11
1986	93	242	168,994	70	54	39	26	42	11
1987	99	246	187,934	72	59	43	27	40	5
1988	103	245	180,174	66	54	48	27	43	7

Year	Largest Assets Size ($M)	Smallest Assets Size ($M)	Number of Offices				
			F	G	I	S	X
1980	6,566	0.4	11	111	21	130	–
1981	19,893	1.2	25	109	21	142	54
1982	22,016	2.3	30	107	25	161	98
1983	21,304	2.1	39	106	28	171	110
1984	17,484	0.1	46	104	29	176	123
1985	17,815	0.3	35	101	35	183	124
1986	12,121	0.2	47	103	34	191	130
1987	15,058	0.3	47	99	34	194	129
1988	12,882	0.2	41	95	33	204	127

Source: Calculated from Board of Governors of the Federal Reserve System,
Structural Data for U.S. Offices of Foreign Banks, 1980-88. See
Table 2.3 for definition of codes.

Note: Western Europe consists of Austria, Belgium, Denmark, Finland, France,
Germany, Greece, Ireland, Italy, Luxembirg, Netherlands, Norway,
Portugal, Spain, Sweden, Switzerland, Turkey, United Kingdom, Yugoslavia,
and other Western Europe (multi-country banks).

Table 8.6

Types of Offices and Location of Western European Banks in the United States

Year	Agencies	Branches	Subsidiary Commercial Banks	Investment Companies	Banking Edge	Total
1980	44	71	14	5	7	141
1981	51	82	15	6	13	167
1982	57	94	18	8	15	192
1983	60	108	20	8	15	211
1984	64	118	20	9	16	227
1985	68	118	25	9	-	220▪
1986	76	121	24	10	11	242
1987	75	128	26	9	9	246
1988	73	136	21	9	7	245

Cities	1980	1981	1982	1983	1984	1985	1986	1987	1988
Atlanta	6	6	8	9	9	9	9	9	7
Chicago	22	23	25	24	24	23	21	24	25
Houston	2	4	5	7	7	-	16	11	10
Los Angeles	15	16	21	23	25	25	24	25	24
Miami	9	14	21	21	21	19	23	24	24
New York	68	78	83	91	101	100	107	107	115
San Francisco	12	16	16	18	19	18	16	16	15
Others	7	10	13	18	21	26	26	30	25
Total	141	167	192	211	227	220	242	246	245

Source: Derived from Board of Governors of the Federal Reserve
System, **Structural Data for U.S. Offices of Foreign
Banks**, 1980-88.
▪ Excluding Edge banks.

the group is Brazil, with an excellent trade record but limited financial power. By year-end 1988, Latin American banks established 80 offices from 46 family banks. Out of the total, 16 family banks and 27 offices belong to Brazil, and another 6 family banks and 14 offices are owned by Mexico. Some 71 percent of these offices are small, with assets of less than $250 million; very few have assets exceeding $500 million. The largest bank held assets of $700 million in 1988 (see table 8.7).

The historical trend indicates that nearly one-third of these Latin American countries did not have banking representation in the United States until 1982. These countries are Chile, the Dominican Republic, Ecuador, El Salvador, and Peru. Their international banking functions were conducted via correspondent relationships, with very limited activities. Currently, 38 percent of Latin American banks in the United States are federally chartered but very few are insured by the FDIC or have retail banking business. The majority are established as international banking facilities. Latin American banking offices are mainly divided between agencies and branches, with 10 percent in the subsidiary form of organization. Among the countries, Mexico is inclined toward the agency form of offices while Brazil's preference is with branching offices. Others show no exclusive pattern. About 26 percent of the offices are grandfathered under the IBA of 1978, all of which belong to Argentina, Brazil, and Mexico. One-half are based in New York, one-fourth in Miami, and the rest located in Los Angeles, with San Francisco and Chicago as the last choices. In summary, the strength of the region rests with Brazil and Mexico, each of which controls 31 percent of all the assets, numerous offices, and a sizeable proportion of the large-size banks. Argentina ranks number 3, and the rest show no financial domination (see table 8.8).

Asia and the Middle East

The Asian and Middle Eastern region represents a strong competitive force in the U.S. banking market. Overall, their investment activities have bypassed other regions, indicating a power that deserves to be recognized. This region is represented by 104 family banks with 275 offices. They collectively control 41 percent of the foreign banking offices and 63 percent of the foreign banking assets in the United States. Historically, with the exception of Hong Kong, Japan and Israel, all are newcomers. Most have opened offices in the United States since the 1960s, and have become a progressive power in today's modern banking system. In fact, the two strong wings of the region, Japan and Israel, were not even dominant forces in the first half of the twentieth century. They grew since 1970 to a powerful size via trade expansion, and took advantage of the lax regulatory opportunities to expand rapidly in the U.S. banking industry.

From the total of 275, 130 banking offices, or 47 percent of the total, have assets below $250 million. Another 74 offices, or 27 percent of the total, each hold assets exceeding $1 billion, as of December 31, 1988 (see table 8.9). This enormous financial power has ensured these foreign banks a prominent place in financial markets, a force to be reckoned with far beyond the traditional international banking activities of trade financing and bank-customer relationships. The largest bank in the group, Dai-Ichi Kangyo Bank of Japan, carries assets of $21.6 billion. Within the region, 80 percent

Table 8.7
Total Assets and Number of U.S. Banking Institutions Owned by Latin American Entities

Year	Number of Family Banks	Number of Bank Offices	Total Assets ($M)	Number of Offices in Assets Size ($M) <100	100–250	250–500	500–1000	>1000	Not Reported
1980	21	42	11,454	15	14	5	4	3	1
1981	30	57	10,957	29	18	3	6	1	–
1982	41	74	11,056	39	24	5	4	1	1
1983	46	80	11,631	44	26	4	3	2	–
1984	47	79	11,339	45	20	6	5	2	1
1985	44	65ᵃ	11,602	29	21	8	4	1	2
1986	46	80	12,676	36	23	12	6	–	3
1987	44	77	12,816	31	27	13	4	–	2
1988	46	80	13,691	30	27	11	7	–	5

Year	Largest Assets Size ($M)	Smallest Assets Size ($M)	Number of Offices				
			F	G	I	S	X
1980	1,493	4.7	1	29	3	41	–
1981	1,515	1.2	14	28	4	43	22
1982	1,004	3.2	30	26	5	44	57
1983	1,217	3.2	35	23	5	45	65
1984	1,242	1.6	35	22	5	44	64
1985	745	3.0	20	22	6	45	53
1986	811	0.0[b]	31	22	9	48	62
1987	991	0.0[b]	29	22	8	48	62
1988	704	0.9	30	21	8	50	63

Source: Calculated from Board of Governors of the Federal Reserve System, Structural Data for U.S. Offices of Foreign Banks, 1980–88. See Table 2.3 for definition of codes.

Note: Latin America consists of Argentina, Brazil, Chile, Colombia, Dominican Republic, Ecuador, El Salvador, Mexico, Panama, Peru, Uruguay, and Venezuela.

a Excluding Edge banks.
b Less than $100,000.

Table 8.8

Types of Offices and Location of Latin American Banks in the United States

Year	Agencies	Branches	Subsidiary Commercial Banks	Investment Companies	Banking Edge	Total
1980	32	5	3	1	1	42
1981	36	11	3	1	6	57
1982	36	23	5	-	10	74
1983	35	27	5	-	13	80
1984	31	29	5	1	13	79
1985	30	28	6	1	-	65ᵃ
1986	32	29	7	1	11	80
1987	33	27	8	-	10	78
1988	36	26	8	-	10	80

Cities	1980	1981	1982	1983	1984	1985ᵃ	1986	1987	1988
Chicago	1	2	2	2	2	2	2	2	1
Los Angeles	8	9	9	8	6	6	7	7	9
Miami	6	10	15	19	19	21	20	18	20
New York	23	32	41	44	45	43	44	43	42
San Francisco	3	3	3	3	3	3	4	4	4
Others	1	1	4	4	4	4	3	4	4
Total	42	57	74	80	79	65ᵃ	80	78	80

Source: Derived from Board of Governors of the Federal Reserve
System, **Structural Data for U.S. Offices of Foreign
Banks**, 1980-88.
ᵃ Excluding Edge banks.

of Asian and Middle Eastern banks are state-chartered banks, nearly one-fourth of which choose affiliation with the FDIC. More than half elect to operate as international banking facilities and 40 percent were grandfathered under the IBA of 1978.

During the 1980s, Asian and Middle Eastern banks, as a group, concentrated on development of branches and subsidiary commercial banking forms of organization to conduct their foreign banking activities. In this period, branch and subsidiary offices doubled in number, while agencies stayed relatively unchanged. The only investment company controlled by this region belongs to a Japanese bank. It became operational in 1985. Like Western European banks, this group owned nine Edge banking facilities, but is growing more rapidly in rank than other regions. These banks tend to select New York and Los Angeles as their preferred cities for locating offices, with San Francisco and Chicago their next most likely choices. The cities of Houston, Miami/Miami Beach, Seattle, and Washington, D.C., were recently marked as prospective new areas of prosperity and were selected for future banking investments (see table 8.10). In general, one major distinction between Western European and Asian/Middle Eastern banks is their preference in location of new bank offices. While both groups select New York City as their primary choice, Western European banks are more inclined toward East Coast money-center cities. On the other hand, the Asian counterparts favor the West Coast region. The Middle Eastern group also follows the Western European pattern of favoring eastern U.S. city centers.

Like the Latin American region, Asian and Middle Eastern banking strength lies in the hands of a small number of participating countries. However, there are major differences among the members of this region. For example, despite the fact that the banking forces from the three major countries of Hong Kong, Japan, and Israel show substantial financial strength, the differences among them are quite wide. These three control 64 percent of the region's banking offices and 95 percent of the region's assets. The other countries in the region control the remaining 36 percent of the banking offices, with 5 percent of the region's assets. Among the three powerful countries of Hong Kong, Japan, and Israel, the Japanese banks hold the upper hand. The banking establishments from Japan operate 122 offices with assets equal to $361 billion. These represent 44 percent of all the banking offices in the region with 87 percent of all the assets. Such strength and power is unique in this form, creating a major difference between this region and any of the other three foreign banking regions in the United States.

The oldest bank from this region, the Hong Kong and Shanghai Bank Corporation, opened an office in New York in 1880. The Israel Discount Bank of New York became operational in 1922. Japan started its American banking adventure in 1916 with Sumitomo Bank, followed by Mitsubishi Bank in 1920. Fifty years later, Japan took the world by surprise with its first assault on the U.S. consumer market, establishing a strong market presence in automobiles, electronics, motorcycles, cameras, and photographic accessories. The second assault, directed toward the financial industry, began in 1977 with concentration on the banking segment of the financial market. Over time, the Japanese methodology and technique has remained unchanged as Japanese firms have pursued the policy of attacking a small segment of the vulnerable market and spreading along the line to other related businesses. The newest move is in the area of the securities

Table 8.9
Total Assets and Number of U.S. Banking Institutions Owned by Asian and Middle Eastern Entities

Year	Number of Family Banks	Number of Bank Offices	Total Assets ($M)	Number of Offices in Assets Size ($M)						Not Reported
				<100	100-250	250-500	500-1000	>1000		
1980	61	160	92,203	73	20	14	20	27		6
1981	69	177	109,843	76	25	15	20	33		8
1982	75	191	142,154	77	29	17	18	41		9
1983	84	207	162,225	78	34	19	21	44		11
1984	91	220	186,845	84	42	15	17	52		10
1985	93	231	221,686	81	47	15	15	58		15
1986	98	249	296,345	89	39	19	12	69		21
1987	99	264	343,389	81	46	29	12	75		21
1988	104	275	413,842	83	47	30	21	74		20

Year	Largest Assets Size ($M)	Smallest Assets Size ($M)	Number of Offices				
			F	G	I	S	X
1980	11,088	0.0ᵃ	8	134	35	152	–
1981	11,890	0.2	14	125	43	163	74
1982	15,286	0.3	22	123	44	169	111
1983	18,249	0.0ᵃ	32	116	46	174	128
1984	15,421	0.3	40	116	51	179	139
1985	20,549	0.3	39	116	52	191	144
1986	20,484	0.0ᵃ	52	115	55	197	152
1987	20,345	0.1	51	115	58	214	159
1988	21,610	0.1	54	112	71	221	163

Source: Calculated from Board of Governors of the Federal Reserve System, **Structural Data for U.S. Offices of Foreign Banks**, 1980–88. See Table 2.3 for definition of codes.

Note: Asia and the Middle East consist of Bahrain, China, Hong Kong, India, Indonesia, Iran, Israel, Japan, Jordan, Kuwait, Malaysia, Pakistan, Philippines, Qatar, Saudi Arabia, South Korea, Taiwan, Thailand, and the United Arab Emirates.

  ᵃ Less than $100,000.

175

Table 8.10

Types of Offices and Location of Asian and Middle Eastern Banks in the United States

Year	Agencies	Branches	Subsidiary Commercial Banks	Investment Companies	Banking Edge	Total
1980	75	65	18	–	2	160
1981	72	82	19	–	4	177
1982	74	91	20	–	6	191
1983	67	109	22	–	7	205
1984	61	125	25	–	8	219
1985	67	136	27	1	–	231
1986	67	142	30	1	9	249
1987	73	147	34	1	9	264
1988	75	154	36	1	9	275

Cities	1980	1981	1982	1983	1984	1985	1986	1987	1988
Chicago	14	15	15	15	15	16	17	21	22
Houston	–	2	3	2	2	2	4	5	5
Los Angeles	38	46	49	50	51	53	54	56	59
New York	70	73	79	89	97	107	115	123	126
Miami/ Miami Beach	3	5	5	5	5	4	6	5	6
San Francisco	16	17	18	20	23	22	24	23	23
Seattle	6	7	6	6	6	7	6	6	6
Wash., D.C.	1	4	3	4	4	2	3	4	4
Others	12	8	13	14	16	18	20	21	24
Total	160	177	191	205	219	231	249	264	275

Source: Derived from Board of Governors of the Federal Reserve System, **Structural Data for U.S. Offices of Foreign Banks**, 1980-88.

Note: Other cities consist mainly of Atlanta, Honolulu, Philadelphia, and Portland.

market, as the Japanese have started to acquire large-sized brokerage firms to solidify their financial positions.

The following are some examples of what the Japanese have accomplished in the past ten years. The number of offices has grown by 100 percent with nearly 400 percent growth in the assets base. While their growth has been in every assets-size category, the major increase came in the category of banks with assets above $1 billion. The number of banks in this category tripled to an all-time high of 67, or 55 percent of all the Japanese banking offices in the United States, paving the road for a major battle between American and Japanese banks in the U.S. credit market. Furthermore, Japanese banks have made a major move in recent years to open inroads into the retail banking market as they shift their emphasis from the agency form of organization to branching and subsidiary commercial banking types of structure. From 1980 to 1988, the number of agencies grew narrowly from 27 to 32 offices, while their branch banking offices grew from 29 to 59 and subsidiary commercial banks from 12 to 24 offices. At the same time, the offices with assets under $250 million grew only from 16 to 21, while those with assets above $500 million increased from 42 to 80. This situation has generated a tremendous financial power far beyond anyone's expectation.

This rapid expansion alarmed various legislators and banking concerns. However, the size of foreign banking investments in the United States is relatively small compared with the overall size of the U.S. banking industry; therefore, no major attempt has been made to correct the advancement beyond the IBA of 1978. It is also appropriate to consider the benefit of foreign-owned institutions as they participate in market competition and contribute to the flow of funds in the U.S. credit market. Their contribution to the hiring and training of the labor force, the introduction of work ethics, and general public expenditures of various sorts are examples of positive contributions to the prosperity of the U.S. economic system.

Other Regions

The other regions group consists of Australia, Bermuda, Canada, Cayman Islands, Egypt, Multiple Countries, New Zealand, and South Africa. This group is dominated by a single country, Canada, which controls 86 percent of the total assets and 67 percent of all the region's offices. Despite the fact that Australia is a strong agricultural and exporting state, its banking establishment in the United States is not a progressive one. Other countries' representation is mainly a necessity, and not motivated by investment opportunities, as these banks provide financial transactions to facilitate government and business trade and foreign exchange markets.

Overall, the numbers of family banks and offices of these regions grew steadily over time. Today, they hold 74 offices with total assets of $46 billion. Half of these offices are small, with assets of less than $250 million; but another 27 percent have assets exceeding $500 million, mostly above $1 billion. In comparison with the other groups, banks from these countries more often elect to be federally chartered, have FDIC insurance, and have fewer international banking facility forms of organization than other com-

Table 8.11
Total Assets and Number of U.S. Banking Institutions Owned by Selected Countries

Year	Number of Family Banks	Number of Bank Offices	Total Assets ($M)	Number of Offices in Assets Size ($M)					Not Reported
				<100	100-250	250-500	500-1000	>1000	
1980	16	48	16,877	20	7	10	5	5	1
1981	17	54	23,151	12	10	6	7	8	5
1982	17	56	25,294	13	10	13	6	7	7
1983	18	56	29,806	13	11	13	5	9	5
1984	20	71	41,238	20	15	11	10	9	6
1985	19	68	44,271	11	18	13	8	9	9
1986	20	72	48,919	18	17	15	5	11	6
1987	20	72	50,342	15	17	14	4	13	9
1988	20	74	45,532	25	12	12	6	13	6

| | Largest Assets | Smallest Assets | Number of Offices | | | | |
Year	Size ($M)	Size ($M)	F	G	I	S	X
1980	2,670	3.6	6	36	7	42	–
1981	3,624	11.2	10	34	6	44	4
1982	3,710	4.9	12	32	7	44	14
1983	4,224	4.6	14	30	7	42	17
1984	6,282	1.7	22	29	14	49	22
1985	6,714	1.8	22	25	15	46	22
1986	7,703	1.3	23	25	14	49	22
1987	7,637	0.9	23	25	15	49	22
1988	8,006	0.8	23	23	16	51	23

Source: Calculated from Board of Governors of the Federal Reserve System, **Structural Data for U.S. Offices of Foreign Banks**, 1980–88. See Table 2.3 for definition of codes.

Note: Selected countries consist of Australia, Bermuda, Canada, Cayman Islands, Egypt, Multiple Countries, New Zealand, and South Africa.

parable sets of countries. The main reason is that, with the exception of
Canada, the countries within this region have very few banks in the United
States, and these are utilized to take advantage of flexibility of branching to
perform their financial transactions. Tables 8.11 and 8.12 present the structural organization and financial strength of this group by assets size, type of
office, and locations. Since 1984, this group has expanded in the subsidiary
form of banking office, with very little progress in other forms of offices.
The dominant office location is New York, followed by Los Angeles, Chicago, and San Francisco.

Canada, the third largest foreign banking establishment in the United
States, has a long history of trade and financial transactions with the United
States. The first Canadian bank, the Bank of Montreal, was chartered in

Table 8.12
Types of Offices and Location of Selected Countries' Banks in the United States

Year	Agencies	Branches	Subsidiary Commercial Banks	Investment Companies	Banking Edge	Total
1980	27	1	9	–	–	47
1981	26	19	9	–	–	54
1982	23	25	9	–	–	57
1983	20	28	9	–	–	57
1984	20	33	16	–	2	71
1985	17	33	18	–	–	68
1986	20	32	18	–	2	72
1987	20	32	18	–	2	72
1988	22	31	19	–	2	74

Cities	1980	1981	1982	1983	1984	1985	1986	1987	1988
Atlanta	3	3	3	3	3	3	4	4	3
Chicago	–	2	5	6	8	9	9	9	9
Los Angeles	4	5	5	5	6	7	8	8	10
New York	19	22	22	22	26	24	25	25	26
Portland	5	5	5	4	4	3	3	3	3
San Francisco	10	9	10	10	9	7	7	7	4
Others	6	8	7	7	15	15	16	16	19

Source: Calculated from Board of Governors of the Federal Reserve
System, **Structural Data for U.S. Offices of Foreign
Banks**, 1980–88.
Note: Selected countries are Australia, Bermuda, Canada, Cayman
Islands, Egypt, Multiple Countries, New Zealand, and
South Africa.

New York in 1859. By the end of 1988, Canadian banking investment amounted to $39 billion, composed of relatively large-size banks, with 12 banks having assets exceeding $1 billion. Canadian banks' structural organization consists of 50 offices from seven family banks. These offices are subdivided into 14 agencies, 17 branches, 18 subsidiaries, and 1 Edge bank. One major strength of the Canadian form of organization is their selection of the subsidiary form of office to conduct their banking activities. This flexibility provides them with opportunities to infiltrate the domestic, retail banking market, if other activities provide less than desired returns.

Traditionally Canada has been one of the strongest U.S. allies, economically and politically. Their trade relationship is two-tiered and growing. To finance trade is one of the oldest and most prominent forms of banking relationship, a foundation for other forms of financial activities. In a survey of specialization of Canadian banks, from limited respondents, it appears that Canadian banking offices are more inclined toward traditional forms of banking services, trade financing, corporate and retail banking, and less in joint venture and investment banking and security market activities. The large number of entities that select the subsidiary form of organization testifies to the importance that Canadian banks place on being part of U.S. banking activities rather than being an agent of foreign entities. They select the state-chartered form of organization for their offices, with 30 percent providing FDIC insurance. Some 38 percent are grandfathered under the IBA of 1978, and only 18 percent elect to operate as international banking facilities.

NOTES

1. James V. Houpt, "International Trends for U.S. Banks and Banking Markets," Staff Study No. 156, Board of Governors of the Federal Reserve System, May 1988, p. 25.

2. Geoff Brouillette, "Foreign Subsidiaries Are Fastest Growing Segment of California Banking," *American Banker*, Vol. 140, No. 148, July 30, 1975, p.1.

3. "Foreign Banks in the United States," *American Banker*, Special Report, Vol. 154, No. 44, March 6, 1989, p. 6A.

4. Ibid.

5. James V. Houpt, "Foreign Ownership of U.S. Banks: Trends and Effects," *Journal of Bank Research*, Volume 14, No. 2, Summer 1983; and United States Senate, "Foreign Takeovers of United States Banks," Committee on Banking, Housing, and Urban Affairs, July 1980.

6. David C. Cates and Frederick C. Wiegold, "Foreign Banks Are Cracking the Facade of U.S. Banking," *Fortune*, August 28, 1978.

7. Henry C. Wallich, "Perspective on Foreign Banking in the United States," Member, Board of Governors of the Federal Reserve System, Conference on Foreign Banking in the United States – the Economic, Legal, and Regulatory Environment, March 1, 1982.

8. Calculated from data provided by *American Banker*, Vol. 153, No. 36, February 23, 1988, and Vol. 154, No. 44, March 6, 1989, Table 9A.

9. "The Profitability of Insured Commercial Banks in 1987," *Federal Reserve Bulletin*, July 1988, pp. 403–405.

10. David K. Eiteman and Arthur I. Stonehill, *Multinational Business Finance*, Addison-Wesley Publishing Company, Reading, Mass., 1986, p. 459.

9   International Trade and Banking Developments

Economic historians often write about the link between trade and finance. The nations with high levels of exportation prosper with the wealth acquired from those who seek importation. The prosperity of a nation is derived from the ability of a country to sacrifice today's consumption in order to save, invest, and export for future return. The existence of an abundance of natural resources within a country could provide an impetus for cheaper production and sales, and reward the producing nation with wealth and an inflow of cash for further development. On the other hand, the less fortunate nations with limited resources could become recipients of goods through importation and could face an outflow of funds in financing trade transactions.

Since financial imbalances exist among exporting and importing countries, trade financing has become a means for the movement of goods and services on a worldwide basis. It is not coincidental that countries with a strong export orientation are also those that provide financial assistance. However, other factors also play a role in the determination of a territory being established as a monetary center for international trade financing. The success of Switzerland as a dominant banking center is attributed to the political neutrality the Swiss government sought during World Wars I and II. Other factors, such as port facilities, historical civilization, and the introduction of innovative approaches to international banking have also contributed to the development of a territory as an international money center.

A review of the historical development of international banking, as presented in chapter 1, shows the link between trade and finance as evolved during the early centuries. Merchant banks were engaged in trade financing and money exchange activities as early as the thirteenth century. The cities of Venice, Amsterdam, and Antwerp prospered for years as port cities instrumental in the movement of large quantities of goods and busy in financing exports-imports and in participating in trade venture loans.

The trend continued in modern times, as the British, Americans, and Japanese began their trade domination. The situation that has concerned Americans in recent years, in light of large U.S. trade deficits and the unusual expansionary attitudes of the foreign investors in the United States, is the widening of the gap between export-import movement and the extent of banking and other investment activities of the trading nations. Do trade relationships among the nations necessitate a strong banking connection? Does the wealth of a nation determine and necessitate international financial involvement? Or is there a correlation between the two?

Answers to these questions are quite complex, determined by a combination of numerous factors. For instance, the wealth of the OPEC nations and their strong trade relationship with the United States did not transfer into an influx of large sums of investments in the United States during the 1970s. The U.S. political alliance with Israel and the fear of political reprisals from the American government prohibited Arab nations from considering the U.S. market as a haven for their investments. On the other hand, Switzerland's lack of export diversification and second grade trade relationship with the United States did not prevent it from becoming a major investor in the U.S. banking market in recent years. It is natural and clear that there is a positive correlation between trade and international business-financial investments. However, the extent of investment is determined by other factors such as government regulations, the economic status of the donor and recipient countries, opportunities within the acquired market, and the political stability of the host country and its relationship with the investor nation.

DEVELOPMENTS IN WORLD TRADE

The years 1987 and 1988 were characterized by continued expansion in world output and trade. A period of decline from 1980 to 1983 had given way to a more sustained rate of growth both in developed and developing nations. The volume of world trade expanded by 5.7 percent in 1987, the second highest expansion in the decade compared with the 8.9 percent expansion in 1984. Developing countries, especially non-oil producers, improved more rapidly than developed countries in the area of exports and were able to depend less heavily on importation of goods and services. As illustrated in table 9.1, both developed and non-oil exporting developing nations were able to increase exports uninterruptedly since 1983, with developing nations having better control over importation to improve their undesirable balance-of-payment deficits. The sharp decline in the price of oil exports and the worldwide reduction of oil consumption had a severe impact

Table 9.1
Summary of World Trade Volume Expansion
(Percentage Growth)

	Average 1970-79	1980	1981	1982	1983
World Trade: Volume	6.5	1.4	1.2	-1.8	3.0
Exports:					
Industrial Countries	6.6	4.2	3.8	-2.1	3.0
Developing Countries	4.9	-3.9	-5.6	-7.1	3.2
Oil Exporters	2.6	-13.2	-14.9	-16.6	-3.7
Non-oil Exporters	7.1	8.8	6.2	2.9	8.6
Imports:					
Industrial Countries	6.5	-1.5	-1.7	-0.6	4.7
Developing Countries	8.4	8.0	8.5	-2.5	-2.3
Oil Exporters	13.7	13.5	19.1	-1.4	-10.4
Non-oil Exporters	6.8	5.9	4.0	-3.0	1.9

	1984	1985	1986	1987
World Trade: Volume	8.9	3.0	4.8	5.7
Exports:				
Industrial Countries	9.9	4.7	2.7	5.0
Developing Countries	7.5	1.1	10.9	8.6
Oil Exporters	0.8	-5.7	13.9	-0.5
Non-oil Exporters	12.2	5.4	9.9	12.1
Imports:				
Industrial Countries	12.5	4.7	8.8	6.7
Developing Countries	3.3	-0.3	-3.9	4.4
Oil Exporters	-6.1	-10.9	-21.9	-11.1
Non-oil Exporters	7.6	4.0	3.0	8.9

Source: International Monetary Fund, **Annual Report**, 1988, p. 16.

on the oil producing nations' consumption pattern, causing curbs on imports to balance their tremendous loss of revenues. This event, while slowing the growth of these nations, forced them to become more fiscally responsible, which could benefit their internal industries over the long run.

On the demand side, the growth of imports in the developing countries decelerated in 1982, 1983, 1985, and 1986, but increased moderately in 1984 and 1987. The deceleration was mainly a result of the decrease in importation by oil producing countries and the decline in the value of their exports. As a result, these countries adjusted importation volumes in response to export limitations. The industrialized countries, on the other hand, grew more rapidly from 1983 to 1987, at an average rate of 7.5 percent, with minor deceleration in 1985 and 1987. The deceleration in 1987 occurred mainly as a result of the slowdown in the growth of the volume of U.S. imports.

The pattern of supply also changed significantly. A major improvement occurred among non-oil developing countries, where export growth increased steadily during the 1980s to a record high of 12.2 percent in 1984 and 12.1 percent in 1987. The OPEC nations, on the other hand, showed limited growth in 1984 and a positive jump in 1986, but, overall, ended in the negative column for the decade of the 1980s. The industrial nations' increase in volume of exports in 1987 was due to the strong export growth of the United States, which accounted for nearly half of the increase in the industrial countries' exports.

Foreign Trade of the United States

The United States of America historically has been a consuming nation. The existence of an abundance of resources (energy and food) and vast and diversified internal markets provided an environment for mass production and consumption. From 1945 to 1960, the United States had an open opportunity to export and expand internationally to take advantage of the existing vacuum in world exporting markets. This opportunity arose because other exporting nations, especially those of Europe and Japan, were engaged in rebuilding their industrial bases, which were damaged during World War II. However, the U.S. export market expansion did not take off as expected. On the contrary, during the 1960s and 1970s, there existed an environment of even greater dependency on foreign imports due to the Vietnam War, internal political turmoil, the OPEC energy crisis, strong foreign competition, and the inability of the U.S. government to foresee and deal with the crisis. U.S. manufacturers also failed to adjust to the new environment and produce quality products.

The record of foreign trade of the United States from 1970 to the present reveals that U.S. exports increased from $43.2 billion in 1970 to $232.9 billion in 1981, but lost steam and contracted from 1982 on, until it regained momentum in 1987 (see table 9.2). In the same period, imports grew from $40 billion in 1970 to $448.8 billion in 1988, with a brief halt in 1982 and 1983 (see table 9.3). As a result, the 1980s were marked with rapid expansion of imports and high trade deficits. The trade imbalance reached an all-time

Table 9.2
Foreign Trade of the United States — Exports
(Billions of U.S. Dollars)

Region and Country	1970	1975	1980	1981	1982	1983	1984	1985	1986	1987	1988[a]
By Geographical Regions:											
Africa	1.6	5.0	9.1	11.1	10.3	8.8	8.8	7.4	6.0	6.3	7.4
Asia	10.0	28.3	60.2	63.9	64.9	63.8	64.6	60.7	64.5	73.3	98.1
Australia & Oceania	1.2	2.4	4.9	6.5	5.7	4.8	5.7	6.4	6.6	6.6	5.7
Europe	14.8	32.7	71.4	69.7	63.7	58.9	62.2	60.0	63.6	71.9	89.8
Northern N. America	9.1	21.8	35.4	39.6	33.8	38.3	46.5	47.3	55.5	59.8	68.0
Southern N. America	3.3	8.3	21.3	24.4	18.4	15.2	18.6	20.0	19.1	21.9	27.5
South America	3.2	8.8	17.4	17.7	15.3	10.6	11.4	11.0	11.9	13.0	14.8
Total	43.2	107.6	219.7	232.9	212.3	200.4	217.8	212.8	227.2	252.8	311.3
By Leading Countries:											
Australia & New Guinea	1.1	1.8	4.1	5.3	4.6	4.0	4.8	5.5	5.6	5.5	6.4
Brazil	0.8	3.1	4.3	3.8	3.4	2.6	2.6	3.1	3.9	4.0	4.3
Canada	9.1	21.8	35.4	39.6	33.8	38.3	46.5	47.3	55.5	59.8	68.0
Egypt	0.0[b]	0.7	1.9	2.2	2.3	2.8	2.7	2.3	2.0	2.2	2.3
France	1.5	3.0	7.5	7.3	7.1	6.0	6.0	6.1	7.2	7.9	9.9
Italy	1.4	2.9	5.5	5.4	4.6	3.9	4.4	4.6	4.8	5.5	6.6
Japan	4.7	9.6	20.8	21.8	21.0	21.9	23.6	22.6	26.9	28.2	37.2
Mexico	1.7	5.1	15.1	17.8	11.8	9.1	11.9	13.6	12.4	14.6	19.6
Republic of So. Africa	0.6	1.3	2.5	2.9	2.4	2.1	2.3	1.2	1.2	1.3	1.7
Soviet Union	0.1	1.8	1.5	2.4	2.6	2.0	2.3	2.4	1.2	1.5	2.7
United Kingdom	2.5	4.5	12.7	12.4	10.6	10.6	12.2	11.3	11.4	14.0	18.0
Venezuela	0.8	2.2	4.6	5.4	5.2	2.8	3.4	3.4	3.1	3.6	4.4
West Germany	2.7	5.2	11.0	10.3	9.3	8.7	9.1	9.1	10.6	11.7	14.1
Total	27.0	63.0	126.9	136.6	119.3	114.8	131.8	132.5	145.8	159.8	195.2

Source: **Survey of Current Business**, March 1971 to November 1988.
Note: Numbers may not add up to total due to rounding.
  a Estimated base on January to September data.
  b Less than $100 million.

Table 9.3

Foreign Trade of the United States — Imports

(Billions of U.S. Dollars)

Region and Country	1970	1975	1980	1981	1982	1983	1984	1985	1986	1987	1988[a]
By Geographical Regions:											
Africa	1.1	8.3	32.3	27.1	17.8	14.4	14.4	12.0	10.3	11.9	11.0
Asia	9.6	27.1	78.8	92.0	85.2	91.5	120.1	131.9	153.9	174.5	192.1
Australia & Oceania	0.9	1.5	3.4	3.1	3.1	3.0	3.6	3.8	3.7	4.1	5.6
Europe	11.4	21.5	47.7	53.4	53.4	55.2	73.1	81.7	91.8	97.4	106.2
Northern N. America	11.1	21.8	41.5	46.4	46.5	55.1	66.5	69.0	68.3	71.1	82.7
Southern N. America	2.9	8.9	22.7	23.5	23.5	25.7	26.8	26.0	23.5	26.5	29.2
South America	3.0	7.2	14.4	15.5	14.4	16.0	21.0	20.9	18.5	20.4	22.0
Total	40.0	96.3	240.8	261.3	243.9	260.9	325.5	345.3	370.0	405.9	448.8
By Leading Countries:											
Australia & New Guinea	0.6	1.2	2.6	2.5	2.3	2.2	2.7	2.9	2.7	3.0	3.6
Brazil	0.6	1.5	3.7	4.5	4.3	4.9	7.6	7.5	6.8	7.9	9.4
Canada	11.1	21.7	41.5	46.4	46.5	52.1	66.5	69.0	68.3	71.1	82.7
Egypt	0.0[b]	0.0[b]	0.5	0.4	0.5	0.3	0.2	0.0[b]	0.1	0.5	0.2
France	0.9	2.1	5.2	5.9	5.5	6.0	8.1	9.5	10.1	10.7	12.2
Italy	1.3	2.4	4.3	5.2	5.3	5.5	7.9	9.7	10.6	11.0	11.4
Japan	5.9	11.3	30.7	37.6	37.7	41.2	57.1	62.8	81.9	84.6	92.7
Mexico	1.2	3.1	12.5	13.8	15.6	16.8	18.0	19.1	17.3	20.3	23.1
Republic of So. Africa	0.3	0.8	3.3	2.4	2.0	2.0	2.5	2.1	2.4	1.3	1.5
Soviet Union	0.0[b]	0.3	0.5	0.3	0.3	0.3	0.6	0.4	0.6	0.4	0.5
United Kingdom	2.2	3.8	9.8	12.8	13.1	12.5	14.5	14.9	15.4	17.3	19.0
Venezuela	1.1	3.6	5.3	5.6	4.7	4.9	6.5	6.5	5.1	5.6	5.4
West Germany	2.1	5.4	11.7	11.4	12.0	12.7	17.0	20.2	25.1	27.1	28.9
Total	27.3	57.2	131.6	148.8	149.8	161.4	209.2	224.6	246.4	260.8	290.6

Source: **Survey of Current Business**, March 1971 to November 1988.

Note: Numbers may not add up to total due to rounding.

[a] Estimated based on January to September data.

[b] Less than $100 million.

Table 9.4

Summary of Payment Balances on U.S. Trade Accounts, 1970–88

(Billions of U.S. Dollars)

Region and Country	1970	1975	1980	1981	1982	1983	1984	1985	1986	1987	1988[a]
By Geographical Regions:											
Africa	0.5	-3.3	-23.2	-16.0	-7.5	-5.6	-5.6	-4.6	-4.3	-5.6	-3.6
Asia	0.4	1.2	-18.6	-28.1	-20.3	-27.7	-55.5	-71.2	-89.4	-101.2	-94.0
Australia & Oceania	0.3	0.9	1.5	3.1	2.6	1.8	2.1	2.6	2.9	2.5	0.1
Europe	3.4	11.2	23.7	16.3	10.3	3.7	-10.9	-21.7	-28.2	-25.5	-16.4
Northern N. America	-2.0	0.0	-6.1	-6.8	-12.7	-16.8	-20.0	-21.7	-12.8	-11.3	-14.7
Southern N. America	0.4	-0.6	-1.4	0.9	-5.1	-10.5	-8.2	-6.0	-4.4	-4.6	-1.7
South America	0.2	1.6	3.0	2.2	0.9	-5.4	-8.6	-9.9	-6.6	-7.4	-7.2
Total Surpluses (Deficits)	3.2	11.0	-21.1	-28.4	-31.8	-60.5	-106.7	-132.5	-142.8	-153.1	-137.5
By Leading Countries:											
Australia & New Guinea	0.3	0.6	1.5	2.8	2.3	1.8	2.1	2.6	2.9	2.5	2.6
Brazil	0.2	1.6	0.6	-0.7	-0.9	-2.3	-5.0	-4.4	-2.9	-3.9	-5.1
Canada	-2.0	0.1	-6.1	-6.8	-12.7	-13.8	-20.0	-21.7	-12.8	-11.3	-14.7
Egypt	0.0[b]	0.7	1.4	1.8	2.4	2.5	2.5	2.3	1.9	1.7	2.1
France	0.6	0.9	2.3	1.41	1.6	0.0	-2.1	-3.4	-2.9	-2.8	-2.3
Italy	0.1	0.5	1.2	0.2	-0.7	-1.6	-3.5	-5.1	-5.8	-5.5	-4.8
Japan	-1.2	-1.7	-9.9	-16.8	-16.7	-19.3	-33.5	-40.2	-55.0	-56.4	-55.5
Mexico	0.5	2.0	2.6	4.0	-3.8	-7.7	-6.1	-5.5	-4.9	-5.7	-3.5
Republic of So. Africa	0.3	0.5	-0.8	0.5	0.4	0.1	-0.2	-0.9	-1.2	0.0	0.2
Soviet Union	0.1	1.5	1.0	2.1	2.3	1.7	1.7	2.0	0.6	1.1	2.2
United Kingdom	0.3	0.7	2.9	-0.4	-2.5	-1.9	-2.3	-3.6	-4.0	-3.3	-1.0
Venezuela	-0.3	-1.4	-0.7	-0.2	0.5	-2.1	-3.1	-3.1	-2.0	-2.0	-1.5
West Germany	0.6	-0.2	-0.7	-1.1	-2.7	-4.0	-7.9	-11.1	-14.5	-15.4	-14.8
Total Surpluses (Deficits)	-0.5	5.8	-4.7	-13.2	0.5	-46.6	-77.4	-92.1	-100.6	-101.0	-96.1

Source: Calculated from Tables 9.2 and 9.3. Trade account is equal to exports minus imports.

Note: Numbers may not add up to total due to rounding.

a Estimated based on January to September data.

b Less than $100 million.

189

high of $153.1 billion in 1987 but saw some improvement in 1988 (see table 9.4).

Geographically, the U.S. trade relationships have been very diversified and continuous. On the demand (import) side, the leading U.S. trade partners in rank are Japan, Canada, West Germany, Mexico, the United Kingdom, France, and Italy. Imports from these countries amounted to $290.6 billion or 65 percent of the value of all imports in 1988. Similarly, the supply (exports) from the United States to leading trade partners was significant, reaching $195.2 billion or 62 percent of the value of all U.S. exports in 1988. Overall, the major beneficiary of the U.S. trade account has been Japan with $55.5 billion in trade surplus in 1988. The accumulated surpluses exceeded $300 billion during the past two decades, and is expected to grow further if no action is taken to change the course. Japan's fortune is followed by that of West Germany and Canada, each with a surplus trade record of $15 billion in 1988 and accumulated gains of $80 billion each since 1970. The newcomer is South Korea with a surplus trade record of $12 billion in 1988.

The enormous outflow of dollars due to the negative U.S. trade account provided unprecedented opportunities for the surplus nations to reinvest a large portion of the excess funds back into the United States. The rechannelling of funds has been conducted in an orderly manner to take advantage of the opportunities that existed in the U.S. banking and financial market, and to prevent destabilization of foreign exchange conduct. The continuation of the U.S. government budget deficits and limitations on the part of policymakers to change the direction of the market without further escalating the troubled course of world affairs presented a dilemma that has yet to be resolved.

DEPENDENCY BETWEEN TRADE AND FOREIGN BANKING INVESTMENT

Historically, countries with positive trade balances prosper as accumulated inflows of funds stimulate further progress and upgrade the standard of wealth of a nation. Conversely, the countries with deficits in their balance of trade face an outflow of funds that may generate impediments to their internal development. The first group of nations would become net creditors and the second group would become net debtors. Due to limitations of their internal markets, the net creditor countries seek international investments in which to channel their excess surpluses, often within the territorial control of their trading partners. The area and market for investment varies according to the opportunities that exist in the acquisition market and the law of the land governing the target country. One such opportunity prevailed in U.S. financial markets during the 1970s when the banking industry faced a situation characterized by a lack of regulations, a large number of financially troubled banks, and, in some respects, depressed bank stock prices.

During the 1960s and early 1970s, the Vietnam War generated a mass production market environment far beyond the normal absorptive capacity of the U.S. economy. The competition intensified as some industrial nations, such as Japan, West Germany, and Canada, energized to take advantage of the booming U.S. economy, by participating to capture a share of the American domestic market. Better quality, lower prices, and differentiated products, along with aggressive marketing techniques geared toward a specific segment of the population, successfully accomplished the exporters' goals. In regard to the automobile industry and market, both Japanese and West German manufacturers targeted young, middle- and lower-income families in presenting their products to fit their budget. Volkswagen and Toyota produced small, efficient, high-quality, low-price products to attract this segment of the market and presented their products in a fashionable manner. Similar bona fide attempts were made in the manufacturing and marketing of electronic equipment, radios, televisions, and cameras that captured the imagination of American consumers at the expense of the American producers. The result was money in Japanese and German banks and a massive market exploration for further development. Unfortunately, the inability of U.S. producers to foresee the changes in the shopping patterns of American families left the market open and, in turn, further accelerated the advancement of foreign participation in U.S. commercial markets.

Trade Revenue and Banking

The foreign investment and trade pattern and balance of U.S. current and capital accounts reveal that trade imbalances and financial investments have always coexisted between the United States and selected countries in Europe, Asia, and North and South America. What is significant today is the change in the magnitude and direction of imbalance among the beneficiaries. For example, U.S. trade deficits with Canada, Japan, and West Germany are continuous, substantial, and growing. On the other hand, trade deficits with Mexico and Venezuela are small in magnitude and show no particular pattern. The trade relationships with the Middle Eastern OPEC countries are minicyclical, narrow, and very balanced. In fact, these countries, during certain cycles, have contributed relatively more to the inflow of funds into the United States than other countries with the same or higher export revenues. Similar patterns have been observed in regard to foreign banking investments of these countries in the United States. Table 9.5 shows the major U.S. trading partners and banking investors in recent years.

As a whole, five patterns of correlation and dependency have been observed in regard to foreign banking investments and trade relationships. The

Table 9.5

U.S. Trade Balance and Foreign Banking Investments in the United States by Assets (Billions of U.S. Dollars)

	1980	1985	1986	1987	1988[a]
		U.S. Trade Status			
Major Trading Partners:					
Australia	1.5	2.6	2.9	2.5	2.6
Brazil	0.6	-4.4	-2.9	-3.9	-5.1
Canada	-6.1	-21.7	-12.8	-11.3	-14.7
France	2.3	-3.4	-2.9	-2.8	-2.3
Italy	1.2	-5.1	-5.8	-5.5	-4.8
Japan	-9.9	-40.2	-55.0	-56.4	-55.5
Mexico	2.6	-5.5	-4.9	-5.7	-3.5
United Kingdom	2.9	-3.6	-4.0	-3.3	-1.0
Venezuela	-0.7	-3.1	-2.0	-2.0	-1.5
West Germany	-0.7	-11.1	-14.5	-15.4	-14.8
		Foreign Banking Investments by Assets			
Major Investors:					
Brazil	4.4	4.0	4.4	4.2	4.3
Canada	15.7	39.5	42.4	44.2	39.2
France	12.9	20.6	22.4	24.6	29.2
Hong Kong	11.9	23.3	24.9	25.6	25.7
Ireland	0.3	4.5	5.5	5.6	6.4
Israel	4.1	7.8	8.1	8.4	9.2
Italy	9.2	29.1	36.4	41.0	39.8
Japan	72.5	179.0	246.0	295.0	360.8
Mexico	3.9	3.9	3.6	4.2	4.4
Netherlands	3.7	7.1	8.5	8.7	10.1
South Korea	2.2	3.3	3.6	3.9	4.6
Spain	2.2	3.9	4.5	5.2	6.1
Switzerland	11.3	18.3	24.5	23.0	23.9
United Kingdom	25.1	57.0	40.6	43.7	32.7
West Germany	7.3	8.8	11.0	13.5	13.0

[a] Estimated, based on January to September data.

characteristics and attitudes of each country and group represent the progressive manner in which each may approach its banking investments in the United States. The differences among the countries can be attributed to their degree of economic strength, along with their wealth, in pursuit of the desired markets for future investment.

Aggressive and Industrialized. This group consists of major industrialized, market-seeking countries with strong independent economies. The countries in this category have been historically progressive and export oriented with advanced multinational banking structures. This classification consists of Canada, France, Italy, Japan, the United Kingdom, and West Germany. They rank highest both in trade and banking investments in the United States, with the strongest correlation between these two economic factors, in comparison with the other categories. Among them, Canada, Japan, and West Germany present the strongest trade ties with the United States and have accumulated the largest trade surpluses. On the banking investment side, the situation is almost the same. The countries of Japan, Italy, Canada, the United Kingdom, and France rank 1 to 5 in banking investment with West Germany ranking 8. The reason is clear. For a long time, Japan has seen the American market as a dominant place for future expansion. The young, vast, diversified, market-oriented economy and the open-market attitude of American business provides a receptive atmosphere for major expansion, unmatched by any other area or country. The family-oriented economic environment of Europe, in contrast, has discouraged Japanese exporters and, in a way, has forced them to concentrate on the U.S. industrial and financial markets. Japanese attempts to gain a foothold in Europe have failed, despite enormous amounts of expenditures on advertising and promotions.

Canada has been the closest U.S. ally and trading partner. The country was a pioneer in the establishment of banking offices in the United States. The banking investment from this neighboring North American country was always justified due to the close trade relationship and economic interdependency. This investment was never considered a threat to the United States because both trade and banking interests between the two have been mutual and reciprocal. These circumstances separate Canada from Japan, whose banking and trade relationship is more one sided. American banking investments in the Japanese financial market are relatively small due to Japanese structural limitations that restrict foreign competition and entry into domestic markets. On the other hand, West Germany's limited interest in presenting true competition in banking investments in the United States is perceived by many to be due to the country's strong desire to be a dominant force in the European market community. Concentration in both European and American markets simultaneously may not be technically possible nor financially achievable, given the force of market demand and the cost of operation in the present world environment.

France, Italy, and the United Kingdom have been active in trade and investment in the United States since colonial times. Traditionally, the volume of trade among the partners is level. But in the 1980s, exportation to the United States surpassed the importation value by a margin of $2 billion to $5 billion. As a result, an imbalance was created. Similarly, banking interest from these countries is strong and growing. The most progressive among the three is Italy, which improved her position from number 7 in 1980 to number 2 in 1988 with a strong desire to close the gap for better position by the year 1990 and thereafter. Italy's strong interest in the U.S. financial market is derived in part from internal market weakness characterized by high inflation and interest rates and a weakening export economy.

One major factor that separates this and the next group from other groups with respect to their trade and banking investment is the correlation and dependency between the degree of increase in exports and the degree of increase in banking investments. With a minor exception, the growth of U.S. banking assets of this category, on average, increased twice that of the changes in the value of exports in the 1980s, signaling a strong desire for these nations to continue their financial activities beyond traditional forms of export financing. Developing countries and those with weaker export transactions with the United States demonstrated a balancing act between exports and bank asset growth.

Industrialized with Moderate Potential. This group consists of the industrialized countries with progressive, export-oriented market attitudes, which are not as aggressive as the first group. These countries are less strong due to their inability to infiltrate international markets with a high volume or a wide variety of merchandise suitable for worldwide distribution. Thus, their market approach is more segmented, as demonstrated in their trade relationships with the United States. Their trade with the United States is moderate, ranging from $300 million to $2.1 billion, and with small trade account imbalances. The products imported from these countries are secondary and tertiary in importance; thus they provide no competition and are of no threat to any crucial segment of the U.S. industrial complex. However, these countries provide first-grade banking presence in the United States. This classification includes the Netherlands, Switzerland, Hong Kong, Spain, Israel, and Ireland.

Hong Kong, Switzerland, and the Netherlands have historically presented strong banking networks with worldwide distribution centers, and with a strong interest in the U.S. financial markets. They ranked numbers 6, 7, and 9 in 1988, with U.S. banking assets of $25.7 billion, $23.8 billion, and $10.1 billion, respectively. Similarly, Israel, Ireland, and Spain ranked 10, 11, and 12 with U.S. banking assets of $6.1 billion to $9.2 billion. The balance between trade transactions and U.S. banking investments of this group is similar to the first group, in which the growth in banking assets of these countries in the United States far surpassed the degree of increase in export activities. Among the countries mentioned above, the Netherlands is one of the largest investors in real estate in the United States.

Progressive with Financial Limitations. The two countries in this category, Mexico and Brazil, have close trade ties with the United States and manage moderate banking assets to support their trade transactions. The correlation between these two elements is strong and growing. Second only to Canada, Mexico has been a strong U.S. trading partner since 1970, with two-way trade in the range of $4 billion to $40 billion. During the 1970s, the United States held the upper hand with a trade surplus in the range of $500 million to $4 billion. But the tide reversed itself in the 1980s with Mexico's increase in the exportation of oil, resulting in an average surplus of $5.3 billion. Mexico's banking assets in the same period averaged $3.9 billion. These banking activities in the United States are essential to encourage exports and foreign exchange trading, and to promote U.S. financial transactions with Mexico. Overall, both trade and banking activities complement each other as they increase proportionally over time.

Brazil also presents similar trends. Despite its position as one of the top ranked exporting nations in the world, its foreign banking activity is not very progressive. Brazil ranks number 15 in banking investment in the United States, with assets of $4.3 billion. At the same time, its exports reached a high of $9.4 billion, resulting in a record trade surplus of $5.1 billion. Like Mexico, the banking activities of Brazilian banking offices in the United States are limited to the general international banking practices of trade financing, foreign exchange trading, and bank-client relationship services.

Overall, this group represents a progressive trade relationship with a secondary banking establishment. The correlation between trade and banking assets growth is high but with moderate changes. Neither of the two factors overshadows the other. In essence the banking concentration is complementary and a by-product of trade transactions.

Newcomers with Potential. This category consists of newly industrialized nations and the progressive wing of developing countries. Most are newcomers to the export market, but have good potential for future progress. In general, the group has developed a good foundation for strong trade relationships with the United States and collectively scored positive in their trade balances with the United States in recent years. However, variation and differences exist among the members. This group consists of countries from Asia, plus Australia and South Africa. During the past five years, the countries of Malaysia, the Philippines, Singapore, South Korea, Taiwan, and Venezuela collectively recorded a surplus trade account with the United States in the range of $8 billion to $25 billion per year, a new historical position unforeseen in the 1970s. On an upbeat note, the U.S. trade account shows a positive trade surplus with Australia in the range of $2.5 billion, and, on average, a nearly level export-import balance with the Republic of South Africa. On the banking investment side, South Korea, Australia,

Taiwan, and Venezuela represent the progressive wing of the group, ranking numbers 13, 16, 18, and 20 respectively, as measured by assets size. The other members rank low: Malaysia number 41, Singapore number 42, the Philippines number 43, and South Africa number 55.

As a result of the diversity among the members, the countries of this group present a mixed bag of dependency between trade and banking investment. While on one hand there is a positive correlation between the level of trade and foreign banking activities of the majority of the progressive wing of the group, the moderate trade surpluses of Malaysia and the Philippines, on the other hand, have not been transformed into further desire on the part of these two nations to increase banking presence in U.S. financial markets. There are two reasons behind this development. First, the weak domestic economic condition of the two countries necessitates that revenues be consumed for domestic investment in preference to foreign investments. Second, their banking industry lacks the strong financial reserves and technical expertise necessary to operate multifunctional banking services outside home territories.

The South African situation supports the hypothesis that there is a positive and upward correlation between the progressive export attitude of a country and its banking investment strength. The low banking investment of South African nationals coincides with the low balance of trade of this country with the United States. A similar but reversed pattern has been observed with respect to China. As the two-way trade relationship between China and the United States approaches the $2 billion mark, China's interest in the U.S. banking market intensifies. Since 1980, the total assets of China's banking investment in the United States increased from almost none to $964 million, changing its rank from 52 to 29, indicating strong positive progress for a developing country with a limited financial power.

The circumstances surrounding OPEC countries' trade and banking participation in the United States differs from others. The U.S. dependency on OPEC oil imports has been substantially reduced to a mere 5 percent, supplied exclusively from a few friendly members: Venezuela, Kuwait, and Saudi Arabia. The worldwide revenues of these exporting nations has also declined to half or less during the 1980s, due to the reduction in the worldwide price of oil and the glut of supply in response to more prudent demands. In addition, domestic affairs, such as the war between Iran and Iraq and Libyan confrontations with the United States, further hindered the development of better trade and investment relationships between these countries and the United States in recent years. Since the energy crisis of 1973, Arab OPEC countries have not felt comfortable investing extensively in the United States, especially in the sensitive area of banking, due to the political attitude generated by the U.S. government's strong support of Israel.

As a result, trade and banking investment relationships have not developed along their normal routes to permit free developmental prospects. These circumstances caused OPEC banking investment in the United States to rank low, with the exception of Venezuela, Bahrain, and Kuwait, despite moderate trade relationships among the countries concerned. The highest-ranked among the countries in this group, measured by banking assets in the United States in 1988, were Venezuela number 20, Bahrain number 27, and Kuwait number 28. Others ranked lower: Saudi Arabia number 37, United Arab Emirates number 46, and the remaining countries with no representation or ranked at the bottom. There is a positive correlation between the deterioration in ranking of the OPEC nations' banking investment and the decline in their trade activities with the United States in recent years.

Developing Countries with Low Potential. This group consists of countries that neither developed strong trade relationships nor have a strong banking presence in the United States. They are mainly developing countries with a limited potential for exports and a weak economic condition. Nearly one-fourth of the countries with some form of trade and banking investment with the United States fall into this category, illustrating the importance of export revenue and a positive trade balance in the pursuit of international banking activities. The countries in this category are Bermuda, the Cayman Islands, Chile, the Dominican Republic, Ecuador, El Salvador, Jordan, Panama, Peru, Egypt, the Soviet Union, and others.

Egypt and the Soviet Union are in this group because their trade transactions with the United States are mostly one-sided and motivated by political decisions rather than the force of a free market mechanism. Egypt's imports from the United States surpass exports, causing a U.S. trade surplus balance of $2 billion per year. However, a large proportion of the Egyptian trade deficits are compensated by U.S. foreign aid in various types and forms. Considering the limited banking assets of Egyptian national banks in the U.S. banking industry ($175 million in 1988, exhibiting a decreasing trend since 1985), the Egyptian case, like other members of this group, supports the fact that an interrelationship exists between exports and the desire for banking activities in a foreign trading country. Lack of either one results in the inactivity of the second component.

The Russian trade relationship with the United States is also discontinuous and limited to political communication between the superpowers. On the average, since 1975, Soviet exports to the United States were $400 million, while their imports from the U.S. averaged $2 billion. The outcome results in a $1.6 billion trade surplus in the favor of the United States. On the banking investment side, financial interrelationship is mutually nonexistent. As a result, the correlation between the factors cannot be established since the cause of the relationship is political.

TRADE FINANCING

One of the traditional functions of multinational banks is to facilitate international trade and payments between trading partners. To achieve this goal, national banks began establishing foreign offices to initiate contacts in serving home-market clients and to facilitate the financing of imports from foreign markets. A survey of foreign banks in the United States points to the importance of trade financing, specifically for small- and medium-sized banks and banks from developing countries with limited international banking services. As a result, the development of an equally diverse and highly sophisticated system of trade financing and banking services is essential in today's competitive market environment of the bank service industry and in aiding the flow of funds across national borders.

Historical Development

The major instruments of trade financing developed in England during the nineteenth century, reaching their peak in the second half of the twentieth century. In the early stage, U.S. banking laws did not permit the issuance of letters of credit. The Federal Reserve Act of 1913 authorized banks to issue letters of credit under specific guidelines. Despite this development, European multinational banks continued to set the pace in the development and usage of trade credit instruments until after World War II. Thereafter, the United States took charge in the acceleration of the development of instruments to accompany the increasing pace of trade transactions.

After World War II, the balance of power shifted from Europe to the United States, as American goods and services were exported to offset shortages in supplies throughout the world. The outcome significantly changed the structural market and the role of American banks in providing the instruments for financing export transactions. From 1945 to 1960, the United States remained the largest supplier of goods, as well as the largest purchaser of foreign products. This new development signaled the importance of the American market in world trade and finance and the beginning of a new era in international banking activities and investments. To respond to the new challenge, foreign banks started to concentrate on the U.S. market by setting up shop immediately thereafter.

As American banks' international activities intensified, they began pioneering new forms of international instruments. Improvements in technique and presentation of new instruments to fit different trade patterns continued into the 1980s with the United States holding top rank in the issuance of drafts and letters of credit. However, as Japan has risen to a formidable rank in world trade and has become the world's number one creditor nation, replacing the United States, there is a strong expectation that Japanese banks will take over the U.S. dominance in trade financing shortly before the year 2000.

Instruments of Trade Financing

The instruments of trade financing consist of the documentation of financial techniques in the presentation of sales and shipments of merchandise across national boundaries. These documentations illustrate the means of payment and the institutional transactors involved in delivery of goods to their final destination. There was no uniform interpretation or practice for these instruments until 1962. At that time, a system of uniform customs and practices for documenting credit was formulated with the formation of the International Chamber of Commerce in Paris in cooperation with other national chambers of commerce and banks. The new rules went into effect in July 1963, and were revised in 1974 and again in 1984 to accommodate changes in international trade and transport techniques.

The fundamental objective of trade financing instruments is to provide assurance against risk of noncompletion of a transaction by either side, whether buyer or seller. In essence, the document assures the seller of payment and the buyer of receipt of merchandise, within a time frame established in the bylaws of the contract. The second function of the instrument is to provide a means of financing and protection against foreign exchange risk. The document presents a predetermined exchange rate and payment guarantees to protect the buyer against risk of foreign exchange fluctuations, and also provides the seller with a marketable document in case the applicant seeks to liquidate the note prior to its maturity date. As a result, these instruments play a central role in the world of international banking and finance.

Types of Instruments

Three types of instruments have been used in international trade financing: (1) letters of credit, (2) drafts, and (3) bills of lading. In addition to the above instruments, all international transactions contain documentation of "certificates of insurance," indicating that insurance has been obtained for the parcel as stipulated in the instrument of credit; a "certificate of origin," specifying the origin of the goods; and a "certificate of shipment," indicating the character of the shipment, and the weight and contents of individual packages.

Letters of Credit. A letter of credit is a bank instrument issued at the request of the buyer (importer) to the credit of the seller (exporter), authorizing a fixed amount of payment upon presentation of the document specified under the terms of the agreement. The letter authorizes the beneficiaries to draw drafts on the issuing banks or via correspondent banks in accordance with the amount specified in the letter, at the specified contract date. A letter of credit usually includes the amount of credit authorization, the date of withdrawal, the shipping date, the contents of merchandise, and the date of arrival of the shipments. The contract reduces the risk of non-completion by either party. The payment is insured against paper documents rather than the actual merchandise, and the documentation insures that all conditions are met in accordance with specified obligations. By obtaining the obligation of a bank, the exporter is almost assured that the payment will be honored by the bank as soon as the goods are shipped and documents are delivered. Similarly, the importer is also assured that the payment will be released only after the documents are delivered as specified under the terms of the contract.

In international trade, most letters of credit are "commercial letters of credit," which means that they are used for the financing of commercial transactions. The letters of credit can be either "revocable" or "irrevocable." A revocable letter of credit can be cancelled, changed, or amended at any time prior to payment. It is intended to serve as a means of arranging payment but not as a guarantee of payment. An irrevocable letter of credit cannot be cancelled or changed without the consent of all parties. It can be in the form of "confirmed" or "unconfirmed." A confirmed letter of credit is typically issued by one bank and endorsed by another bank in either the buyer's or seller's country. The endorsement by a second bank makes both banks obligated to honor the draft. However, if the credit is the only obligation of the issuing bank or if the second bank acts as agent of the seller (exporter) in checking or accepting the document, then the letter of credit is unconfirmed. Normally if exporters have doubts about the foreign bank's credit standing or ability to pay the obligation, or they expect noncompletion due to political instability in the importer's market, exporters may request a confirmed letter of credit cosigned or endorsed by a domestic bank in their home country.

A letter of credit may be "revolving" or "nonrevolving." If the letter of credit is valid for only one transaction, it is nonrevolving. But if the authorization to draw drafts is continuous daily, weekly, or monthly, it is revolving. If the revolving credit permits the drawee to carry over in a later period an undrawn amount of the current or a past period, the credit is called "cumulative revolving credit;" otherwise, it is "noncumulative." The revolving letter of credit may be used when the shipment of goods is to be made over a period of time, or when the volume of credit is so large that no bank or buyer wants to have it outstanding.

On occasion, the drawee obtains "transferrable letters of credit," which designate the buyer as the creditor, but permit credit transferability in its entirety or in part to another person(s), normally the seller, within the time frame and provision of the draft. On the other hand, the seller may request a "standby letter of credit," payable upon presentation of a draft against the

Table 9.6
Instruments of Trade Financing

Letters of Credit

Revocable Letters of Credit

Irrevocable Letters of Credit
Confirmed
Unconfirmed

Revolving Letters of Credit
Cumulative
Noncumulative

Nonrevolving Letters of Credit

Standby Letters of Credit

Negotiable Letters of Credit

Foreign Currency Letters of Credit

Time Letters of Credit

Back-to-Back Letters of Credit

Red Clause Letters of Credit

Green Clause Letters of Credit

Drafts

Sight Drafts: Clean or Documentary

Time Drafts: Clean or Documentary
Bankers' Acceptances
Trade Acceptances

Bills of Lading

Straight or To Order
Clean   On-Board   Foul
Received-for-Shipment

issuing bank if the clauses in the contract are not met or if the contractor (buyer) defaults on its obligation. The risk to the bank is very high with this form of credit because there is the possibility that the beneficiary (seller) may fraudulently notify the issuing bank of default.

If the letter of credit permits third-party involvement in which the beneficiary's draft can be purchased by other than the major party involved, it is called a "negotiable letter of credit." The third party involved may be a bank that purchases the beneficiary's draft at a discount for future collection. Furthermore, letters of credit that are expressed in the national currency of other countries are known as "foreign currency letters of credit." This document transfers the risk of currency fluctuation from seller to buyer of the goods, as the exporter demands receipt of the payment in the desired currency of the home country or other currency. If the exporter wishes to extend credit to the importer or provide more lenient credit terms than the bank, then it is customary to use "deferred-payment letters of credit" or "time letters of credit." This type of credit defers the payment beyond the designated term of the draft but still guarantees payment by a bank.

Other types of letters of credit used by banks in international trade financing are "back-to-back letters of credit," and "red and green clause letters of credit." A back-to-back letter of credit involves a third party acting as agent between a buyer and seller, using the buyer's credit as its own. It consists of two letters of credit that have similar documentation requirements. Two different prices will be shown on the letter of credit and the invoices. The difference is the agent's profit. The two drafts and two prices often invite discrepancies and concern; therefore, safeguards are required by the bank.

When a letter of credit contains a provision permitting the advance of partial payment of the credit to the exporter, the letter of credit is known as a "red clause letter of credit" with the special clause printed in red. The advance payment is permitted to facilitate performance by the beneficiary in regard to shipment or for other uses associated with the transaction. The red clause line is used when the importer has faith in the exporter, thus permitting the bank to make an advance of partial payment. This situation normally occurs when it is essential that the exporter pay subcontractors on the spot for assembled goods or the agent prior to the shipment. A related but more restricted form of letters of credit is the "green clause," in which the terms require the merchandise to be stored under the bank's control until shipment is made. This form prevents the sellers of bad faith from noncompletion of the term of contract by failure to ship the merchandise on time. This also prevents or reduces the buyer's risk of nondelivery.

Drafts. A "draft" is a written order to pay a specified amount of money at a specified point in time to a given person or to the bearer. The parties involved in a draft are the drawer (exporter), the drawee (importer's bank), and the payee (importer). Domestic transactions are normally more informal than international transactions. In domestic practice, no formal document indicating the obligation to pay is required prior to the buyer's obtaining possession of the merchandise. Domestic laws protect the seller, and delivery documents testify to the actual transaction. However, the issuance of drafts and means of payment should already be in order to clarify the method of payment. In international practice, advance payment or a formal promise to pay is required before the buyer can obtain the merchandise. Thus, there is less trust involved, and use of negotiable instruments is often necessary to facilitate the transaction.

There are two types of drafts. A "sight draft" requires immediate payment to the drawee upon presentation of the document. The "time draft" or "usance draft," in contrast, allows a delay in payment. It is a deferred payment bill, allowing payment in the future as specified in the draft to the drawer or the beneficiary upon presentation of the draft. A time draft that is endorsed and accepted by a bank is a "bankers' acceptance"; when it is accepted by a business firm, it is a "trade acceptance."

A banker's acceptance matures in 90 days; however, other forms of time drafts may have maturities of 30, 60, 90, or other specified numbers of days. When a draft is presented to a bank, the bank will review the inscription shown on the draft, the signature, and other specific legalities before accepting the document. Upon completion of the review and acceptance of the draft, the bank stamps the draft; thus it becomes a bankers' acceptance. There is a secondary market for bankers' acceptances. The market is a discount market providing liquidity for the beneficiary. In contrast, a trade acceptance has no secondary market and is not as liquid as bankers' acceptances.

In the United States, bankers' acceptances have developed a significant market. In essence, they are products advanced by American bankers as opposed to the European form of sight drafts. The document can be in the form of either an "eligible" or "ineligible" draft, indicating its marketability and liquidity process. An ineligible bankers' acceptance is a sound and marketable instrument, but it does not hold the specific characteristics that are required for discount and liquidity by the Federal Reserve System. An eligible bankers' acceptance requires a maturity of less than six months for discount and less than nine months for purchase. It must be a by-product of domestic or international trade, and be self-liquidating. Eligibility dictates that the financing be used for goods already shipped or in storage, secured by a warehouse receipt. In general, most international trade letters of credit are eligible within this classification, due to tight controls and regulatory restrictions applied to reduce the risk of noncompletion.

Drafts are also classified as "clean" or "documentary." A clean draft, normally used for domestic trade and for shipment to affiliates, will be honored by order of the buyer when presented after shipment of the merchandise. It is unaccompanied by any other documents, and can be in the form of sight or time draft. On the other hand, a documentary draft is usually accompanied by invoices, bills of lading, insurance papers, and consular invoices. A documentary draft is often used for international trade, requiring the buyer to honor the draft by payment or by acceptance prior to receiving title to the goods. Thus, the system is safeguarded against non-completion of the transaction to the benefit of all parties involved.

Bills of Lading. A bill of lading is prepared for the exporter by a shipping company, indicating title to the goods. It is five documents in one. It specifies receipt of the merchandise by the shipper; the conditions and consigned terms of delivery; the destination, weight, and dimensions of the cargo; the contract and document of title; and the terms and conditions of delivery to the recipient (buyer). If shipping charges are paid in advance, the bill of lading is "freight paid"; otherwise, the carrier maintains a temporary lien on the merchandise until the freight is paid. The bill of lading is either "straight" or "to order." A straight bill of lading directs delivery of merchandise directly to the buyer, with a no-transfer clause (nonnegotiable). Delivery does not automatically transfer the title of the goods, nor is it good collateral for loans. Therefore, in international transactions, a straight bill of lading is used only when the goods have been paid for in advance, or when the shipment is to an affiliate, or when the exporter initiates financing of the transaction.

With the order bill of lading (negotiable), the exporter (seller) retains title to the merchandise until such time as the payment is received. Upon payment, the exporter releases title to the party making the payment, usually to the importer's bank. The seller often consigns the goods to the order of the shipper, who transfers the title and delivers the goods upon payment to the buyer or a designated agent at the port of arrival.

A bill of lading can be "clean," "foul," "on board," or "received-for-shipment," depending on the condition of the merchandise received. A clean bill of lading indicates that goods were received by the carrier and loaded in apparently good condition. Similarly, a foul bill of lading indicates that the merchandise suffered some damage before being received for shipment, thus informing the buyer of the condition of the merchandise prior to final payment. Other considerations and information regarding the status of the condition and delivery period of the goods may be desirable both for the drawee's bank and the importer. In this regard, "on-board" and "on-dock" bills of lading may be used to explain the shipping status of the merchandise. For instance, an on-board bill of lading indicates that the merchandise has been placed on board the vessel whose name appears on the trade document. On the other hand, a received-for-shipment or on-dock bill of lading specifies that the goods are not on the vessel, but sitting on the dock at present and might be there for some time. The procedures and use of certain bills of lading provide valuable information to both the buyer and seller regarding the process and duration of their transactions.

10 Impact of Foreign Banks and Future Prospects

Following the end of World War II, two events redirected world attention concerning international banking transformation. First, the general perception was that Americans were coming and soon U.S. multinational banks would take over from the European domination. In fact, there was some truth to this notion as U.S. banks increased their activities and presence overseas. Second, after the Japanese assault on world industrial markets, almost exclusively in the United States, the banking environment changed with the Japanese invasion of credit markets. Interestingly enough, the U.S. dollar played a key role in both events. At first, the U.S. dollar aided the rebuilding of the European economy, and then the outflow of the dollar provided the Japanese with an opportunity to rechannel their funds to build a banking base in the U.S. market.

The combination of U.S. budget and trade deficits and its dependency on capital inflows, along with the significant increases in debt rescheduling and the default of several developing countries, have left many to wonder about the international strategies of multinational banks. However, the past trend leaves no doubt about the future prospects and impact of foreign banks in the United States, signaling an upward trend as world attention turns toward the exporting nations of Japan, West Germany, and South Korea. Unquestionably, this evolution raises questions about the complexity of the subject and related factors that shift the benefit to a new generation of creditors. At the same time, the complexity has made it virtually impossible to forecast accurately about the future prospects of international banking, specifically the banks' continued surge into the U.S. domestic market.

Recognizing an era of coexistence, U.S. concern has shifted to the impact and importance of foreign banks' presence in the United States. The responses that most benefit the banks as well as the general public are those that address potential benefits of foreign banking investment and concern about the future direction of U.S. banking institutions in association with foreign banking presence and growth.

IMPACT OF FOREIGN BANKS

The study of foreign banking in the United States is young and consequently produces very preliminary results. Advanced studies are handicapped by lack of extensive and comprehensive data. Despite the Federal Reserve collection of data since 1972 and the publication of structured data on foreign banks in the United States, present information lacks in-depth presentation of characteristics comparable to the ones available for U.S. commercial banks. As a result, studies that argue in favor of or against the effects of foreign banking investments lack detailed data to clearly support their arguments.

Impact on the U.S. Economy

The remarkable speed with which foreign banks grew so large in a short period of time in comparison with U.S. banks has created apprehension about the economic effects of these institutions on the overall U.S. economy. The socioeconomic impact associated with the influx of jobs, taxation, provision of managerial skill, and flow of capital to local communities is positive and supportive of the U.S. economy. During the 1970s and early 1980s, various states welcomed foreign banks as a means of promoting local economies. Investments by foreign entities and banking agencies contributed to the development of local markets and aided revenue for state governments as foreign banks expanded their operation with state licensing.

The American bank management who acquired positions with foreign banking entities after years of work with local banks have expressed pleasure in working with foreign employers. Their satisfaction is derived from better working environments, higher earnings, and broader challenges than in their previous positions. An example of a foreign takeover that reflects a positive impact on the local community is the merger between the Bank of Tokyo and the Southern California First National Bank. The merger increased the California bank's financial strength and market participation, increased the number of services available to local customers, created additional jobs, and opened a new dimension for the Southern California First National Bank in the area of commercial and international lending services.

Another example of success is the case of the First American Bank of Virginia. The bank, formerly known as Valley National Bank of Harrisonburg, Virginia, was acquired in 1983 by a foreign-owned bank holding company of six commercial banks and saving institutions from Virginia, Maryland, and Washington, D.C. The inflow of funds improved the status of the acquired bank, causing assets to triple in five years, placing the institution in a better competitive position to serve its community and state, with access to the larger markets of the nearby cities of Baltimore and Washington, D.C.

The work ethic and managerial skill associated with foreign banks also contribute toward a new teaching environment for American employers as well as for other banks serving the same markets. For example, natives of Japan, Hong Kong, and Korea are known as a group with a stronger work ethic, whereas Europeans are thought to be more diversified in services and more technically advanced in international financial approaches. The transfer of technology gives Americans a new dimension and opportunity in the area of international lending and a chance to increase market participation by learning from other cultural approaches.

Impact on Competition

Many foreign banks in the United States are large in terms of assets, deposits, and the magnitude of their worldwide activities. These banks are among the world's 500 largest banks, with numerous banks from Canada, Hong Kong, Japan, and Western Europe among the top 100. Banks of this magnitude are considered to be a strongly competitive force within the U.S. market. The concern is whether foreign banks experienced unfair advantages over U.S. banks, thus reducing competition. On the contrary, studies conducted by the staff of the Federal Reserve and reported to Congress indicate that foreign banks have contributed positively to the force of competition by providing many important benefits to the U.S. banking market.

Former Governor Henry C. Wallich of the Federal Reserve Board summarized the U.S. government view on the competitive influence of foreign banks by proclaiming their benefits. In the domestic sphere, they (1) have introduced innovation and have increased competition; (2) have introduced new pricing techniques, such as LIBOR; (3) have contributed to the capitalization of U.S. banks by providing a flow of home-office capital into banks' deposits and in turn to the U.S. balance of payments capital account; (4) have tried to create a stronger dollar base for their own international operations, and have helped to solidify the international role of the dollar as well as having enhanced the American banking market as the world financial center, thus contributing to the general betterment of the U.S. economy and the competitive banking market; and (5) with respect to the acquisition of problem banks, have helped to resolve problems created by the U.S. law that prohibits interstate mergers and acquisitions within individual states, and provided a better competitive environment in the markets that those weak banks served.[1]

Most foreign banks in the United States are concentrated in the large metropolitan areas, in which they compete with similarly large American banks. In these markets foreign banks and affiliated agencies are involved in international trade financing, foreign exchange activities, and money market transactions, with very limited retail banking. As a result, their activities and market participation provide a larger supply of funds and more diversified competitive services. This interaction gives American international bank lenders opportunities to infiltrate foreign markets by providing better services to foreign clients involved in the U.S. export-import market.

Foreign banks' retail banking operations intensified in the 1970s and 1980s as foreign banks concentrated on subsidiary forms of organization, thus acquiring or merging with local banks. Foreign banks with retail banking operations (especially Japanese banks) concentrated in the California market. Two of the larger purchases were the Lloyd Bank Ltd. of London acquisition of the First Western Bank & Trust Co., then the eighth largest California bank in terms of deposits (96 offices), and the purchase of 19 branches of the Bank of California by Sumitomo Bank of Japan. Despite Japanese banks' success in infiltrating California's retail banking market (4 percent) and business lending services (13 percent), the overall impact has been minimal.

In the California market, these banks are perceived to be relatively small, especially when compared with the Bank of America, one of the giants in the world of international banking, with 1,000 branches in California alone. Furthermore, FDIC investigations on foreign banks' market penetration found no cause for concern and ruled that the competitive impact of the acquisition and merger in each case would not be negative.[2] In conclusion, there is no evidence to support arguments about the negative impact of competition by foreign banks in the United States. A study by the staff of the Federal Reserve Board presented to the U.S. Senate Committee on Banking, Housing, and Urban Affairs supports FDIC findings and cleared doubt about any detrimental impact of foreign banking competition in the United States.[3]

Impact on Monetary Policy Control

Apprehension regarding the impact of foreign banks on U.S. monetary policy was felt mainly by U.S. multinational banks that were overwhelmed by foreign competition. In reality the assets of the foreign institutions were historically less than 8 percent of the U.S. money supply, with less than 3 percent of the retail banking market. Their market penetration is mainly limited to a few banks from Canada, Western Europe, and Japan. Others provide no challenge overall, nor do they present any significant influence in determining monetary policy. For example, in 1988, from the foreign banks' lending share of the U.S. market of 27.5 percent, 18.6 percent was by the three countries of Japan, the United Kingdom, and Canada. The remaining 53 countries' lending activities were limited to only 8.9 percent.[4] Similarly the assets ownership of foreign banks was controlled by a few banks from industrialized nations. As a result domination is not uniform, nor is it unified to favor foreign interests.

The Federal Reserve monetary policy is traditionally conducted on the basis of inflation and credit market expansionary trends, disregarding foreign investments. There is no indication that any lending or investment pattern of foreign banks has ever influenced U.S. monetary policy nor were those patterns ever considered significant enough to require regulatory measures. The concern over any such impact was addressed under the International Banking Act of 1978. As a result, the fear of monetary policy impact appears to be unjustified. The Federal Reserve's and FDIC's periodic inspections under the regulatory requirements have found no reason for concern nor any justification for further reform.

The global law of international relations dictates that foreign banks in the United States be treated neither differently nor more severely than U.S. banks' treatment abroad. The inflow and outflow of funds through foreign banks should not be subject to limitations other than those that apply to U.S. banks. The monetary policy decisions regarding foreign exchange market activities are subject to the "managed float" exchange system, regulated by the law of supply and demand for currency. Occasional interference by single or collective governmental actions occurs only in severe situations in which the monetary stability and trade policy of a country or region are shattered without any reinforcement. The recent decline in the value of the U.S. dollar, spurred by the U.S. government policy to stimulate exports, in fact promoted foreign investments and banking activities, which further stabilized the current exchange rate and pricing mechanism in the United States.

CONCERN ABOUT FOREIGN BANKS

Banking is a sensitive business. This is documented by heavy regulation. Foreign ownership touches sensitive nerves in many places. Two major concerns have been expressed regarding the regulatory environment, impact, and treatment of foreign banks. First, regulatory concern is related to the open policy of the United States in the banking area, arguing that, despite the IBA of 1978, foreign banks still enjoy unique advantages over American banks. Second, socioeconomic concern addresses the responsiveness of foreign banks to the needs of the local community, cost advantages of foreign banks, the lack of similar treatment of U.S. banks abroad and the potential ownership by foreigners of a significant proportion of U.S. capital.

Regulatory Concern

A bank supervisory problem would exist if a foreign acquirer of a U.S. bank were engaged in unsafe or unsound banking practices. The practices might include the deliberate use of the resources of the bank to enhance business interests, disregarding the interests of the depositors or other creditors of the bank. This could be the case when individual investors, rather than a bank, acquire interest in a local banking entity. The situation could result in actions containing provisions to make loans and investments in certain companies with favorable terms, engaging in foreign exchange contracts with favorable rates, or paying higher interest on certain deposits. Another related concern is about the influence of a foreign government on the foreign banking entities, resulting in harmful actions against the interest of the American community and policies.

Under the Bank Holding Company Act, the Federal Reserve has authority to supervise foreign-owned banks.[5] Since the passage of the IBA of 1978, all acquisitions require the approval of the regulatory authorities, as is the case with U.S. banks. When a foreign investor is an individual rather than a bank or holding company, the standards for approval of acquisition are the same as the rules stipulated in the IBA of 1978. The act requires that individuals seeking to acquire control of a bank give the federal bank regulatory agency 60 days' prior notification. The proposed application will be approved on the grounds that the acquisition would not substantially lessen competition, would not create banking monopoly, and would not jeopardize the financial stability of the acquired bank and community involved. By the end of 1987, the individual investors' share of foreign-owned U.S. banks was estimated at $28.7 billion, relatively small in relationship to total investments.[6]

Once a bank has been acquired by a foreign investor, the Federal Reserve Board has the same supervisory powers over the foreign bank that it has over domestic owners. On the subject of the ability of the Federal Reserve to achieve its monetary policy objectives, most large, foreign-owned banks have accepted membership in the Federal Reserve System and are subject to reserve requirements and other instruments of monetary policy. Because more than half of the foreign banks in the United States are small and are active in limited banking transactions, their overall monetary impact is negligible and has not been considered a threat or cause of any disruption.

Supervisory Power. Executive Order 11858 states the U.S. government policy regarding foreign government investments. The order calls for advance consultation by a foreign government on prospective major foreign governmental investments in the United States. This process provides an opportunity to deal with any potential trouble and guarantees that the proposed investment is in line with activities permissible by banking laws. On the matter of individual investors, there are very few cases that cause concern due to management problems that may have led to bank failure or merger with another bank. Two notable cases are the Franklin National Bank of New York and the American Bank and Trust, both of whose owners were foreign individuals, and their failure was due to management problems. In most cases, the problems facing foreign banks are similar to the problems encountered by American banks.

Grandfathering. Another regulatory concern is expressed in regard to the grandfathering aspect of foreign banks and the acquisition of large American banks by foreign bank holding companies. The claim here is that the practice of grandfathering has given some foreign banks competitive advantages over both American banks and foreign banks that entered after the IBA of 1978. Certainly this concern can neither be denied nor disputed. However, as foreign banks start to practice broader ranges of financial services, such as retail banking, and reach the statutory limitation in assets size of above $1 billion, in order to be competitive and active in the market, the regulatory environment requires the institution to become a member bank, insured by the FDIC. Thus, many waive the grandfather right to receive regulatory permission for the proposed activities. The Federal Reserve Structural Data report reveals the decline in the number of foreign banks with grandfathered provisions since 1980. The number decreased by 20 percent in the past eight years, most notably among the foreign banks from Asia and Latin America.

Acquisitions. Regarding the acquisition of large American banks by foreign bank holding companies, the Federal Reserve Board found that there is no statutory authority in the BHC Act for taking into account the nationality of the acquired company. Similarly, the Community Reinvestment Act does not apply to transactions in which the acquiring banking organization has no presence in the United States. Therefore, the board, upon approval of a merger, has looked only at the merits of each case and has not considered nationality as a material factor in arriving at its decision. Actually, federal regulatory authorities have reluctantly preferred foreign acquisition of domestic banks as a means of increasing competition and reducing concentration of power. Table 10.1 lists the major acquisitions from 1974 to 1982, in which, in each case, the foreign bank infused capital into an acquired bank in order to improve its deteriorating financial standing.

Prior to acquisition, acquired banks had three general characteristics: (1) with a few notable exceptions, the acquired banks were mainly small- to medium-sized, with most having assets below $100 million, and were located primarily in New York and California; (2) they either had low profitability, experienced losses, or were in receivership; (3) they generally had low liquidity, higher proportions of loans to total assets, and a greater reliance on money markets for their funding than did other banks in their peer groups.[7]

Socioeconomic Concern

The socioeconomic concern addresses two areas. First, it is attentive to foreign banks' lack of sensitivity to the needs of the local community and the lack of similar opportunities for U.S. banks abroad. A related concern is over a possible reorientation of an acquired bank away from serving the local credit or deposit needs of its traditional customers and market areas and toward international prospects.

Table 10.1
U.S. Banks Acquired by Foreign Parties with Domestic Assets Exceeding $500 Million (Millions of U.S. Dollars)

Bank	Year Acquired	Total Domestic Assets Preceeding Acquisition
First Western Bank and Trust, L.A., CA	1974	1,334
Franklin National Bank, N.Y., NY	1974	3,805
Southern CA First National Bank, L.A., CA	1975	884
Bank of CA, San Francisco, CA	1976	2,698
Bank of Commonwealth, Detroit, MI	1977	925
Union Bank, L.A., CA	1979	5,125
National Bank of North America, N.Y., NY	1979	3,642
Lasalle National Bank, Chicago, IL	1979	920
Marine Midland Bank, N.Y., NY	1980	10,514
Crocker National Corporation, L.A., CA	1981	19,000
Long Island Trust Company (LITCO), L.I., NY	1982	1,100

Source: United States Senate, "Foreign Takeovers of United States Banks,"
July 1980; and other reports.

Experience to date shows no marked shift in the business orientation of acquired banks. On the contrary, the foreign acquisitions of small banks have in fact been attempts toward retail banking. In regard to the large-sized banks and metropolitan banks, the reorientation of a bank's business could be from retail to wholesale banking or from domestic to international banking. But either could occur regardless of the nationality of the acquirers.

The second concern is in regard to the lower cost of funds and higher earning ratio of the foreign-owned U.S. banks in comparison with their U.S. counterparts. The cost advantage is derived from lack of regulations necessitating that all foreign banks meet reserve requirements. The other advantages of these institutions are the ability to use differential interest rates in borrowing funds in international money markets and the infusion of capital from parent holding companies with favorable currency exchange rates. While the illusion seems convincing, the reality presents a different scenario. Nearly half of the foreign banks are small with limited potential. They are neither involved in retail banking nor strongly fed by parent banks to achieve superiority. The main activities of foreign banks from developing countries are trade financing and foreign exchange trading for internal markets. No evidence exists to suggest the extensive involvement in investment banking transactions that are prerequisites for market penetration.

The success of some large- and medium-sized foreign banks in the United States is credited to the opportunities developed during the past 15 years in U.S. banking markets and the decline in the value of the dollar. The outcome has boosted the value of foreign capital, not only in the financial market, but similarly in real estate and tourism, to the point of apprehension over the expansion. By October 1988, foreign banks' assets climbed to 22 percent of those of U.S. commercial banks, and approximately 16 percent of all U.S. banking deposits.[8]

U.S. banks abroad also play a positive role in international finance. As of September 1988, assets of U.S. offices of American banks abroad were estimated at $490.6 billion. Their portfolios consisted of 153 family banks with 902 branches and $350 billion in assets, and 860 subsidiaries with $132.2 billion in assets.[9] These institutions have played a prominent role in the economy of their local communities and have raised the same concern in foreign markets that foreign banks display in the United States today.

FUTURE OF INTERNATIONAL BANKING

During the past few years, the default of many Third World debtors on their private debt and the changing of the guard in the world supply of credit from the United States to Japan and West Germany have contributed to the prediction that the nature of international banking operations will soon undergo some major change. Dominant economic and regulatory issues are likely to decide the fate of the future. First, economic austerity in Third

World nations and imbalances in trade in many countries may determine whether the crisis will lead to further economic deterioration and may also indicate whether the raising of barriers will invoke retaliation and protectionist measures in the trade war between the United States, Japan, and European allies.

Second, the question of oil prices and the future of OPEC domination is the other issue economically affecting developed and developing countries as they await the possible reemergence of OPEC as a force in the world oil distribution market. However, the new hostile regime in Iran and the Iran-Iraq war have provided a crisis of confidence in oil exporting nations concerning their ability to provide uniform pricing and policies toward consuming nations.

Overproduction and undercut pricing have generated oversupply of oil in the world market, causing prices to falter from $33 per barrel to an average of $20. The decline in oil price brought temporary relief to developing nations, allowing them to improve their trade balances. Whether or not the end to the hostilities between Iran and Iraq and among other OPEC countries will result in a unified front and control of oil production remains to be seen. Certainly the outcome will have a global impact on economic as well as international banking environments, if the wealth of the nations shifts back to the OPEC market with different financial and banking prospects.

The third challenge of modern times is the feasibility of continuing austerity measures implemented by the IMF in the 1980s, which provide fiscal responsibility among developing countries receiving loans from IMF general funds. Whether the policy will succeed in its continuity is a question pondered by many international bankers. The problem is derived from the realization that IMF social and economic pressures may not coincide with real economic development needs in the developing markets, thus in turn disrupting the flow of funds to commercial banks. This outcome would add further to the debt crisis and more than ever limit the scope of credit granting in the world of international banking.

Faced with a severe debt crisis in 1985, Mexico and Peru, followed thereafter by other Latin American countries, announced that they could not meet the terms agreed to with the IMF and requested rescheduling of interest payments. The pressure finally forced industrial nations, at the initiative of the United States, to find a solution in terms of debt rescheduling. Some U.S. multinational banks called off their unpaid interest and principal, declared default, and sought tax credit compensations. Other banks participated in the program by rescheduling debts and even providing further funds to relieve the pressure, in hope of better economic prosperity for debtor nations.

Finally, American banking deregulation is expected to spread worldwide, opening undisclosed markets for international banking approaches. The principle of reciprocity implemented by New York State banking laws forced the Australian monetary authority to reform its laws to permit foreign branch activities and deregulate the restricted club membership. The target now is to open the restricted Japanese market to counteract the effects of U.S. trade deficits that have reached their peak with Japan in recent years. Given the interconnection between banking and insurance, real estate, and brokerage, it is expected that any future banking deregulation will have a great impact on related banking activities.

In summary, the broad economic and political conditions surrounding a bank operation, and international banking services generally, may not suddenly change, but it is certain that recent world financial events will have a great impact on the future implications of global banking. By the year 2000, the dimensions of international banking will be broader, more competitive, and uniform. Furthermore, the role of banks in fostering worldwide economic development is becoming more crucial, and advanced telecommunications and innovative approaches are becoming more essential in banks' loan distributions. Competition will produce new services and cooperation will replace the banks' cartel, with multinational banks continuing to gain momentum at the expense of smaller domestic banks.

FUTURE OF FOREIGN BANKS IN THE UNITED STATES

There is a general belief that the present broad economic and political environment in which foreign banks in the United States operate is likely to remain unchanged. For the next five to ten years, foreign banks will continue to expand. No one is clearly forecasting the status of these banks, especially in regard to the Japanese moves. Two sets of factors, external and internal, will combine to determine the prevailing conditions. The external forces are by-products of the expansion in world output and trade, and the economic progress of developing and debtor countries. The internal forces are determined by the status of the U.S. dollar, U.S. trade and budget deficits, the present crisis of confidence in U.S. savings and loan associations, and the possible regulatory action to slow or impede foreign banks' expansion in the United States.

External Factors

The strong momentum of growth has continued among both industrialized and developing nations since 1986. The major industrialized countries have made important strides toward promoting sustained growth with low inflation and reducing external debt. The economic turnaround in the year 1987 and the first half of 1988 led these countries to believe that growth with low inflation is attainable and forthcoming, despite minor setbacks during the second half of 1988. The nominal GNP for the seven major industrial countries rose by 7.3 percent; given the GNP inflationary deflector of 3 percent, the real GNP expanded by 4.3 percent. The reduction of the federal budget deficit in the United States to 1.4 percent of GNP is one of the most important policy achievements of this period.[10]

Among the developing countries, rapid export growth permitted a strengthening of external positions and declines in debt-to-export ratios. But there were substantial differences in performance among groups of countries. The non-oil exporting nations benefited from vigorous export growth, which was accompanied by a partial recovery of export prices. This activity was stronger among Asian manufacturing exporters than others. The Saharan African countries suffered from a rise in output below the population growth, causing further erosion in their standard of living. Meanwhile, the economies of oil exporting countries remained stagnant, reflecting the continuing adjustments to the decline in oil export earnings.

International Economy Accords. Overall, world trade expanded by 5.7 percent in 1987 and by 4.5 percent in the first half of 1988. The recent accords on the international economy by the group of seven have in part contributed to this positive record. On February 22, 1987, in "The Louvre Accord," the finance ministers of the six major industrial countries of Canada, France, the Federal Republic of Germany, Japan, the United Kingdom, and the United States agreed at the Palais du Louvre in Paris to intensify efforts at economic policy coordination to promote more balanced, low-inflationary economic growth and to reduce existing imbalances. They further agreed to cooperate to foster stability of exchange rates around current levels.

At the Venice Economic Summit on June 8–10, 1987, in Venice, Italy, the heads of governments of seven major industrial countries agreed to strengthen the surveillance of their economies by using coordinated economic indicators, by developing medium-term objectives, and by continuously reviewing and testing current economic trends to determine the course required for remedial actions. Further, in the Toronto Economic Meeting on June 21, 1988, the heads of state of seven major industrial countries affirmed the need for resisting protectionism and supporting an open, multilateral trading system. They welcomed progress in the area of exchange rate stability, and agreed to help the poorest developing countries to resume sustained growth.

Despite the progress, it appears that industrialized nations have failed to present a specific agenda and program to address the needs of the poorest countries. Most international declarations and communiques point to the problems but present no remedies. The interaction among the governments of the major industrial countries address the specific needs of the major seven in relationship to world affairs, but fail to recognize the long-term economic strategy needed for the small, low-income developing countries and those heavily indebted, middle-income countries.

The low-income, developing countries lack the basic infrastructure to sustain economic growth. The middle-income countries, on the other hand, are economically prudent, but have borrowed so heavily from private sectors that the existing debts have constrained their economic agenda and progress. In either case, further deterioration in these markets, in turn, would hamper world economic progress and have a direct affect on international banking as debtor countries begin to fail once again to repay their loan obligations. The outcome would have a negative effect on the performance of multinational banks around the world and those involved in U.S. banking activities.

Internal Factors

The success of foreign banks in the United States in the 1990s will depend, to a large extent, on the internal factors that constitute U.S. domestic strength. Unquestionably, the evolution of international banking and foreign investments in the 1970s and 1980s was shaped by a host of complex and interrelated factors that will remain unmatched. But its continued viability is dependent on the cooperation and communication links between foreign and U.S. banks, and the extent to which expansionary moves may jeopardize the national sovereignty of the United States. Five internal factors provide clues to the future of foreign banks in the United States.

Confidence in Banking. The structure of the American banking system has changed significantly since the mid-1970s. Over the past ten years, the number of banking organizations has declined considerably, while the share of banking assets controlled by the largest banks has increased sharply. Bank ownership has changed hands more frequently and foreign investment in U.S. financial markets has intensified. At the same time, banks have expanded beyond traditional geographical borders, becoming involved more in related nonbanking activities (real estate, trusts, insurance, and securities); and differences between commercial banks and thrift institutions have diminished.

Structural changes have affected the operating efficiency of banks, causing changes in costs, pricing, and, subsequently, profits. The changes in costs were attributed to the changes in size and market demand for different types of services. The increase in costs, in turn, contributed to the increase in the number of bank mergers and acquisitions, as unprofitable and inefficient banks were forced to seek partners to become competitive in providing financial services. These mergers and acquisitions, along with the increase in foreign investments in banking offices, consequently caused increases in the aggregate concentration of economic resources in banking. Between 1976 and 1988, the number of banks declined by 8 percent from 14,399 to 13,122, a net decrease of 1,277 banks, while their assets quadrupled. Of the banks that failed since 1976, only 41 percent actually ceased operations.[11] Most failed banks were acquired by other institutions, under the supervision of the FDIC.

A recent, disturbing event is the unprecedented crisis of confidence in savings and loan institutions (S&Ls) and the reaction of depositors to this situation. Within the first quarter of 1989, nearly $10 billion has been withdrawn from thrift institutions and channeled to commercial banks and money market mutual funds. A study reveals that nearly 1,000 marginal S&Ls are in danger of foundering in the next five years.[12] In 1988 alone, 350 S&Ls faced seizure under the Bank Board plan and the FDIC took control of 222 thrifts that were insolvent, for an estimated bailout of $100 billion.[13]

Whether the S&L crisis will spread to banks is a concern to various experts. It is certain that the number of S&Ls will decrease by 5 to 10 percent and a good proportion will be acquired by foreign entities or institutions with foreign banking affiliations. As the crisis of confidence in domestic banking management increases, the probability of foreign banks' participation in domestic banking also intensifies.

Budget and Trade Deficits. Despite vast improvements in the U.S. trade picture in 1988, many analysts see few signs that the gap will shrink much further. The trade deficit for 1988 narrowed to $137.5 billion, almost a 10 percent reduction from 1987; but most of the improvements came during the first half of the year. Exports grew a stunning 26 percent in 1988, while imports continued their steady climb, rising by 8 percent. A disturbing factor was the reversal of the declining trend of the first half with an unusual rise in the second half. For the month of December, imports reached a record $41.09 billion, leaving the month with trade deficits of $12 billion.[14]

The reason for the climb, in part, was the rise in the price of petroleum imports and, in part, the general increase in demand for imported seasonal merchandise. The December figure also revealed that the United States improved its trade deficits over the previous month, with Canada, Western Europe, and the newly industrialized countries (Singapore, Hong Kong, Taiwan, and South Korea). However, on an individual basis, the deficits with Japan and South Korea increased during the same period.

The December increases in trade figures overshadowed improvements in the merchandise trade deficit in 1988, which had narrowed for the first time since 1980 (see table 10.2). To combat the trade deficits, a combination of factors is essential. First, the dollar exchange rate should remain low (see table 10.3). Second, a substantial improvement should be made in upgrading the quality of U.S. manufactured products and also in raising the productivity of U.S. factories to around 90 percent of capacity. During the past ten years, American consumers have become acquainted with the quality of foreign-made products and have shown signs that they are willing to pay a higher price for more durable merchandise. The bias against foreign products is softening.

The federal budget deficit should also continue to decrease by a moderate rate. A decline would further stabilize the value of the U.S. dollar and

Table 10.2
U.S. Merchandise Trade Deficits
(Billions of U.S. Dollars)

	1984	1985	1986	1987	1988
Canada	16.6	17.8	15.0	13.8	14.8
EEC[a]	11.5	20.8	25.2	22.9	12.7
Japan	33.9	46.6	59.1	57.1	53.1
NICs[b]	30.2	33.4	37.3	44.8	37.9
OPEC[c]	13.0	11.3	9.1	13.2	9.2
Other	0.5	0.7	6.4	6.4	1.4
World	105.7	130.6	152.1	158.2	129.1

Source: United States International Trade Commission,
International Economic Review, April 1989,
p. 22.
[a] European Economic Community includes:
Belgium, Denmark, France, Greece, Ireland,
Italy, Luxemburg, the Netherlands, Portugal,
Spain, the United Kingdom, and West Germany.
[b] Newly industrialized countries include:
Brazil, Hong Kong, Mexico, Singapore, South
Korea, and Taiwan.
[c] Organization of Petroleum Exporting Countries
includes: Algeria, Ecuador, Gabon, Indonesia,
Iran, Iraq, Kuwait, Libya, Nigeria, Qatar,
Saudi Arabia, the U.A.E., and Venezuela.

interest rates for more sustained economic growth. The continuation of the Gramm-Rudman-Hollings Balanced Budget Act will provide the necessary regulatory force to reduce the deficit, but the key to effectiveness is the speed at which the reduction will occur. A $25 billion reduction would wipe out the deficit in five or six years, a contribution that would have an immediate positive impact on the market interest rate and in fueling the economy as a whole.

Bank Regulation. Banking deregulation served financial institutions well by establishing a more competitive framework and reducing the artificial barriers created by previous regulations. But deregulation failed to achieve its ultimate goal of a more sound and efficient banking environment because the regulatory organizations governing these institutions were not reformed to the new climate surrounding the banks and thrift institutions. The separation of the regulatory authorities for commercial banks from

Table 10.3
Index of Weighted Average Exchange Value of U.S. Dollars Against Currencies of Other G-10 Countries and Switzerland

1979	88.09	1984	138.19
1980	87.39	1985	143.01
1981	102.94	1986	112.22
1982	116.57	1987	96.94
1983	125.34	1988	95.28*

Source: Board of Governors of the Federal Reserve System, **Federal Reserve Bulletin**, December 1982, 1985, and 1988.
Note: G-10 countries consist of: Belgium, Denmark, France, Greece, Ireland, Italy, Luxemburg, the Netherlands, the United Kingdom, and West Germany.
* Estimate, based on May to October 1988 data.

those for thrift institutions created difficulty in coordination and establishing harmony among activities of these institutions. In the past, the focus of attention was devoted to commercial banks under the Federal Reserve and FDIC authorities. The Federal Home Loan Bank Board (FHLBB), the governing body of thrift institutions, especially savings and loans, failed to protect thrifts because of poor judgments, causing a crisis that never would have occurred if there were stronger check and balance guidelines and inspections.

Table 10.4
U.S. Budget Deficits and Surpluses
(Billions of U.S. Dollars)

1950	-3.1	1985	-212.3
1960	0.3	1986	-220.7
1970	-2.8	1987	-149.7
1980	-73.8	1988	-140.5

Source: United States Department of Commerce, **Survey of Current Business**, January 1988; and **Statistical Abstract of the United States**, 1988.

The crisis of confidence in banks' management raised questions about the future of the banking industry in the United States. Legislators, as well as some bankers, have called for reregulation to provide better control of the activities of banks and thrifts and to minimize bad management judgments. In fact, what is needed is not reregulation, but centralization of banking and thrifts under the supervisory authorities of the Federal Reserve and FDIC. The elimination of FHLBB and other agencies with banking supervisory functions is essential for more efficient and uniform inspections. Foreign banks and affiliated institutions should also become subject to the same rules and inspection criteria as domestic-owned banks. Any mismanagement by American bankers provides an opportunity for foreign banks to fill the gap created by the crisis of confidence. Whether the U.S. government monetary authorities would reverse the course of action, to slow or impede foreign banks' growth pattern under present circumstances, is doubtful.

FOREIGN BANKS' CURRENT STATUS
AND PROJECTIONS

One of the key indicators of the future progress of foreign banks in the United States is the success of these institutions in utilization of their lending share of the U.S. market. The current status presents a mirror of future success. Based on C&I loans outstanding, foreign banks' lending share of the U.S. market reached an all-time high of 27.5 percent of the total U.S. market in 1988. The rise is a 10 percent increase since 1980 and is more than triple the level of the mid-1970's. A study by the research office of the *American Banker*, a daily financial services newspaper, reveals that business loans grew nearly five times faster at U.S. offices of foreign banks than at American-owned banks in 1988.[15]

The reason behind the surge of business loan activities of foreign-owned, U.S.-based multinational banks is the sell-off of substantial portions of business loan portfolios by a large number of U.S. banks. This sell-off is the result of American banking institutions' need for liquidity as they attempt to better manage, restructure, and bring to balance their assets-liabilities accounts. The chief buyers have been Japanese banks. In 1988, Japanese banks led the surge in business loans and accounted for 77 percent of the growth in business loans by all foreign banks in the United States.

Since 1980, the three countries of Canada, Japan, and the United Kingdom together provided 60 to 68 percent of the total business lending posted by all foreign banks in the United States. While both Canada's and the United Kingdom's share declined since 1982, the Japanese share doubled. In 1988, the Japanese lending share swelled to 50 percent of all foreign banks' business lending and 13.9 percent of all U.S. banks' business lending.

What may signal the future course of action is not the size of foreign-owned U.S. banks' market lending share, per se, but the dimension and elements that are responsible for this progress. For example, foreign banks' business lending share increased by 2.5 percent from 22.3 percent in 1986 to 24.8 percent in 1987. The Japanese share of this market increased at the same time by 2.6 percent. Similarly in 1988, the increase in the Japanese share of U.S. banks' lending market increased faster than all foreign banks' shares—2.9 percent for Japanese banks versus 2.7 percent for all other banks, indicating Japan's progress at the expense of others. It is expected that the trend will continue without much change into the next decade.

Foreign banks' progress was not limited to business loans alone but was also supported by progress in deposits and assets categories. From 1982 to 1988, foreign banks' U.S. deposits and assets, as a proportion of total U.S. banks' deposits and assets, rose from 11.2 percent to 16.2 percent in deposits and from 15.5 percent to 21.8 percent in assets. While this increase may be attributed in large part to Japanese banks' aggressive marketing approach, other industrialized countries also showed formidable advancement.

Crystal Ball Projection

Due to the complexities of modern economic life, an accurate projection of the foreign banking status in the year 2000 is technically impossible except under some guided assumptions. Two scenarios may occur. First, based on historical trends, a mild or moderate progress may prevail. Under this scenario, the foreign banks' expansionary movement will continue without any extensive change in direction, but with more emphasis on retail banking operations by the industrialized and progressive wing of foreign banks. The system would continue to serve its paramount functions of providing trade financing, foreign exchange trading, and money market activities. Corporate and retail banking would remain secondary but progressive. By the end of this century, the foreign banks' lending, deposits, and assets share of the U.S. market is expected to reach 30, 18, and 28 percent, respectively.

The second scenario is based on the more progressive approach adopted by these institutions in the past five years. Under these circumstances, corporate banking and money market activities would supersede trade financing and foreign exchange activities, with special emphasis on retail banking and other bank-related activities. The area of development and expansion would be in security underwriting, venture capital, and security trading, given the statutory limitation guidelines of the Federal Reserve Board. On January 18, 1989, the board broke down a wall that had separated banking and securities, allowing banking companies to raise money for corporations in the bond market.

Banking companies have also asked the Federal Reserve to allow them to underwrite and sell new issues of corporate stocks. The Federal Reserve has withheld a decision on the ruling for a year, pending a review of the banks'

Table 10.5
Status of Foreign Banks in the U.S. Market
(Percentage)

	1982	1984	1986	1987	1988
Business Loans					
U.S.-Owned U.S. Banks	78.5	79.6	77.7	75.2	72.5
Foreign-Owned U.S. Banks	21.5	20.4	22.3	24.8	27.5
By Country:					
Canada	2.4	2.2	2.4	2.4	2.2
Japan	7.2	7.4	11.0	8.4	13.9
United Kingdom	3.5	3.3	2.5	2.5	2.5
Other	8.4	7.5	9.0	8.9	8.9
Assets and Deposits as % of Total U.S. Banks					
Deposits	11.2	14.9	14.2	16.3	16.2
Assets	15.5	17.7	18.4	20.9	21.8

Source: **American Banker**, Special Reports, 1985-89.

activities. Given the prospects in the security market and convenience of retail banking operations, there is a strong possibility that these two elements will further boost foreign banks' activities in the United States and, in fact, strongly encourage expansion in related banking services. In this situation, the foreign banks' lending, deposits, and assets shares of the U.S. market may reach an unprecedented 40 percent, 24 percent, and 30 percent, respectively, by the year 2000. It is uncertain whether U.S. banking authorities, legislators, and banks management would remain silent to such an outcome. However, it is certain that the legislation governing foreign banks would be more restricted and scrutinizing than ever before.

Among the participating banks, the foreign banks from industrialized countries will play a key role in the integration and future developmental cooperation between the U.S. and foreign banking entities. Among the progressive wing of the foreign banks, four countries deserve special attention. These key players are Japan, Italy, Israel, and South Korea. Japanese banking investments in the United States will continue as long as the trade deficits between the two nations favor Japanese manufacturers. Similarly,

South Korea's recent surge in trade surplus with the United States demands actions to facilitate trade financing and corporate banking services. Italy's and Israel's progressive banking practices, despite second-grade trade relationships with the United States, have left no doubt of the intention of the two to establish strong banking presences.

Japanese-U.S. Banking Ventures

The United States and Japan hold significantly different economic views. U.S. notions of economic freedom and growth stem from Adam Smith's view that consumption derives from growth. The U.S. concept of a fair and open market encourages competition. Production entices internal consumption. Japan, on the other hand, concentrates its efforts to support industries that produce sophisticated products with fast growth potential. This effort requires that Japan coordinate, protect, and subsidize the designated industries and markets for exportation in order to generate additional funds for further investments.

The Japanese economic system sees growth through exportation as a means of improving in its national economy. The economic foundation was built up after World War II through devotion to high-quality, low-profit margin exports. What was once a country that learned management and production techniques from the United States is now a country that consistently outmanages and outproduces American industry across the board.

The yen has been surging against the dollar for more than four years. In the early 1980s, the yen traded against the dollar at ¥355 to $1. In 1989, it is ¥140 to $1, a gain of nearly 153 percent in value. The U.S. government is trying to lower the value of U.S. currency in order to reduce the American trade deficit. Just as the weak dollar has made American exports cheap, the strong yen has made Japanese products expensive in foreign markets. But Japan successfully counters variation in the foreign exchange rate by spurring its domestic demand to continue growth, and producing quality products at a marginal cost to retain international markets, specifically the U.S. domestic markets. As a result, Japan has successfully maintained a large trade surplus with the United States. However, in the first half of 1989, sales have been leveling off for the first time, due to large, unsold inventories.

Japanese Influence on U.S. Financial Markets. The Japanese have followed the same strategy to expand in U.S. banking and financial markets that they used to conquer the U.S. automobile market. The essence of their strategy was to concentrate on a segment of the market, and develop high volumes with low profit margins. At first, the banking target was California's market. As of December 1988, Japanese banks owned 13 percent of California banking assets and business lending, 4 percent of the state's retail banking, and four of the ten largest California banks. Similar success has been observed in regard to the state of Hawaii, and the expansion is spreading into other markets.

Overall, Japanese banks control 55 percent of all foreign banks' assets, 13.9 percent of foreign banks' lending share of the U.S. market, 18 of the top 38 foreign banks in the United States with more than $1 billion in business loans outstanding, and 122 offices or nearly 18 percent of all the foreign banking offices in the United States.

With their success in the banking industry, the Japanese have turned their attention to U.S. securities and real estate markets. Their strategy is aimed at becoming one of the top brokerage houses on Wall Street and at the same time developing broad diversification in financial markets. The long-term goal is to sell financial products to U.S. customers. In both banking and security markets, the Japanese have begun to purchase U.S. firms in order to make inroads in the U.S. domestic market without changing the managerial operation of the firms. By using American management, those who understand the intricacies of the U.S. system, the Japanese guarantee daily operation without interruption. There was no need to import managerial skill and know-how, nor is there a need for temporary disruption.

Perhaps the area where the Japanese have had the biggest influence in the United States has been in the U.S. bond market. The United States currently relies heavily on Japanese purchases of U.S. government bonds to fund the huge budget deficit. Since 1985, the top four Japanese security firms have generated as much as $20 billion a day in bond holding and sales, acquiring and managing 20 percent of the long-term U.S. government bonds trading and 5 to 10 percent of all trading on the New York Stock Exchange.[16] In 1988, the Japanese multinational corporations started to broaden their conservative low-margin strategy into the more dynamic areas of mergers, leveraged buy-outs, and venture capital.

Similarly, interest in real estate ownership has recently intensified. As a result of the increase in the value of the yen, U.S. prime property has become relatively cheap compared with similar property in Japan. From 1985 to 1989, Japanese ventures in the U.S. real estate market ranged from $4 billion to $10 billion per year in major cities across the nation. Prime property from the portfolio of Japanese purchases include a Bank of America property in San Francisco for $500 million, a portion of Citicorp Tower in New York City for $670 million, and Westin Hotel and Resorts with a price tag of $1.5 billion. In March 1989, Sony negotiated to purchase MCA, a holding company that owns Universal Studios and a large prime property in California, for an undisclosed price, estimated at near $2 billion.

Despite Japanese inroads in the real estate market in the United States, the Japanese fascination with banking and related areas is continuing. In February 1988, the Bank of Tokyo agreed to acquire the Union Bank of Los Angeles from Standard Chartered PLC of London for $750 million. Its rival, Fuji Bank, acquired equity investment in Heller International Corporation, a Chicago-based commercial finance company, for $425 million. In March 1989, Fuji Bank began a joint venture with Wolfensohn, an investment banker, to provide strategic financial advice to U.S. and Japanese corporations in regard to acquisitions of other companies in the United States and Japan. Other such joint ventures include Nikko Securities Company with the Blackstone Group, Nomura Securities Company with Wasserstein Perella & Co., and Yamaichi Securities with Lodestar Partners.[17] These actions signal Japanese interest and intention to broaden participation in financial institutions, and indicate the future direction in which Japanese banks consider growth-oriented markets.

Future Outcome. Given the current Japanese $361 billion banking investments and $100 billion related financial acquisitions, it is certain that the trend will continue upward. The question and concern is related to the velocity and direction of future expansionary movements. Japanese banking assets currently account for 9 percent of total U.S. banking assets. Based on current growth, the Japanese banking assets should reach 15 percent of the total U.S. banking assets, and 25 percent of the commercial bank assets in California, before the year 2000. Considering investments in securities and the real estate market, total investment should then reach three-fourths of one trillion dollars, an amount unprecedented by any country at any time in the history of civilization.

More moderate and wiser forecasting points to increased Japanese participation in the retail banking market and moderate growth in overall assets and deposits. The Japanese style of management has never been confrontational in the U.S. market. Their banking investment patterns always followed the situation wherein little competition or genuine interest existed among American investors because of regulatory limitations or the pricing structure of the acquisition. Most acquisitions reveal that Japanese acquirers paid a fair or above-market price, and also supplied additional capital to stimulate the troubled institutions. There has been a strong interest in joint ventures and cooperative programs between Japanese and American counterparts in the areas of student loans, real estate, and projects related to the financing and development of roads, bridges, and shopping centers. A cooperative effort should be made between state and local governments and Japanese financial entities in the financing of community projects. This form of developmental activity would benefit both countries in forming better business relationships.

The Japanese now realize that their position as the world's largest creditor requires direct participation in international financial affairs through soft loans, donations, and the opening of its boarders to more competitive environments. In fact, in the past few years, the foundation for this strategic decision has already begun as Japan's contribution for construction of various projects around the world has surpassed $200 million. The projects include a $50 million opera house in Cairo, Egypt; a $20 million trade center in Beijing, China; and a $6 million computer center for computerized air traffic control in Manila, Philippines.

Other signs of the opening of the Japanese market to U.S. commercial banks is the recent success of Citicorp (Citibank of New York) in capturing part of Japan's rapidly expanding credit market. At present, the Japanese maintain 0.7 credit cards per capita. This number is expected to increase to 1.7 credit cards per capita in the near future. Citicorp's strategy is to capture a large proportion of this expanding market. With the Japanese population at 120 million, Citibank hopes to issue as many as one million new credit cards. To pave the way for future expansion, Citibank has joined forces with the Dai-Ichi Kangyo Bank of Japan in operating automated teller machines (ATMs), and has gained customer access to 1588 ATMs.[18]

Within the next 10 to 20 years, Japan's financial market will be forced to move toward more deregulated environments. Upon opening the borders to foreign banks and other financial organizations, the circumstances will automatically invite a more competitive environment within the Japanese market. In addition, the fear of losing the domestic market to foreign competitors may dampen their rapid expansionary movement in other international markets. As a result, the current rapid growth of the Japanese infiltration of the American market may slow and even decline by the year 1995 and thereafter.

The decline in the U.S. budget and trade deficits would also have an impact on lowering the market rate of interest and restoring the real value of the dollar, and thereby may contribute to lowering some of the attractiveness of the U.S. financial markets. Overall, the United States needs to become more familiar with the idea of globalization of the world's financial markets, and must also adopt a long-term economic philosophy to regain its momentum and position as the world's largest creditor.

NOTES

1. Henry C. Wallich, "Perspectives on Foreign Banks in the United States," Member, Board of Governors of the Federal Reserve System, Conference on Foreign Banking in the United States—the Economic, Legal, and Regulatory Environment, Washington, D.C., March 1, 1982, pp. 3–4.

2. Federal Deposit Insurance Corporation, "Basis for Corporation Approval, B-27," August 28, 1975, and "Re: The Sumitomo Bank of California, San Francisco, California, Basis for Corporation Approval, B-45," October 25, 1977.

3. United States Senate, "Foreign Takeovers of United States Banks," study by the staff of the Federal Reserve Boards, Committee on Banking, Housing and Urban Affairs, Washington, D.C., July, 1980, pp. 1–75.

4. "Foreign Banks in the United States," *American Banker*, Special Report, Vol. 154, No. 44, March 6, 1989, p. 1A.

5. United States Senate, "Foreign Takeovers of United States Banks," pp. 24–33.

6. James V. Houpt, "International Trends for U.S. Banks and Banking Markets," Staff Study No. 156, Board of Governors of the Federal Reserve System, May 1988, p. 25.

7. James V. Houpt, "Foreign Ownership of U.S. Banks: Trends and Effects," *Journal of Bank Research*, Vol. 14, No. 2, Summer 1983; and United States Senate, "Foreign Takeovers of U.S. Banks," pp. 3–18.

8. "Foreign Banks in the United States," *American Banker*, Vol. 153, No. 36, February 23, 1988, p. 2A.

9. Board of Governors of the Federal Reserve, *Federal Reserve Bulletin*, Vol. 75, No. 1, January 1989, p. A57; and James V. Houpt, "International Trends for U.S. Banks and Banking Markets," pp. 7 and 11.

10. International Monetary Fund, "Developments in the World Economy," *Annual Report*, 1988, pp. 1–6.

11. Board of Governors of the Federal Reserve System, "Trends in Banking Structure Since the Mid-1970s," *Federal Reserve Bulletin*, Vol. 75, No. 3, March 1989, pp. 123–124.

12. "Study Says, 1000 Marginal S&Ls Could Collapse," *American Banker*, Vol. 154, No. 26, February 7, 1989, p. 2.

13. "FDIC Takes Control of 222 S&Ls," *American Banker*, Vol. 154, No. 27, February 8, 1989, pp. 1 and 16.

14. United States Department of Commerce, *Survey of Current Business*, 1987–88 issues; and "Trade Picture Isn't Improving, Analysts Say," *Wall Street Journal*, February 21, 1989, p. A2.

15. "Foreign Banks in U.S. Boost Loan Purchases," *American Banker*, Vol. 153, No. 36, February 23, 1988, p. 1; and "Foreign Banks in the United States," *American Banker*, Vol. 154, No. 44, March 6, 1989, p. 1.

16. "The Big Four Japanese Brokerage Houses," *Business Week*, September 7, 1987, p. 42.

17. "Fiji Bank Sets Joint Advisory Venture with Wolfensohn, an Investment Banker," *Wall Street Journal*, March 14, 1989, p. A6; and "Bank of Tokyo Unit to Acquire California Bank," *Wall Street Journal*, February 17, 1988, p. 2.

18. "Citibank Brandishes Gold Citicard to Charge into Japan's Retail Front," *American Banker*, Vol. 152, No. 130, July 6, 1987, p. 1.

Selected Bibliography

Agmon, Tamir, and Donald Lessard. "Investor Recognition of Corporate International Diversification," *Journal of Finance*, September 1977, pp. 1049–1055.

Ahorani, Yair. *The Foreign Investment Decision Process*. Boston: Harvard Graduate School of Business Administration, Division of Research, 1966.

"AID Statement of Organization, Functions, and Procedures," *AID Handbook 17*, Trans. Memo No. 17:402. August 26, 1987.

Aliber, Robert. "A Theory of Foreign Direct Investment," in Charles P. Kindleberger (ed.), *The International Corporation*. Cambridge, Mass.: MIT Press, 1970, pp. 17–34.

_____. "Toward a Theory of International Banking," *Economic Review*, Federal Reserve Bank of San Francisco, Spring 1976, pp. 5–8.

American Bankers Association. *A Banker's Guide to Financing Exports*. New York: Credit Policy Committee, 1966.

Anderson, Gerard H. "Current Developments in the Regulation of International Banking," *Economic Review*, Federal Reserve Bank of Cleveland, January 1980, pp. 1–15.

Arpan, Jeffrey S., Edward B. Flowers, and David A. Ricks. "Foreign Direct Investment in the United States: The State of Knowledge in Research," *Journal of International Business Studies*, Spring–Summer 1981, pp. 137–154.

Arvan, Alice. "Those Fabulous Japanese Banks," *Bankers Monthly*, Vol. 105, No. 1, January 1988.

Asian Development Bank. *Annual Report*, Singapore, 1985–87.

Averyt, William F. "Canadian and Japanese Foreign Investment Screening," *Columbia Journal of World Business*, Vol. 22, No. 4, Winter 1986.

Baker, James C., and John K. Ryan, Jr. "An Evaluation of U.S. Federal Regulation of Foreign Bank Operations," *Issues in Bank Regulation*, Vol. 10, No. 4, Spring 1987, pp. 28–35.

"Bank Holding Company Act Amendment of 1970," Public Law 91-607, H.R. 6778, December 31, 1970.

"Bank Holding Company Act Amendments of 1956," Public Law 511, H.R. 6227, May 9, 1956.

"Bank of Tokyo Unit to Acquire California Bank," *Wall Street Journal*, February 17, 1988.

Bayalic, Arthur E. "The Documentation Dilemma in International Trade," *Columbia Journal of World Business*, Spring 1976, pp. 15–22.

"The Big Four Japanese Brokerage Houses," *Business Week*, September 7, 1987.

Bloch, Henry S. "Export Financing Emerging as a Major Policy Problem," *Columbia Journal of World Business*, Fall 1976, pp. 86–95.

Board of Governors of the Federal Reserve System. "Data Series on Foreign-Owned U.S. Banks," *Federal Reserve Bulletin*, Vol. 60, No. 10, 1974, pp. 741–742.

———. *Federal Reserve Bulletin*, various issues, 1970–89.

———. "Foreign Branches of U.S. Banks: Balance Sheet Data," *Federal Reserve Bulletin*, Vol. 75, No. 1, January 1989, Table 3.14, p. A57.

———. *Regulation K: International Banking Operations*, 12 CFR 211, October 24, 1985.

———. "Regulation K: International Banking Operations," *Press Release*, Docket No. R-0610, August 12, 1987.

———. "Statement of Policy on Supervision and Regulation of Foreign Bank Holding Companies," *Press Release*, February 23, 1979.

———. *Structural Data for U.S. Offices of Foreign Banks*, 1980–1988.

———. "Trends in Banking Structure Since the Mid-1970s," *Federal Reserve Bulletin*, Vol. 75, No. 3, March 1989.

Brady, Donald L., and William O. Bearden. "The Effect of Managerial Attitudes on Alternative Export Methods," *Journal of International Business Studies*, Winter 1979, pp. 79–94.

"Britain in the European Community," Central Office of Information Reference Pamphlet No. 73/86, London, July 1986.

Brouillette, Geoff. "Foreign Subsidiaries Are the Fastest Growing Segment of California Banking," *American Banker*, Vol. 140, No. 148, July 30, 1975.

Buckley, Peter J., and Mark Casson. *The Future of the Multinational Enterprise*. London: Macmillan Publishing Company, 1976.

Calvet, A. Louis. "A Synthesis of Foreign Direct Investment Theories and Theories of the Multinational Firm," *Journal of International Business Studies*, Spring–Summer 1981, pp. 43–59.

Cargill, Thomas F., and Gillian G. Garcia. *Financial Deregulation and Monetary Control*. Stanford, Calif.: Hoover Institution Press, Stanford University, 1982.

Cates, David C., and Frederick C. Weigold. "Foreign Banks Are Cracking the Facade of U.S. Banking," *Fortune*, August 28, 1978.

Caves, Richard E. "International Corporations: The Industrial Economics of Foreign Investments," *Economica*, February 1971, pp. 1–27.

Celi, Louis J., and I. James Czechowicz. *Export Financing, A Handbook of Sources and Techniques*. Morristown, N.J.: Financial Executives Foundation, 1985.

Chew, Ralph H. "Export Trading Companies: Current Legislation, Regulation, and

Commercial Bank Involvement," *Columbia Journal of World Business*, Winter 1981, pp. 36–47.

Cho, Kang Rae, Suresh Krishnan, and Douglas Nigh. "The State of Foreign Banking Presence in the United States," paper presented to the Academy of International Business, London, England, 1986.

"Citibank Brandishes Gold Citicard to Charge into Japan's Retail Front," *American Banker*, Vol. 152, No. 130, July 6, 1987.

Commission of the European Communities. European Communities Information Publications, 1987.

_____. "Steps to European Unity," European Documentation Series, 1985.

Crane, Dwight B., and Samuel L. Hayes III. "The Evolution of International Banking Competition and Its Implications for Regulation," *Journal of Bank Research*, Spring 1983, pp. 39–58.

Cumming, Christine M. "Federal Deposit Insurance and Deposit at Foreign Branches of U.S. Banks," *Quarterly Review*, Federal Reserve Bank of New York, Autumn 1985, pp. 30–38.

Czinkota, Michael R., and George Tesar. *Export Management: An International Context*. New York: Praeger Publishers, 1982.

Dame, Robert F. (ed.). *Foreign Acquisition of U.S. Banks*. Richmond, Va.: The Comptroller of the Currency, Administration of National Banks, and Robert F. Dame, Inc., 1981.

Davidson, William H. "The Location of Foreign Direct Investment Activity: Country Characteristics and Experience Effects," *Journal of International Business Studies*, Fall 1980, pp. 9–22.

Deak, Nicholas L., and JoAnne C. Celusak. *International Banking*. New York: New York Institute of Finance, Prentice-Hall, Inc., 1984.

"Depository Institutions Deregulation and Monetary Control Act of 1980," Public Law 96-221, H.R. 4986, March 31, 1980.

"Direct Eximbank Loan to Continue," *Journal of Commerce and Commercial*, Vol. 365, August 12, 1985.

Dufey, Gunter. "Institutional Constraints and Incentives on International Portfolio Investment," *International Portfolio Investment*, U.S. Department of the Treasury, OASIA, 1975.

_____, and Ian H. Giddy. "Innovation in the International Financial Markets," *Journal of International Business Studies*, Fall 1981, pp. 33–51.

Dun, Angus, and Martin Knight. *Export Financing*. London: Euromoney Publications, 1982.

Dunning, John H. "The Determinants of International Production," *Oxford Economic Papers*, November 1973, pp. 289–336.

_____, and Alan M. Rugman. "The Influence of Hymer's Dissertation on the Theory of Foreign Direct Investment," *American Economic Review*, May 1985, pp. 228–232.

Edwards, Franklin R., and Jack Zwick. "Foreign Banks in the United States: Activities and Regulatory Issues," Research Paper No. 80, Columbia University, New York, January 22, 1975.

Eiteman, David K., and Arthur I. Stonehill. *Multinational Business Finance*. Reading, Mass.: Addison-Wesley Publishing Company, 1986.

Ely, E. S. "Dawn of New Age," *Institutional Investor*, March 1987.

Emden, Paul H. *Money Powers of Europe in the Nineteenth and Twentieth Centuries*. London: Garland Publishing, Inc., 1983, pp. 1–63.

Eng, Maxima. *U.S. Overseas Banking—Its Past and Future*. New York: Business Research Institute, St. John's University, September 1970.

European Communities. *Steps to European Unity*, Catalogue No. CB-42-84-250-EN-C, Luxemburg, 1985.

"Eximbank Aid Slashed by Congress," *Journal of Commerce and Commercial*, Vol. 366, December 16, 1985.

"Eximbank Target of OMB Knife—Is the Threat Serious?" *United States Banker*, Vol. 96, March 1985.

"Export-Import Bank Makes Policy Changes to Help Boost U.S. Exports," *Journal of Commerce and Commercial*, Vol. 371, March 6, 1987.

Export-Import Bank of the United States. *Annual Report*, 1987.

———. "Engineering Multiplier Program," The Office of Public Affairs, Washington, D.C., 1984.

———. "Exim News," The Office of Public Affairs, Washington, D.C., March 31, 1987.

———. "Eximbank Programs and Small Business," The Office of Public Affairs, Washington, D.C., 1984.

———. "Eximbank Programs Summary," The Office of Public Affairs, Washington, D.C., 1984.

———. "Export-Import Bank: Financing for American Exports—Support for American Jobs," Washington, D.C., 1980.

———. "Working Capital Guarantee Programs: The Basics," Washington, D.C., 1984.

"FDIC Takes Control of 222 S&Ls," *American Banker*, Vol. 154, No. 27, February 8, 1989.

Federal Deposit Insurance Corporation. "Basis for Corporation Approval, B-27," Washington, D.C., August 28, 1975.

———. "Re: The Sumitomo Bank of California, San Francisco, California, Basis for Corporation Approval, B-45," October 25, 1977.

———. "Statement of the Federal Bank Regulatory Agencies Concerning the International Banking Act of 1978," *News Release*, PR-114-78, November 16, 1978.

Federal Financial Institutional Examination Council. *Country Exposure Lending Survey December 1982*, Washington, D.C., December 1983.

"Federal Reserve Act," Public Law No. 43, S. 2689, December 22, 1913.

Federal Reserve Bank of Boston. *Key Issues in International Banking*, Boston, 1977.

Feis, Herbert. *Europe: The World Banker, 1870–1914*. New York: W. W. Norton and Company, 1965.

Fieleke, Norman S. "The Growth of U.S. Banking Abroad: An Analytical Survey," *Key Issues in International Banking*, Federal Reserve Bank of Boston, Conference Proceedings in International Banking, October 1977, pp. 9–40.

"Fight Fire with Fire—Treasury Department Proposes $300 Million Export Credit Fund," *United States Banker*, Vol. 97, April 1986.

"Fiji Bank Sets Joint Advisory Venture with Wolfensohn, an Investment Banker," *Wall Street Journal*, March 14, 1989.

"Fiscal 1987 Request Cuts Eximbank Direct Loans," *Aviation Week*, Vol. 124, February 27, 1986.

"Foreign Banks and the Federal Reserve," *Fedpoints 26*, Federal Reserve Bank of New York, August 1982.

"Foreign Banks Complain About Exclusion From State Interstate Banking Laws," *Washington Financial Reports*, Vol. 46, No. 1, January 6, 1986, pp. 5–6.

"Foreign Banks in U.S. Boost Loan Purchases," *American Banker*, Vol. 153, No. 36, February 23, 1988.

"Foreign Banks in the United States," Special Report, *American Banker*, Vol. 154, No. 44, March 6, 1989.

"Foreign Banks in the United States: Foreign Office Roundup and Profitability of Foreign Banks," *American Banker*, Vol. 153, No. 36, February 23, 1988.

Foreign Credit Insurance Association. "The FCIA Bank Letter of Credit Policy," New York, August 1987.

_____. "The FCIA Multi-Buyer Export Credit Insurance Policy," New York, May 1987.

_____. "The FCIA New-to-Export Policy," New York, December 1987.

_____. "The FCIA Operating and Financing Lease Policies," New York, September 1988.

_____. "The FCIA Short-Term Single Buyer Export Credit Insurance Policy," New York, November 1986.

_____. "The Political Risks Policy," New York, June 1987.

_____. "Your Competitive Edge in Selling Overseas," New York, May 1988.

Franko, Lawrence G. "Foreign Direct Investment in Less Developed Countries: Impact on Home Countries," *Journal of International Business Studies*, Winter 1978, pp. 55–65.

Gaynor, Ranon L. "Trends in U.S. Regulation of Foreign Banks," *The Banker*, February 1981, pp. 98–104.

Giddy, Ian H. "The Demise of the Product Cycle Model in International Business Theory," *Columbia Journal of World Business*, Spring 1978, pp. 90–97.

_____. "The Theory and Industrial Organization of International Banking," in Robert G. Hawkins, et al. (eds.), *The Internationalization of Financial Markets and National Economic Policy*, JAI Press, Vol. 3, 1983, pp. 195–243.

Gisselquist, David. *The Political Economics of International Bank Lending*. New York: Praeger Publishers, 1981, Chapters 1–4.

Goddin, C. Stewart, and Steven J. Weiss. "U.S. Banks' Loss of Global Standing," The Office of the Comptroller of the Currency, June 1980.

Gross, Robert. "The Theory of Foreign Direct Investment," *Essays in International Business*, Center for International Business Studies, University of South Carolina, Columbia, December 1981.

Grubel, Herbert. "A Theory of Multinational Banking," *Quarterly Review*, Banca Nazionale del Lavoro, December 1977, pp. 349–363.

Gruson, Michael, and Timothy E. Flanigan. "The Breaux Amendment: A Severe Limitation on Foreign Investments," *Banking Expansion Reporter*, Vol. 6, No. 9, May 4, 1987, pp. 1 and 12–15.

Gruson, Michael, and Jonathan M. Weld. "Nonbanking Activities of Foreign Banks

Operating in the United States," *University of Illinois Law Forum*, Vol. 129, 1980, pp. 129–162.

Hervey, Jack L. "Bankers' Acceptances Revisited," *Economic Perspective*, Federal Reserve Bank of Chicago, May/June 1983, pp. 21–31.

Hooke, A. W. *The International Monetary Fund: Its Evolution, Organization, and Activities*, IMF Pamphlet Series No. 37, 2nd ed., Washington, D.C., 1982.

Houpt, James V. "Foreign Ownership of U.S. Banks: Trends and Effects," *Journal of Bank Research*, Vol. 14, No. 2, Summer 1983.

———. "International Trends for U.S. Banks and Banking Markets," Board of Governors of the Federal Reserve System, Staff Study No. 156, May 1988.

———. "Performance and Characteristics of Edge Corporations," Board of Governors of the Federal Reserve System, January 1981.

Hymer, Stephen. *The International Operations of National Firms: A Study of Direct Foreign Investment*. Cambridge, Mass.: MIT Press, 1976.

Inter-American Development Bank. *Annual Report*, Washington, D.C., 1987.

"International Banking Act of 1978," Public Law 95-369, H.R. 10899, September 17, 1978.

International Chamber of Commerce. *Uniform Customs and Practices for Documentary Credits*, Brochure No. 190 (1974 Revision) and No. 400 (1984 Revision).

International Financial Corporation. *Annual Report*, Washington, D.C., 1988.

International Monetary Fund. *Annual Report*, Washington, D.C., 1988.

———. "Development in the World Economy," *Annual Report*, Chapter 1, 1988, pp. 1–34.

———. *International Financial Statistics*, various issues, 1962–81.

Jacobs, Klaus Peter. "The Development of International and Multinational Banking," *Columbia Journal of World Business*, Vol. 10, No. 4, Winter 1975, pp. 33–39.

"Japanese Banks in California," *Western Banker*, Vol. 79, No. 4, April 1987.

Kennedy, Patrick H. "The Role of Foreign Banks in a Changing U.S. Banking System," *The Banker*, February 1982, pp. 101–103.

Key, Sydney J., and James M. Brundy. "Implementation of the International Banking Act," *Federal Reserve Bulletin*, October 1979, pp. 785–796.

Khambata, Dara M. *The Practice of Multinational Banking*. New York: Quorum Books, 1984.

Khoury, Sarkis J. *Dynamics of International Banking*. New York: Praeger Publishers, 1980.

Kindleberger, Charles P. *American Business Abroad: Six Lectures on Direct Investment*. New Haven: Yale University Press, 1969.

Klopstock, Fred H. "Foreign Banks in the United States: Scope and Growth of Operations," *Monthly Review*, Federal Reserve Bank of New York, June 1973, pp. 140–154.

Korth, Christopher M. "The Evolving Role of U.S. Banks in International Finance," *The Bankers Magazine*, July–August 1980, pp. 68–73.

Kozolchyk, Boris. *Commercial Letters of Credit in the Americas: A Comparative Study of Contemporary Commercial Transaction*. Albany, N.Y.: Matthew Bender Publishing, 1966.

Lees, Francis A., *International Banking and Finance*. New York: Holstead Press, John Wiley and Sons, 1974.

"Letters of Credit: Current Theories and Usages," Commentary, *L.A. Law Review*, No. 39, Winter 1979, pp. 581–622.

Mathis, F. John (ed.). *Offshore Lending by U.S. Commercial Banks*. Philadelphia: Bankers' Association for Foreign Trade, Washington, D.C., and Robert Morris Associates, 1981.

Melton, William C., and Jean M. Mahr. "Bankers Acceptances," *Quarterly Review*, Federal Reserve Bank of New York, Summer 1981, pp. 39–52.

Mintz, Ilse. *Deterioration in the Quality of Foreign Bonds Issued in the United States, 1920–1930*. Washington, D.C.: National Bureau of Economic Research, 1951.

Mirus, Rolf. "A Note on the Choice Between Licensing and Direct Foreign Investment," *Journal of International Business Studies*, Spring–Summer 1980.

Monetary Authority of Singapore. *Annual Report*, 1984–86.

Morgan Guarantee Trust Company. *World Financial Markets*, New York, 1983–1987.

"The 1987 Foreign Banking in America Directory," *Institutional Investor*, Vol. 21, No. 9, September 1987, pp. 303–325; and Vol. 22, No. 9, September 1988, pp. 259–289.

"The 100 Biggest Banks," *Fortune*, Vol. 118, No. 3, August 1, 1988

"The 100 Largest Commercial Banking Companies," *Fortune*, Vol. 117, No. 12, June 6, 1988.

Oppenheim, Peter. *International Banking*, 3rd rev. ed. Washington, D.C.: American Bankers Association, 1979.

Organization for Economic Cooperation and Development. *Activities of OECD in 1987*, report by the secretary general, Paris, 1988.

———. "Costs and Margins in Banking — An International Survey," *Financial Market Trends*, June 1980, pp. 93–108.

Overseas Private Investment Corporation. *Annual Report*, 1987.

———. *Investment Finance Handbook*, Publication 1187, Washington, D.C., 1988.

———. *Investment Insurance Handbook*, Publication 0588, Washington, D.C., 1988.

———. "Overseas Private Investment Corporation," *Programs and Services*, Publication 0688, Washington, D.C., 1988.

Park, Yoon S., and Jack Zwick. *International Banking in Theory and Practice*. Reading, Mass.: Addison-Wesley Publishing Company, 1985.

Polomski, Josephine F. "Voluntary Foreign Credit Restraint Program Spurs Foreign-Based Activities of U.S. Banks," *Business Review*, Federal Reserve Bank of Philadelphia, June 1973, pp. 7–11.

"The Profitability of Insured Commercial Banks in 1987," *Federal Reserve Bulletin*, Vol. 74, No. 7, July 1988.

"Reagan Budget Puts U.S. Loan Programs on Chopping Block," *American Banker*, Vol. 150, No. 25, February 5, 1985.

"Reagan Team Acts to Sway Bankers on Export Credits," *Journal of Commerce and Commercial*, Vol. 367, January 8, 1986.

Ryder, Frank R. "Challenges to the Use of the Documentary Credit in International Trade Transactions," *Columbia Journal of World Business*, Winter 1981, pp. 36–47.

Salehizadeh, Mehdi. "Regulations of Foreign Direct Investment by Host Countries,"

Essays in International Business, Center for International Business Studies, University of South Carolina, Columbia, May 1983.

Schmitthof, Clive. *The Export Trade: The Law and Practice of International Trade*, 4th ed. London: Stevens, 1975.

Shay, Jerome W. "Interstate Banking Restrictions of the International Banking and Bank Holding Company Acts," *Banking Law Journal*, Vol. 97, June–July 1986, pp. 524–566.

"Study Says, 1000 Marginal S&Ls Could Collapse," *American Banker,* Vol. 154, No. 26, February 7, 1989.

Summers, Bruce J. "Foreign Banking in the United States: Movement toward Federal Regulation," *Economic Review*, Federal Reserve Bank of Richmond, January/February 1976, pp. 3–7.

Terrel, Henry S., and Sydney J. Key. "The U.S. Activities of Foreign Banks: An Analytic Survey," *International Finance Discussion Papers*, No. 113, November 1977.

_____. "U.S. Offices of Foreign Banks: The Recent Experience," *International Financial Discussion Papers*, No. 124, September 1978.

"The Top 500 Banks in the World," *American Banker*, Vol. 152, No. 149, July 31, 1987, pp. 1 and 28–35.

"Trade Picture Isn't Improving, Analysts Say," *Wall Street Journal*, February 21, 1989, p. A2.

United States Agency for International Development. *The AID Challenge*. Washington, D.C.: Bureau of External Affairs, November 1988.

_____. *Highlights*, Vol. 5, No. 3, Summer 1988.

_____. *An Investment in Global Growth*, The Administrator's Statement for the Fiscal Year 1989—Congressional Presentation, Washington, D.C., March 1988.

_____. *U.S. Overseas Loans and Grants*. Washington, D.C.: Office of Planning and Budgeting, CONG-R-0105, 1987.

United States Bureau of Census. *Historical Statistics of the United States, Colonial Times to 1957,* Washington, D.C., 1960, pp. 550–552.

United States Congress. "An Act to Amend the Act Approved December 23, 1913, Known as the Federal Reserve Act," S. 2472, 66th Congress, 2nd Session, 1919, pp. 378–384.

_____. House Committee on Banking, Currency, and Housing, *Financial Institutions and Nations and the Nation's Economy (FINE)—Discussion Principles*, 94th Congress, 1st Session, Title VI, 1975.

_____. Joint Economic Committee, *Foreign Banking in the United States*, Economic Policies and Practices, paper No. 9, by Jack Zwick, Washington, D.C., 1966.

United States Council of the International Chamber of Commerce. *Uniform Customs and Practices for Documentary Credits*, New York, 1984.

United States Department of Commerce. *Survey of Current Business*. Washington, D.C.: Bureau of Economic Analysis, 1971–88.

"U.S. Export-Import Bank Claims It's Competitive with Other Nations: Survey View Differs," *Wall Street Journal*, September 24, 1987.

United States International Development Cooperation Agency. *Development Issues*

1988, the Annual Report of the Chairman of the Development Coordination Committee, Washington, D.C., 1988.

United States International Trade Commission. "Composition of the U.S. Merchandise Trade Deficit, 1984-88," *International Economic Review*, Special Edition, Washington, D.C., April 1989.

United States Senate. "Edge Corporation Branching; Foreign Bank Takeovers; and International Banking Facilities," Hearings before the Committee on Banking, Housing, and Urban Affairs, Ninety-Sixth Congress, First Session, July 16 and 20, 1979.

————. "Foreign Takeovers of United States Banks," study by the staff of the Federal Reserve Board, published by the Committee on Banking, Housing, and Urban Affairs, July 1980.

————. "International Banking Act of 1978," Hearing before the Subcommittee on Financial Institutions of the Committee on Banking, Housing, and Urban Affairs, Ninety-Fifth Congress, Second Session, on H.R. 10899, June 21, 1978.

Vernon, Raymond. "International Investment and International Trade in the Product Cycle," *Quarterly Journal of Economics*, May 1966, pp. 190-207.

Volcker, Paul A. "Treatment of Foreign Banks in the United States: Dilemmas and Opportunities," *Quarterly Review*, Federal Reserve Bank of New York, Summer 1979, pp. 1-5.

Wallich, Henry C. "Nonbanking Activities of Foreign Bank Holding Companies," before the Commerce, Consumer, and Monetary Affairs Subcommittee of the Committee on Government Operations, House of Representatives, June 25, 1980.

————. "Perspectives on Foreign Banking in the United States," Conference on Foreign Banking in the United States — the Economic, Legal, and Regulatory Environment, Washington, D.C., March 1, 1982.

White, Betsy B. "Foreign Banking in the United States: A Regulatory and Supervisory Perspective," *Quarterly Review*, Federal Reserve Bank of New York, Summer 1982, pp. 48-58.

Wolf, Frederick D. "Recapitalizing the Export-Import Bank of the U.S.: Why It Is Necessary; How It Can Be Accomplished," testimony before the Subcommittee on International Finance, Trade, and Monetary Policy, House of Representatives, February 25, 1988.

The World Bank. *Annual Report*, Washington, D.C., 1988.

Wright, Richard W., and Gunter A. Pauli. *The Second Wave: Japanese Global Assault on Financial Services*. New York: St. Martin's Press, 1987.

Index

About the Author

FARAMARZ DAMANPOUR is Professor of Finance and Business Law, College of Business, at James Madison University in Harrisonburg, Virginia. He is the author of numerous articles in the area of banking and international finance and business. His recent articles have appeared in the *Columbia Journal of World Business*, the *Journal of Retail Banking*, *Bankers Monthly*, the *Asian Pacific Journal of Management*, and various other national and international publications. He is also president and founder of the Association for Global Business, an educational organization devoted to fostering education and advancing professional standards in the fields of international business and related areas of global concern.